Tinkering toward Utopia

This book has been awarded Harvard University
Press's annual prize for an outstanding publication
about education and society, established in 1995
by the Virginia and Warren Stone Fund.

Tinkering toward Utopia

A Century of Public School Reform

David Tyack &
Larry Cuban

Harvard University Press
Cambridge, Massachusetts
London, England

Library of Congress Cataloging-in-Publication Data

Tyack, David B.
Tinkering toward utopia : a century of public school reform /
David Tyack and Larry Cuban.
p. cm.
Includes bibliographical references and index.
ISBN 0-674-89282-8 (cloth)
ISBN 0-674-89283-6 (pbk.)
1. Educational change—United States—History—19th century.
2. Educational change—United States—History—20th century.
3. Education—Social aspects—United States. 4. Education and
state—United States. 5. Politics and education—United States.
I. Cuban, Larry. II. Title.
LA216.T92 1995
371'.01'097309—dc20
94-47545

To Our Students
Past, Present, and Future

Contents

Prologue

Learning from the Past

We call this book *Tinkering toward Utopia* to highlight the tension between Americans' intense faith in education—almost a secular religion—and the gradualness of changes in educational practices. For over a century citizens have sought to perfect the future by debating how to improve the young through education. Actual reforms in schools have rarely matched such aspirations, however. The words "utopia" and "tinkering" each have positive and negative connotations. Utopian thinking can be dismissed as pie-in-the-sky or valued as visionary; tinkering can be condemned as mere incrementalism or praised as a commonsense remedy for everyday problems. Both positive and negative examples of tinkering and utopian thinking abound in the record of educational reform. At the heart of that history lies the complex interplay between the purposes and processes of institutional change.[1]

Reforming the public schools has long been a favorite way of improving not just education but society. In the 1840s Horace Mann took his audience to the edge of the precipice to see the social hell that lay before them if they did not achieve salvation through the common school. In 1983 a presidential commission produced another fire-and-brimstone sermon about education, *A Nation at Risk*, though its definition of damnation (economic decline) differed from Mann's (moral dissolution). For over a century and a half, Americans have translated their cultural anxieties and hopes into dramatic demands for educational reform.[2]

Utopian thinking about education has been a tapestry woven of many strands. One was political. The new nation declared on its national seal the aim of becoming "The New Order of the Ages." From the Revolution onward, educational theorists have self-consciously used schooling to construct the citizens of that new order. A Protestant-republican ideology of making the United States literally God's country inspired the promoters of the public school movement of the nineteenth century.[3]

The political theorist Hannah Arendt argued that in the United States education has played a "different and, politically, incomparably more important role" than elsewhere, in large part because of "the role that continuous immigration plays in the country's political consciousness and frame of mind." Educational leaders have tried to transform immigrant newcomers and other "outsiders" into individuals who matched their idealized image of what an "American" should be, an effort succinctly portrayed in the accompanying cartoon, first published in *Judge* on April 20, 1901. But the newcomers and "outsiders," of course, were not simply wax figures on which dominant groups impressed their values. Many groups have contested with one another to define and create model citizens through schooling, and this political debate has shaped the course of public education.[4]

Millennial thinking about schooling has also been a favored solution to social and economic problems. In the early twentieth century, educational elites saw themselves as expert social engineers who could perfect the nation by consciously directing the evolution of society. When Lyndon B. Johnson sought to build the "Great Society" and declared war on poverty in the 1960s, he asserted that "the answer to all our national problems comes down to a single word: education."[5]

Americans have thought it easier to instruct the young than to coerce the adult. Debates over how to create perfect citizens through schooling long antedated Miss Manners's *Guide to Raising Perfect Children*. In theory, if the child was properly educated, the adult would need no reform. But if adults did prove wayward—ending up in traffic court, for example—taking a course might set things straight. In 1990, when state legislators in California faced charges of corruption, they passed a law requiring all lobbyists to enroll in a class on ethics.[6]

Repeatedly, Americans have followed a common pattern in devising educational prescriptions for specific social or economic ills. Once they had discovered a problem, they labeled it and taught a course on the subject: alcohol or drug instruction to fight addictions; sex education to combat syphilis or AIDS; home economics to lower the divorce rate; driver education to eliminate carnage on the highway; and vocational training or courses in computer literacy to keep the United States economically competitive.[7]

2

THE AMERICAN POLICY
Bringing the truant boy to the little Red, White and Blue Schoolhouse.

Faith in the power of education has had both positive and negative consequences. It has helped to persuade citizens to create the most comprehensive system of public schooling in the world. Americans have used discourse about education to articulate and instill a sense of the common good. But overpromising has often led to disillusionment and to blaming the schools for not solving problems beyond their reach. More important, the utopian tradition of social reform through schooling has often diverted attention from more costly, politically controversial, and difficult societal reforms. It's easier to provide vocational education than to remedy inequities in employment and gross disparities in wealth and income.

––––

When we speak of educational reforms, we mean planned efforts to change schools in order to correct perceived social and educational problems. Sometimes broad social crises triggered school reforms, and sometimes reforms were internal improvements initiated by professionals. Diagnoses of problems and proposed solutions changed over time. But whatever the reform, it usually entailed a long and complex set of steps: discovering problems, devising remedies, adopting new policies, and bringing about institutional change.[8]

Americans celebrate innovation. In education this penchant for the new has produced, time and again, criticism that educators are mossbacks who resist change. In his studies of educational reforms, Paul Mort concluded that about half a century elapsed between the introduction of a new practice and its widespread implementation; he called the latecomers "laggards."[9]

While some lament that educational reform is an institutional Bermuda Triangle into which intrepid change agents sail, never to appear again, others argue that public education is too trendy, that entirely too many foolish notions circulate through the system at high velocity. Are schools too resistant to change or too faddish? Viewed over the course of history, they may seem to be both. Educators have often paid lip service to demands for reform to signify their alertness to the public will. But their symbolic responses often protected school people from basic challenges to their core practices.[10]

In the last generation reforms have come thick and fast, as educators can testify. Since the value of change is in the eye of the beholder, one set of innovators may seek to undo the results of previous reforms. At one time reformers thought that the graded school—which groups children by age and proficiency—greatly enhanced educational efficiency; later critics sought to create ungraded schools as a way to break the lockstep of fixed grades. Curriculum designers succeeded in substituting easy texts for classic works in English classes for "slow learners," only to find the new curriculum condemned as the educational equivalent of junk food.[11]

Focusing only on change runs the danger of ignoring continuity in the basic practices of schools. The film *Hope and Glory,* about London during the Blitz in World War II, vividly portrays the persistence of familiar routines under the most trying conditions. Crowded in a bomb

4

shelter during an air raid, schoolchildren sit in rows under the stern eye of their instructor as they recite their multiplication tables through their gas masks.

We want to probe the meaning of continuity in schooling as well as to understand change. Change, we believe, is not synonymous with progress. Sometimes preserving good practices in the face of challenges is a major achievement, and sometimes teachers have been wise to resist reforms that violated their professional judgment.

Although policy talk about reform has had a utopian ring, actual reforms have typically been gradual and incremental—tinkering with the system. It may be fashionable to decry such change as piecemeal and inadequate, but over long periods of time such revisions of practice, adapted to local contexts, can substantially improve schools. Rather than seeing the hybridizing of reform ideas as a fault, we suggest it can be a virtue. Tinkering is one way of preserving what is valuable and reworking what is not.

Integrating our own research with the work of many colleagues, we explore some broad interpretive questions about the character of school reform. Typically we pose a puzzle, explore its dimensions and meanings through historical evidence and case studies, and then reflect on the issue in the light of the contemporary situation in education. Here we address some questions about reform that have intrigued us for years:[12]

Why have Americans believed in progress in education for over a century but have come to doubt it in recent years?

How accurate is the common notion that educational reforms come in cycles? Can this be reconciled with the notion of progress?

What is the relation between policy talk, policy action, and institutional trends?

How have schools changed reforms, as opposed to reforms changing schools?

What constitutes "success" in school reform? Why have some "successes" become invisible?

Why has the "grammar of schooling"—the organizational forms that govern instruction—persisted, while challenges to it have mostly been evanescent?

Why have outsiders' attempts to reinvent schooling—break-the-mold strategies—generally been short-lived shooting stars?

We hope that this book, which takes a century as its time span, will contribute to the broader conversation about educational reform today, for improving public schools is everybody's business. And it is a special concern of parents and students, activists and scholars, school board members and federal and state officials, and the millions of educators who work daily in the schools.

Why, given the urgency of educational problems today, should anyone be concerned about the history of educational reform? To judge from the ahistorical character of most current policy talk about reform, innovators may consider amnesia a virtue. And in those rare occasions when reformers do discuss the history of schooling, they often portray the past in politicized, stylized ways as a golden age to be restored or a dismal legacy to be repudiated.

Anyone who would improve schooling is a captive of history in two ways. All people and institutions are the product of history (defined as past events). And whether they are aware of it or not, all people use history (defined as an interpretation of past events) when they make choices about the present and future. The issue is not whether people use a sense of the past in shaping their lives but how accurate and appropriate are their historical maps: Are their inferences attentive to context and complexity? Are their analogies plausible? And how might alternative understandings of the past produce different visions of the future?[13]

History provides a whole storehouse of experiments on dead people. Studying such experiments is cheap (no small matter when funds are short); and it does not use people (often the poor) as live guinea pigs. Many educational problems have deep roots in the past, and many solutions have been tried before. If some "new" ideas have already been tried, and many have, why not see how they fared in the past?

Studies of past reforms confer the benefits of psychological distance on issues obscured by the passions of the present. Consider controversies over providing day care for young children. Generation after generation of Americans have rediscovered that working mothers need help in caring for their children, but they have tended to make patchwork day-care arrangements, assuming that the problem of minding the children would wither away when the family regained its rightful status. Once people recognize that the need for day care is not a new or temporary problem, they might conclude that its permanence is best

6

understood as the result of long-term trends in families and public institutions.[14]

Finally, history provides a generous time frame for appraising reforms. It is not driven by the short-term needs of election cycles, budgets, foundation grants, media attention, or the reputations of professional reformers. Certain reforms may look successful when judged soon after adoption, but in fact they may turn out to be fireflies, flickering brightly but soon fading; the recurrent desire to employ technology as a teacher-proof form of instruction is a case in point. Other reforms may seem of questionable benefit in the short run but effective in the long run. The positive effects of the Head Start program become more obvious when the participants are young adults than when they were in the primary grades. When reforms aim at basic institutional changes or the eradication of deep social injustices, the appropriate period for evaluation may be a generation or more.[15]

Our interpretation of school reform blends political and institutional analysis. A political perspective shows how groups become mobilized to publicize problems, devise remedies, and secure the adoption of policies by school boards and legislatures. Understanding actual implementation of reforms in schools—or lack of implementation—requires insight into the distinctive institutional character of schools.

Not all reforms are born equal; some enjoy strong political sponsors while others are political orphans. But even reforms with strong supporters do not always become embedded in the schools. Outside forces shape the course of school reform, but schools are also in some respects autonomous, buffered institutions. Educators have variously welcomed, improved, deflected, coopted, modified, and sabotaged outside efforts at reform.

Over long periods of time schools have remained basically similar in their core operation, so much so that these regularities have imprinted themselves on students, educators, and the public as the essential features of a "real school." Resistance to change is sometimes dismissed as the result of popular ignorance or institutional inertia, but that oversimplifies. Often teachers have had well-founded reasons for resisting change, as have parents. If reformers have had their plans for schools, people in schools and local communities have had their own ways of dealing with reforms.[16]

The disparities evident in the political economy of the nation have strongly constricted or enhanced what people thought possible or desirable in educational policy and practice. These inequalities have been apparent in regional differences of wealth and economic power; sharp contrasts of life in rural and urban communities; racial, class, and gender discrimination; the honoring of some cultures and the ignoring or dismissing of others; and the great disparities in political power between groups. Life at the bottom of the social system has been far different from life at the top. Many people who claimed that the educational system has been marching up the ladder of progress paid scant attention to what was happening to the students on the lower rungs.[17]

Educational reforms are intrinsically political in origin. Groups organize and contest with other groups in the politics of education to express their values and to secure their interests in the public school. Conflicts in education have arisen over ethnic, religious, racial, gender, and class differences. Controversies over language policies—English only or bilingual instruction—have recurred for over a century, as did contests over racial or gender segregation or the use of the Bible and prayer in schools.[18]

Although many groups have entered school politics, especially in the protest movements of the last half-century, this apparent pluralism is misleading. The politics of education has not been conducted on a level playing field. Policy elites—people who managed the economy, who had privileged access to the media and to political officials, who controlled foundations, who were educational leaders in the universities and in city and state superintendencies, and who redesigned and led organizations of many kinds—gained a disproportionate authority over educational reform, especially during the first half of the twentieth century. These leaders inside and outside education generally shared a common vision of scientific management and a similar blueprint for reorganizing the educational system.[19]

Policy elites often claimed to be "taking the schools out of politics." They sought to do this by centralizing control of schools and delegating decisions about education, wherever possible, to "experts." In the process they did not, of course, eliminate politics, but they acquired formidable powers: to set the agenda of reform, to diagnose problems, to prescribe solutions, and often to influence what should *not* be on the agenda of reform. Their template for structural change in education set the dominant pattern of school reform during the period from 1900 to 1950.

During the last century, there has been much continuity in the structures, rules, and practices that organize the work of instruction. These

organizational regularities, the grammar of schooling include such familiar practices as the age-grading of students, the division of knowledge
into separate subjects, and the self-contained classroom with one teacher.
At the core of the school—in classroom instruction—change was slow.
Reforms took place, but they were largely accretions around that core.
To understand why, consider how different institutions maintain their
distinctiveness. One way is by developing specific rules and cultures to
channel the behavior of people within them. People act in different ways
in armies, churches, and schools because these institutions socialize
individuals to their different organizational norms. People who move
from one institution to another come to take these differences for
granted: children know that they should raise their hands in class to get
the teacher's attention but not during a sermon in church; a rookie in
boot camp does not expect his sergeant to treat him the way his first-
grade teacher did.[20]

Most Americans have been to school and know what a "real school"
is like. Congruence with that cultural template has helped maintain the
legitimacy of the institution in the minds of the public. But when schooling departed too much from the consensual model of a "real school,"
failed to match the grammar of schooling, trouble often ensued. If
teachers did not maintain strict discipline and consistently supervise
students in class, if traditional subjects were neglected, if pupils did not
bring report cards home, reforms might be suspect.[21]

For their part, teachers also have had an investment in the familiar
institutional practices of the school. They learned these as students, and
as they moved to the other side of the desk, they often took traditional
patterns of organization for granted as just the way things were. It was
one thing to add on a popular innovation at the border of the school—
say a new vocational wing or dental examinations—and quite another to
ask teachers, faced with the job of controlling and instructing a large
number of students, to make fundamental changes in their daily routines.
Such alterations in basic practices have increased teachers' workloads,
often without compensatory time or resources. Because teachers retained
a fair degree of autonomy once the classroom door was closed, they
could, if they chose, comply only symbolically or fitfully or not at all with
the mandates for change pressed on them by platoons of outside reformers. Or teachers could respond to reforms by hybridizing them, blending
the old and the new by selecting those parts that made their job more
efficient or satisfying.

The institutional character of the school, then, influenced the chances that a particular reform would be incorporated in the educational system, how it would be implemented, and how the public and teachers would view the results. Both general beliefs in the broader culture about what a "real school" was and the hold of standard operating procedures on staff and students put a brake on innovators who sought basic changes in classroom instruction.

Local educational leaders faced a potential Catch-22 if political demands for innovation conflicted with institutional conservatism. As a public enterprise, the schools might be expected to respond to innovations advocated by politically organized groups. Superintendents who wanted to keep their jobs needed to convince their school boards and policy elites that they were ready to adopt improvements. Among their peers, too, they felt the pressure to be up to date lest they be branded laggards. If the reforms they adopted were add-ons, such as kindergartens or classes in commercial education, few citizens or teachers would complain (except, perhaps, about expense). But if reforms reached into regular classrooms and departed too much from consensual notions of a "real school," protests or foot-dragging might ensue.

———

Change where it counts the most—in the daily interactions of teachers and students—is the hardest to achieve and the most important, but we are not pessimistic about improving the public schools. We think it difficult and essential, above all for the educationally dispossessed. To do this requires not only political will and commitment but also an accurate understanding of schools as institutions.

We favor attempts to bring about such improvements by working from the inside out, especially by enlisting the support and skills of teachers as key actors in reform. This might be seen as a positive kind of tinkering, adapting knowledgeably to local needs and circumstances, preserving what is valuable and correcting what is not. But teachers cannot do the job alone. They need resources of time and money, practical designs for change, and collegial support. And they can succeed best if they do their work in partnership with parents.

Policy talk about educational reform has been replete with extravagant claims for innovations that flickered and faded. This is a pie-in-the-sky brand of utopianism, and it has often led to disillusionment among teachers and to public cynicism. Exaggeration has pervaded these public rituals of dismay and promise.

There is, however, a different kind of utopianism—a vision of a just democracy—that has marked the best discourse about educational purpose over the past century. We believe that debate over educational and social goals has become radically restricted in the past generation. An essential political task today is to renegotiate a pluralistic conception of the public good, a sense of trusteeship that preserves the best of the past while building a generous conception of a common future.

1

Progress or Regress?

"Is the educational utopia in sight?" W. W. Carpenter, an educator in Missouri, the show-me state, asked that question in 1931 amid the joblessness and suffering caused by the Great Depression. He was not being sarcastic or rhetorical. His answer was "yes," for he believed Americans were "approaching with steady progress" the goal of giving every child an appropriate education. In pursuing this goal, he said, "we are carrying on the most important experiment in democracy the world has ever seen, the results of which may determine educational procedures for centuries to come."[1]

Carpenter was not an idiosyncratic optimist. He expressed two opinions common among Americans and nearly axiomatic among educational leaders: that progress was the rule in public education and that better schooling would guarantee a better society. Progress was an animating ideal that gave direction and coherence to reforms. It was also, educators believed, a plain fact documented by trends in educational practice: Americans were gaining not only more schooling but also a better education.[2]

To be sure, America had its share of school haters who believed that the best education was extramural. Also, from time to time some citizens have longed for a return to what they saw as a golden age in the past. But typically when people have proclaimed public education a "failure," as an author did in *Look* magazine in 1946, the chief criticism was that the schools did not match the modern template of progress. When *Life* magazine printed the questionnaire "How Good Is Your School?" in 1950, the items on the checklist of excellence were precisely those sought by up-to-date professional leaders whose program of progress seemed the public's.[3]

Until recently, citizens thought that public schools were good and getting better. Consider the results of public opinion surveys. In 1940 Gallup interviewers asked a large sample of adults their views about public education. Eighty-five percent agreed "that young people today are getting a better education in school than their parents got." At about the same time Swedes were asked a similar question; only 38 percent of fathers in Sweden thought their sons had been better educated than they had. In another Gallup poll in 1946, 87 percent of parents said that they were satisfied with the schools their children attended, up seven points from a similar survey in 1943.[4]

Teachers fared well in early public opinion surveys. In a poll in 1946, 60 percent won top ratings, 29 percent middling, and only 8 percent poor. Recognizing that teachers generally had low salaries and over-crowded classrooms in the mid-1950s, two-thirds of citizens polled said that they would be willing to pay more taxes if the extra money went to higher pay for teachers. In 1957 three-quarters of parents said that they would like to have a daughter become a teacher.[5]

When asked for criticisms of the schools, 40 percent of citizens in 1946 could think of nothing wrong. Nothing. This echoed the results of a poll in 1938 in which citizens were asked, "If you were running the school in this community, what changes would you make?" "None" was the answer of 24 percent, 29 percent did not answer, and from the rest emerged a scatter of minor complaints (only 1 percent called for stricter discipline).[6]

Opinion has changed. Now regress in public schools seems as axiomatic to many people as progress did during the previous hundred years. After 1969—the year when the Gallup organization began systematic yearly surveys of public opinion about public education—it became clear that the doctrine of steady educational progress no longer made sense to most people. As criticisms of education mushroomed, polls revealed lower rankings of the schools and of teachers year by year. On average, citizens rated schools as B– institutions in 1974 and C– institutions in 1981. In 1978, 41 percent of Americans declared that schools were worse than they used to be, and only 35 percent thought they were better; a *New York Times* study five years later found the two opinions evenly balanced at 36 percent.[7]

The most influential school reform report of the 1980s, *A Nation at Risk,* quotes, as if it is obviously true, Paul Copperman's assertion that "for the first time in the history of our country, the educational skills of one generation will not surpass, will not equal, will not even approach, those of their parents." A litany of dismal statistics in the report purports to show that regress, not progress, is the trend in public education.[8]

But the belief that better schools make a better society—the deeply ingrained utopian conviction about the importance of schooling—is alive and well. The accompanying cartoon plays off the notion that the future would be brighter if schools improved and test scores rose.

Schools can easily shift from panacea to scapegoat. If the schools are supposed to solve social problems, and do not, then they present a ready target. In recent years, allegedly worse schools have been blamed for lack of economic competitiveness and other societal problems. Some observers have interpreted the supposed decline of education as a trumpet call to reform public schools. Others, believing that public education is mostly beyond repair, have argued that the way to regenerate schooling is to create a market system of education in which parents can choose their children's schools, either public or private, and pay the tuition through vouchers funded by taxes.[9]

Notions of progress or regress in education and society are, of course, highly debatable, though at any one time they may seem self-evidently true or false. In an epoch of history as tortured as the twentieth century, the very idea of human progress strikes many people as absurd. A sense of progress is always relative—now compared with then, one group compared with others. Since the expectations and experiences of people differ, so do their appraisals of whether things are getting better or worse. If one group advances, its progress may undermine the comparative advantage of another group, so that gain for one can seem loss for another. Thus success in keeping youths from impoverished families in high schools can erode the privilege of prosperous families who once regarded secondary education as their own middle-class preserve.[10]

Beliefs in progress or regress always convey a political message. Opinions about advance or decline in education reflect general confidence in American institutions. Faith in the nation and its institutions was far higher in the aftermath of success in World War II than in the skeptical era of the Vietnam War and Watergate. Expectations about education change, as do media representations of what is happening in schools. And the broader goals that education serves—the visions of possibility that animate the society—also shift in different periods, making it necessary to ask how people have judged progress, from what viewpoints, over what spans of time.[11]

When the issues are framed in this way, it becomes obvious that there

14

"*Just when citywide reading scores were edging up!*"

Drawing by Ed Fisher; © 1991 The New Yorker Magazine, Inc.

is no simple answer to the question whether schooling or the society have gotten better or worse. The notions of progress or regress—the concepts of a golden age in the future or in the past—raise complex puzzles in American educational history. Why did progress once seem plausible, indeed indisputable, to educational leaders and to most of the public? How did policy elites translate the concept of progress into a systematic

15

program of reform? Progress for whom—who was left out of this forward march? How did dispossessed groups create their own politics of
progress or challenge the dominant faith in improvement? How and why
did public opinion about the quality of schooling shift even as the general
faith in its importance to society persisted? And finally, how has the
debate over progress and regress framed political choices and policy talk
about public education in recent years?

Progress as Ideology and "Fact"

We see two interwoven strands in the belief system that decreed that
schools were improving and through them the nation. The first, well
represented by Horace Mann, was the religious and political faith of the
common school reformers of the mid-nineteenth century. They drew on
and appealed to a pervasive Protestant-republican ideology that held that
proper education could bring about a secular millennium, could make
the United States quite literally God's country. In the Progressive era of
the early twentieth century this evangelical enthusiasm became merged
with a second faith that animated educational reformers: that a newly
discovered "science" of education provided the precise tools needed to
guide the course of social evolution.[12]

The rhetoric of Carpenter, the Missourian educator, echoed that of
Mann. No educational task was menial if seen as part of the brightly lit
path of progress. A school planner, absorbed in the details of improving
ventilation and plumbing, found transcendent importance in his work.
The schoolhouse was to America in the 1920s what the cathedral was to
the Middle Ages, he believed: "something of the same spirit . . . is
seeking expression in furnishing to the youth of our land nobler temples
in which their hearts, minds, and bodies may better adjust themselves to
the demands of a practical civic brotherhood." In America even blackboards "are essentially democratic" tools.[13]

"Dull and phlegmatic indeed" must be the person who is not "thrilled
by the progress made in seventy-five years," wrote two prominent educators in 1925, "and by what that progress means to the age-long,
world-wide struggle for the betterment of human living." The modern
public school of Detroit, they believed, "has ceased to be a prison and
is becoming a childish utopia." Schools that ministered "to the whole
nature of the pupil, not simply to his intellect," were producing "a social
revolution as complete and as far-reaching as the progress of democracy
itself." Children were also learning academic subjects better, they said,

despite complaints by some parents that "in the good old days of drill and discipline, the children really learned something."[14]

During the first half of the twentieth century, the chief American architects of reform and arbiters of educational "progress" constituted a policy elite we call the administrative progressives. These reformers were a group unified by similar training, interests, and values. They were the first generation of professional leaders educated in the new schools of education. These white men—few women and almost no people of color were admitted to the inner circle of movers and shakers—carved out lifelong careers in education as city superintendents, education professors, state or federal officers, leaders in professional organizations such as the National Education Association (NEA), and foundation officials. They shared a common faith in "educational science" and in lifting education "above politics" so that experts could make the crucial decisions. Occupying key positions and sharing definitions of problems and solutions, they shaped the agenda and implementation of school reform more powerfully from 1900 to 1950 than any other group has done before or since.[15]

With the confidence of Teddy Roosevelt creating the Panama Canal, these reformers developed a blueprint for educational progress. Though sometimes nostalgic about the values and experiences common in the rural and small town America of their youth, they still located an educational golden age in the future rather than in the past. The pathway to that golden future was punctuated with orderly bumps called "problems" to be smoothed out by experts. The evidence that they were making progress came in equally orderly statistics of success. Those who lived to mid-century had good reason to believe that they had achieved most of their goals, for graphs of institutional trends—the "facts" they enshrined at the center of their faith in educational science—showed steady upward movement.[16]

Their program for progress stemmed from a shared conviction that education was the prime means of directing the course of social evolution. They sought to expand access to education so that more young people could attend schools for longer periods of time. They thought that schooling should be both more differentiated and more standardized: differentiated in curriculum to fit the backgrounds and future destinies of students; and standardized with respect to buildings and equipment, professional qualifications of staff, administrative procedures, social and health services and regulations, and other educational practices. Year by year, decade by decade, they moved confidently forward. In their view, progress was a fact: the schools in 1950 were far superior to those in 1900.[17]

The administrative progressives worked for change at the local, state, and federal levels, collaborating with foundations that shared their blueprints for change. Confronting this "educational trust," the American Federation of Labor complained that education was becoming "Rockefellerized" (John D. Rockefeller's General Education Board had subsidized agents hired by the U.S. Bureau of Education at a dollar a year). The federal government and foundations conducted state and local surveys of schools that were highly prescriptive in character and issued monographs on reforms favored by the administrative progressives. Critics complained of groupthink and suppression of dissenting views.[18]

The new educational ideology of progress through science, efficient management, and professionalism gave the appearance of turning educational policy into a process of rational planning, surely not political bargaining. Take the long view, said an official of the NEA, whose state affiliates were the most powerful lobbyists for school legislation in the state capitols: "An efficient state school system cannot be created overnight, nor does it spring up as the result of incantations and the waving of a magic wand. It is the result always of persistence during a long period of steady effort." An ever present danger was that "the educational forces may be prevailed upon to accept weakening compromises with the opponents of good school conditions . . . 'Be sure that you are right, then go ahead' is a good motto for a program of school legislation." Creating a sound structure of reformed schools demanded long-range planning based on research, "continuous and effective publicity," and "organized unity of purpose in the entire educational profession."[19]

The administrative progressives believed that school governance would be more efficient and expert if it were more buffered from lay control. There *was* something they wanted less of—the influence of school boards, whose members they sometimes accused of being corrupt or ignorant meddlers. In fact, one of the mandarins of the movement, Charles H. Judd of the University of Chicago, argued that local school boards should be abolished. Education should be controlled as much as possible by specially trained professionals certified by the state.[20]

At the beginning of the twentieth century, educational leaders collaborated with business and professional elites to transform the character of urban school politics. They wanted to eliminate ward school committees and to cut the size of central school boards. From 1890 to 1920 the average number of central board members in cities of more than 100,000 inhabitants dropped from twenty-one to seven, and most cities eliminated ward boards. But it was not only the size of the central boards that was a problem; the reformers also wanted to increase the number of prosperous and well-educated members and to adopt a model of policy making patterned on that of business corporations. The board, they believed, should delegate decisions to the superintendent and central staff, experts assumed to serve the interests of all the children. This form of governance increasingly became the expressed norm in city school systems, if not always the actuality.[21]

In the countryside, the consolidation of school districts decimated the number of lay school trustees. Local school districts declined from 127,531 in 1932 to 16,960 in 1973. Between 1930 and 1980 the number of one-room schools nose-dived from 130,000 to less than 1,000. As the number of small town superintendents and rural supervisors of teachers rose steadily, these administrators took over some of the functions formerly performed by lay trustees.[22]

The administrative progressives believed that the U.S. Bureau of Education should take the lead in informing state legislators about what a modern school should be (they lobbied Congress in the early 1920s to make the bureau a *department* of education with expanded powers). In 1919 the Bureau issued *A Manual of Educational Legislation,* addressed to state legislators who served on education committees. It laid out a whole program of state legislation designed to standardize schooling to match the program of "reorganization" (their version of systemic reform) favored by the administrative progressives, treating such topics as school consolidation, increased state financing, physical education, improved school construction, state certification for teachers, and standard textbooks and curriculum. A comparison of that plan with a summary of "state legal standards for the provision of public education" in 1978 shows that most of the recommendations of 1919 were put into practice in the following six decades.[23]

Prodded by professional organizations like the NEA, state legislatures increasingly standardized schools across the nation according to the model of a modern school proposed by the policy elite. To carry out their new regulatory roles, state departments of education increased enormously during the twentieth century. In 1890 there was, on average, one staff member in state departments of education for every 100,000 pupils; in 1974 there was one for about every 2,000. Regulations ballooned: in California the state education code took about two hundred pages in 1900, in 1985 more than twenty-six hundred.[24]

Educators lobbied state governments to require local schools to meet minimum requirements in order to receive state aid. These included the quality and safety of buildings, the qualifications of teachers, the length of the school term, congruence with the state course of study, and even the size of flags and pictures on the walls. University professors developed "score cards"—appealing to a sense of competition—to evaluate schools. These featured precise specifications about playground space and apparatus, pupils' desks, globes and musical equipment, hygiene and sanitation, and even "community spirit." Thirty-four state departments of education managed to "standardize" more than 40,000 schools by 1925 in accord with legislation, regulations of the state board, or rulings of the state superintendents. Private accreditation agencies also insisted on greater institutional uniformity, especially at the secondary level, all in the name of progress.[25]

In elaborate surveys of urban schools, the administrative progressives placed their template of a modern school system on city after city to see how well the existing schools measured up to their ideal of educational "progress." In addition to upgrading the quality of the school plant and the qualifications of teachers, they wanted the standard city system to have a large staff of certified specialists and administrators; elaborate fiscal accounting; uniform student record cards and guidance procedures; standardized intelligence and achievement tests; a diversified curriculum that included vocational training, physical education, and a host of elective courses at the secondary level; and a policy of grouping children by ability.[26]

Basic to their conception of educational science was a conviction that children had different abilities, interests, and destinies in life. Hence schools should treat them differently; this was their concept of equality of educational opportunity. They gave different labels to students who did not fit their definition of "normal," and they created tracks and niches for them. Progress to these experts meant a place for every child and every child in his or her place.[27]

Prodded by a variety of lay reformers to expand social and health services, educational administrators added programs of physical education and recreation and gave instruction in health. Hundreds of cities added vacation schools (later called summer schools), school lunch programs, and medical and dental care, especially for the children of working-class immigrant families. States and urban districts began creating special schools or classes for physically and mentally handicapped students—the number of separate state or district schools for such children increased from 180 in 1900 to 551 in 1930. Cities also created new categories of classes for "misfits"—children who were too "backward" to proceed at the normal rate in graded classrooms or too unruly for the teachers to handle.[28]

To achieve reforms such as these, the administrative progressives believed, schools should become larger. They did. The number of students per school has jumped more than sixfold in the last half-century. The one-room school became a vanishing breed. Early in the twentieth century the modal high school had perhaps 100 students, but by 1986 over half enrolled more than 1,000 students. The total number of high schools remained fairly constant at about 24,000 between 1930 and 1980, but the number of high school graduates jumped in those years from 592,000 to 2,748,000.[29]

A major proof of progress, educational leaders believed, was increased access to schooling for young people for ever longer periods of time. In 1900 only half the population five to nineteen years old were enrolled in school; by 1950, this proportion had increased to nearly eight in ten (and by 1990 to more than nine in ten). The average number of days these students spent in school grew steadily from 99 in 1900 to 158 in 1950, increasing only marginally from then on. Another sign of progress was a tripling of per-pupil expenditures (in constant dollars) from 1920 to 1950; in the following three decades the average sum per student tripled again. Yet another indication of progress was the steady rise in rates of literacy, from 89 percent in 1900 to 97 percent in 1950.[30]

Supremely confident, the administrative progressives all along proclaimed their reforms as being in the national interest and in the interest of the schoolchildren—hence as obvious progress. This progress, they believed, required ever higher costs per pupil. Many school districts and professional associations added publicity departments to persuade citizens that the reforms were worth the money.[31]

In the firm belief that they were the trustees of the public interest, superintendents and other policy elites of the first half of the century tended to dismiss their opponents as ignorant or self-interested. They portrayed the decentralized urban ward boards of education as corrupt and accused them of meddling in professional matters. They regarded the rural foes of school consolidation as backward yokels who did not know what was good for their children. The big school was better because it permitted more differentiation of curriculum, and school boards and parents who did not recognize this fact were behind the times. Teachers who opposed guidance by expert administrators were unprofessional trouble-makers. Such foot-draggers might slow reforms, but the trends were going in the right direction. History was progressive.[32]

Progress for Whom?

Although most groups made some advances in the quality of their schooling—even those who were most subordinated, southern rural blacks—the apparent march of progress to mid-century left many people behind. A probe behind aggregated national statistics and the upbeat rhetoric of the administrative progressives reveals major disparities in educational opportunities. These inequalities stemmed from differences in place of residence, family occupation and income, race, and gender, and from physical and mental handicaps. At mid-century American public education was not a seamless system of roughly similar common schools but instead a diverse and unequal set of institutions that reflected deeply embedded economic and social inequalities. Americans from all walks of life may have shared a common faith in individual and societal progress through education, but they hardly participated equally in its benefits.[33]

The people who suffered most from inequalities—the poor, blacks, working-class immigrants, the disabled, females—had little influence over educational policy. A system of governance and finance rooted in local school boards and state legislatures and professionally guided by the administrative progressives placed most power in the hands of prosperous, white, male leaders born in the United States who tended to assume the correctness of their own culture and policies. In the South, school systems were part of a caste system that legally assigned blacks to a separate and distinctly unequal education; relatively few white educators challenged these inequities. Most educational policymakers did not notice, much less seek to correct, gender inequalities. Although educators did try to create special, usually segregated, niches in the system for children with special needs, hundreds of thousands of physically handicapped and other impaired children were excluded from school as "uneducable." Because New Deal reformers regarded public schools as unresponsive to poor youth, they chose to create their own programs, such as the National Youth Administration, to assist the impoverished. A number of educational leaders were concerned about the highly unequal funding of rural schools and tried to give them more state aid, but such efforts fell far short of their goal of equalizing school finance. Many people remained outside the magic circle of the politics of progress, excluded, segregated, or given an inferior education despite the rhetoric of democracy and equality of educational opportunity.[34]

In 1940 where children lived largely determined the resources available for their schooling. The biggest fiscal dividing line was between urban and rural schools, and this was in turn magnified by gross regional differences in school funding. The young people who needed schooling the most generally received the least. At that time the poorest rural families tended to have the most children. Typically, the communities in which they lived had meager resources to devote to building schools and paying teachers. In 1930 families in the southeastern region of the United States had to nurture and educate one-quarter of the children of the nation on one-tenth of the income. Farmers raised 31 percent of the country's children but received only 9 percent of the national income. By contrast, the urban Northeast commanded 43 percent of the nation's income but had only 30 percent of the children, while the figures for the West were 9 and 5 percent, respectively. The median years of schooling for urban whites aged twenty-five years and over in 1940 were 9.6 but only 8.0 for those in farming communities; among blacks the comparable figures were 6.8 (urban) and 4.1 (rural).[35]

In much of America, rural schools were well supported and effective, but in impoverished regions—much of the South, the Dust Bowl, Appalachia, and the cut-over forest lands of the upper Midwest—families had to struggle hard to provide even the most rudimentary education for their children. Cities spent twice as much per pupil on teacher salaries and school buildings as did rural districts. In 1940 30 percent of city dwellers had completed high school compared with only 12 percent of farmers.[36]

In 1940 about two out of three blacks lived in rural areas, overwhelmingly in the South. Racial oppression compounded inequalities created by the poverty of the region. Disenfranchised, blacks had to make do with the starvation diet of school funds that white officials allocated to the segregated "colored" schools. Blacks constituted over a quarter of the public school students but received only 12 percent of revenues. Half of the black teachers had gone no further than high school, compared with 7 percent of white teachers. They often lacked the most basic aids to learning—textbooks, slates and chalk, or desks—and frequently had very large classes when the children were not needed for farm labor. A visitor to East Texas described a typical black school:

> The building was a crude box shack built by the Negroes out of old scraps and scrap lumber. Windows and doors were badly broken.

The floor was in such condition that one had to walk carefully to keep from going through cracks and weak boards. Daylight was easily visible through walls, floors, and roof. The building was used for both church and school. Its only equipment consisted of a few rough hewn seats, an old stove brought from a junk pile, a crude homemade pulpit, a very small table, and a large water barrel . . . Fifty-two children were enrolled . . . No supplies, except a broom, were furnished the district during the year.[37]

Among whites who lived in cities—generally considered to be the most favored group educationally—class background strongly shaped educational opportunity. In northeastern cities, only 56 percent of youth coming from low-income families entered high school in 1935–36, compared with almost nine in ten who came from prosperous homes. In Maryland in 1938 students' chances of going beyond eighth grade neatly matched the prestige of their fathers' occupations.[38]

Once inside the high school, despite an official ideology that public education should be class-blind, working-class and upper-strata students typically had quite different experiences. In the 1940s Elmtown High School in Illinois, even the hooks for coats were segregated by social class, not by official school policy but by the mores of the students. Within the classroom pupils received an unequal education in college and general tracks. Grades and vocational guidance tended to reflect family status. Forty percent of Americans polled by Gallup in 1940—most of this 40 percent being from low-income groups—agreed with the statement that "teachers favor the children of parents who have the most money or the best position in the community."[39]

Inequality of educational opportunity based on gender was less obvious to most people in 1940 than racial or class disparities, in part because girls and boys had roughly equal access to instruction and performed at roughly similar levels. To the degree that educators paid attention to sex differences among pupils at all, they tended to worry about boys because they seemed to have more trouble learning to read, outnumbered girls in remedial classes, created more discipline problems, and dropped out of high school in somewhat greater numbers. One response was to try to make the schools more attractive to boys by creating sex-segregated vocational courses and tracks, by adopting textbooks attuned to the interests of boys, and by stressing competitive, male-only athletic teams.[40]

At mid-century most people regarded such differentiation by gender and other forms of sex-stereotyped activities as "natural," not as a form of institutional sexism, as reformers twenty years later would claim. Two

24

kinds of gender discrimination did attract some attention, however: the common practice of firing women—but not men—when they married; and the predominance of men in the higher administrative ranks in a profession in which females outnumbered males as teachers by about five to one. The shortage of teachers during World War II undermined the policy of firing married women teachers, but the practice of hiring men for administrative jobs continued unabated in the postwar years.[41]

Programs for handicapped children and those with special needs were pretty much a patchwork in the first half of the twentieth century. In 1938 they served less than 1 percent of all pupils, up substantially from a decade earlier but far short of the 10 percent of children covered by federally funded programs for children with special needs in the 1970s. State legislatures and large urban districts sometimes provided separate schools for pupils who were blind, deaf, or physically or mentally handicapped, but millions of impaired children never saw the inside of a public school. Compulsory attendance laws frequently exempted disabled children, for whom an appropriate education was often regarded more as a charity than as a right. Much of the time the initiative to provide for sick and "crippled" children came not from within the educational system but from women's groups and from parents of affected children.[42]

The largest proportion of "special" students in city schools were placed in ungraded classes for "backward" children and "disciplinary" classes for unruly pupils (almost all students in both of these were boys). Indeed, much of special education was deliberately designed to meet the needs of the organization quite as much as the interests of the "special" children. Such differentiated classes buffered students and teachers in the graded-school mainstream from "misfits," children who did not advance at the expected rate or who caused discipline problems. In such cul-de-sac classes they were kept from receiving a standard education, not excluded from school but segregated.[43]

Progress for whom?—the answers to that question suggest the unevenness of the "progress" achieved by top-down planning by the administrative progressives, however impressive were aggregate trends such as the increasing rate of retention of students or the growing expenditures per student. At mid-century the subordinated or underserved families of the nation probably considered the utopia of equal education to be not just around the corner but at best on a far-distant horizon. Yet soon some groups barred from equal opportunities joined their activist allies to create a new politics of schooling. They challenged society to distribute educational opportunities more fairly and to realize what Gunnar Myrdal called "the American Creed": a commitment to "liberty, equality, justice, and fair opportunity for everybody." Could this rhetoric of hope, the doctrine of progress, really apply to everyone?[44]

A New Politics of Progress

Thesis

In recent decades social protest groups have called attention to discrimination and deprivation and declared injustice mutable, not just the way things are. African Americans, feminists, Hispanics, Native Americans, and parents of handicapped children all entered the arena of educational politics and broke open the "closed system" of governance. In the process they created new goals and strategies of school reform. These groups joined forces in large-scale social protest movements and moved issues of equity to the forefront of the newspapers, the television news, and the agendas of the courts, legislatures, and school boards. People who had been ignored or subordinated demanded to participate in "progress." They developed a new style of activist reform and could take much of the credit for desegregation in the South, new attention to the children of immigrants, attacks on discriminatory gender practices, and better education of children with special needs.[45]

A major catalyst for this campaign for "simple justice" was the Supreme Court's decision in Brown v. Board of Education in 1954. Its immediate target was the racial segregation of students, but its language of justification and its force as a legal and moral precedent encouraged not only blacks but other groups as well to demand educational equity as a right. The Justices maintained that "it is doubtful that any child may reasonably be expected to succeed in life if he is denied the opportunity of an education." That gave protest groups a broad mandate. Activists working for women's rights, for the handicapped, for immigrant students, and for the poor were able to draw on this doctrine that individual and societal progress demanded progress in schooling.[46]

The administrative progressives had envisioned progress as the result of a gradual and expertly designed institutional evolution. There was little legitimate place for social conflict in this model of reform planned and executed largely from the top down. Protest and advocacy groups pushing for equity for outsiders, by contrast, often regarded social conflict as essential to educational advance. When they found, as they often did, that local school boards were unresponsive or unsympathetic to their demands, they organized demonstrations and boycotts to publicize and advance their groups' demands. They also pushed class action suits in the courts and lobbied for legislation and administrative regulations at the state and national levels.[47]

26

At first, many of the groups seeking greater educational opportunity worked to achieve greater access to the mainstream, to share the same resources, to enjoy the equality of opportunity envisaged by the American creed, and to participate in the forms of "progress" already enjoyed by more favored parts of the society. Blacks pressed to desegregate public schools so that they could share the same educational advantages as whites. In part this campaign reflected a desire to erase the stigma of racial oppression and to realize the universalistic goal of equality so eloquently stated by Martin Luther King, Jr., in his famous speech in 1963, "I Have a Dream." Advocates for handicapped pupils argued that an appropriate education for the disabled was a *right,* not a gift. They sought to mainstream those with special needs in regular classrooms in the "least restrictive environment" that was possible for them. No longer should children with special needs be ignored or labeled and warehoused. Feminists sought to abolish all gender distinctions in school policies and practices so that both girls and boys would have the same opportunities and not be restricted by segregation in vocational classes or physical education, by sex-stereotyping by counselors and teachers, and by unequal treatment in competitive athletics. Through Title I of the Elementary and Secondary Education Act of 1965 reformers targeted funds to students from low-income families to prevent poverty from restricting school opportunities and academic achievement. President Lyndon Johnson declared that proper schooling could prevent poverty, not merely ameliorate the lives of the poor, echoing a claim made by Horace Mann more then a century before. A faith in the possibility of progress fueled both protest and federal policymaking in the 1960s.[48]

This attention to equality in the two decades following the *Brown* decision produced progress that looked rapid and impressive if compared with the glacial pace of equalization in previous decades. Consider the experience of blacks, for example. By the end of the 1960s, segregation of the races had been challenged as legal policy across the South, and mostly because of reassignment of students there, the proportion of African Americans in nearly *all-black* schools decreased from two-thirds to one-third from 1968 to 1980 (though most African Americans were still in *majority-black* schools because of residential segregation). In 1967 almost one-third of black high school students across the country dropped out before graduation, but by 1989 this rate had been cut in half and approximated the proportion of whites who quit school. In 1976, after a decade in which the proportion of blacks attending college had more than doubled, almost one-third of black high school graduates enrolled in some form of higher education, about the same rate as for

whites. During the 1980s the gap between whites and blacks on achievement tests in the National Assessment of Educational Progress declined
significantly.[49]

Equalization of opportunity proceeded slowly, however, if compared
not with the pace of change prior to *Brown* but with expectations
aroused by campaigns for social justice in education. Although Johnson's
War on Poverty relied heavily on schools as an agent of reform, actual
redistribution of educational resources lagged far behind need, for "savage inequalities" persisted, particularly in urban and rural schools that
enrolled the poor and people of color. Leaders of protest groups began
to question how much progress in fact had occurred. Did the poor and
people of color really have access to good schools? A spate of depressing
books with titles like *Our Children Are Dying* and *Death at an Early Age*
said no.[50]

Leaders of protest groups also began to redefine what they meant by
progress. Was open access to the mainstream really the solution? Black
activists argued that the schools that their children attended were per-
meated with institutional racism. Hispanics said that immigrant children
encountered cultural imperialism that denied their language and heritage.
Feminists complained that girls had to struggle against a male-dominated
and sexist institution. Perhaps some form of separatism and a pluralistic
definition of progress was needed to replace the older notion of equality
as sameness. Many blacks, dismayed by continuing resistance to desegregation and seeing that demographic changes in cities were making
"minorities" into majorities as white families migrated to the suburbs,
began to think that control of schools in their own communities offered
a more potent lever of advancement than desegregation. Some advocated
all-black and all-male Afrocentric schools. Although Title IX of the 1972
Education Amendments provided activists with legal mandates to secure
identical coeducation, they found it an uphill battle to counter institutional sexism. Instead of trying to equalize coeducational schools, a few
feminists argued for single-sex schools for girls. Some Hispanic leaders
thought that bilingual-bicultural education should aim at preserving
immigrant languages and heritages, not simply serve as a transition to the
English language and an Anglo-dominated curriculum.[51]

Questioning Progress

The pace of social and educational change after *Brown* was entirely too
rapid for many who had benefited most from the older educational order.
Many conservatives opposed busing to relieve racial isolation, affirmative

action, bilingual classes for the children of immigrants, the banning of prayer and Bible reading, the mainstreaming of children with special needs (especially those with emotional problems and learning disabilities), and the feminist agenda for gender equality.

The politics of education, once so predictable that political scientists called school districts "closed systems," erupted in conflicts between contending groups. As the media played up student unrest, violence, drugs, and overcrowded schools, images of blackboard jungles became etched in the public's consciousness. Controversies within the educational profession—strikes, collective bargaining, racial disputes—altered the stereotype of teachers as disinterested public servants. Formerly favored by the top-down governance of the administrative progressives, prosperous whites asked: Was all this turmoil *progress?*[52]

In the abstract, people may favor giving all children a fair chance, but at the same time they want *their* children to succeed in the competition for economic and social advantage. As David K. Cohen and Barbara Neufeld observe, "public schools are one of the few American institutions that try to take equality seriously. Yet their service in this cause has been ambiguous and frequently compromised, for the schools are a public institution oriented to equality in a society dominated by private institutions oriented to the market." When secondary schools succeed in retaining and graduating minorities and the poor, for example, they appear to lessen the advantage once enjoyed by middle-class whites. In an age when "accountability" is measured more and more by scores on standardized tests, "progress" in enrolling previously excluded youth in high schools and colleges seems to lead to "regress" in academic achievement.[53]

At the very time when the poor and people of color were beginning to gain access to more equal schooling, social scientists were starting to question the value of education. Would equality of resources produce equality of results? Was schooling a route out of poverty, a means of redistributing opportunity? While some wondered, "Does schooling make a difference?" others wrote that Americans were becoming "overeducated" for their prospects in the job market. It is perhaps no coincidence that such issues arose just when "nontraditional" students were gaining entry into colleges. Conflicts about the question "progress for whom?" helped to set the stage for public doubts about whether schooling was progressing or regressing. As policy talk about decline shaped the politics of school reform beginning in the mid-1970s, the equity gains of the previous generation were increasingly downplayed or identified as the source of problems.[54]

Public perceptions and expectations of schools, well charted by Gallup polls, have so changed in recent decades that an institution once secure in the public confidence has regressed in public esteem to a point where the 1930s, 1940s, or 1950s seem another world, to some even a golden age, despite the obvious gross inequities of those decades. Opinions about schools reflect a more general enchantment or disenchantment about institutions, both public and private. In 1946 the nine in ten who expressed satisfaction with public schools probably indicated the pride that attended victory in World War II. Just as schools then enjoyed the benefit of patriotic glory, they have suffered, along with most other institutions, a sharp decline of confidence in an era that has produced the Vietnam War, Watergate, Irangate, the ballooning deficit, the S&L scandal, and other debacles. In 1958, 58 percent of Americans said they trusted the government; by 1978, this figure had dropped to 19 percent. The decline of confidence in public schools needs to be juxtaposed to that larger growing cynicism about institutions in general and to a widespread worry of parents that their children's economic future is clouded.[55]

Today the notion of steady improvement of schools is widely rejected, people have no trouble identifying defects, and citizens lack trust in those who would lead in education. Yet all this needs to be seen in context: citizens have not lost their faith in the importance of schooling both for the individual and for society; the nearer the observer is to the schools, the better they look; and confidence in schools is higher than trust in most other institutions. In one poll people placed schools second only to churches as institutions serving the public interest, ahead (in descending order) of local government, state government, the courts, and the federal government. It appears that people trust most the institutions that are closest to hand.[56]

The Gallup polls provide many ways to assess whether people thought the schools were progressing or regressing. When asked whether "children today get a better—or worse—education than you did?" 61 percent of respondents said *better* in 1973 but only 41 percent said so in 1979. In 1969, 75 percent of respondents said they would like a child of theirs to "take up teaching in the public schools as a career" but only 45 percent wanted that in 1983. And in 1974, 48 percent of people polled gave an A or B grade to the schools, but in 1983 (shortly after *A Nation at Risk*) only 31 percent gave A or B grades.[57]

Overall, the polls indicate a fairly consistent and dramatic drop in public confidence in the schools in the 1970s and early 1980s—suggesting a deep-seated questioning of the traditional view of educational progress—and then a slight recovery of esteem for public education later in the 1980s. Public opinion, however, has been somewhat volatile, as indicated in an 11 percent rise from 1988 to 1990 in people who thought that the schools had gotten worse in the previous five years and a 13 percent rise from 1983 to 1988 in respondents who thought teaching a good career for their children.

Important differences appear when responses to the polls are broken down by group. The most disaffected people have been blacks and inner-city dwellers (the two categories overlap considerably, of course). In 1991, 42 percent of the national sample gave A or B ratings to the local public schools but only 28 percent of blacks and 27 percent of inner-city residents did so. In view of the high drop-out rates, violence, inadequate financing, discrimination, and high turnover of teachers and students in urban schools, such low ratings are hardly surprising. These schools *do* desperately need improvement, and local citizens know it.[58]

In general, however, familiarity with local schools seems to breed not contempt but respect. Parents who have children in public schools tend to rate public education much more highly than the average respondent, and those polled have a higher opinion of local schools than they do of schools in general. Parents give high ratings to the particular schools their children attend. Here are the percentages of different groups who gave the schools an A or B in 1985, for example:

Rating of nation's schools by all respondents	27
Rating of local schools by all respondents	43
Rating of local school district by parents	52
Parents' rating of school attended by oldest child	71

A more detailed picture of parents' opinions about the schools emerges when parents say whether the school their oldest child attended matches the definition of "an effective school" developed by educators. These are the percentages of people who said that the description fit the school very or fairly accurately:

Safe, orderly school environment	84
Student progress measured, reported	80
Staff has high expectations, demands achievement	74
Staff, parents agree on school goals	70
Principal helps teachers	54[59]

31

Although breakdowns of the polls show that the schools looked better up close and that parents (who presumably knew the most about public education) had fairly favorable views of their own children's education, the overall decline in confidence is nonetheless striking. Why did this occur? Because nonparents rate schools significantly lower than parents do, changing demographics help to explain why the public ratings of schools dropped so precipitously between 1974 and 1983. The proportion of adults who had children in school fell from 39 percent to 27 percent in those years. In addition, as we have said, the media often presented very negative images and accounts of schools, and there was a general decline in confidence in institutions of all kinds.[60]

The slide in the ratings also resulted, of course, from perceived faults in the schools. From 1969 onward parents had no trouble identifying defects (perhaps in part because they were themselves notably better educated than adults in the 1940s). Each year the pollsters asked people this open-ended question: "What do you think are the biggest problems with which the public schools of this community must deal?" There was remarkable consistency in the answers during the twenty years from 1969 to 1988. If one looks at the top five or six problems, "discipline" was first for sixteen of the twenty years and always included. About 25 percent listed it each year. Next in frequency and intensity, starting in 1976, was drugs. Integration/busing was always in the top five or six "problems" until 1982, when it disappeared from that select circle. Finding and keeping good teachers was almost always on the short list, as was finance. Curriculum/standards appeared in the top five each year beginning with 1976, when "back to basics" became a common plea in policy talk, and persisted in the 1980s as federal officials and commentators in the media reported declines in test scores.[61]

Parents shared the blame with teachers for what the public saw as a pervasive lack of respect for authority among the students. In 1984, 50 percent of the respondents gave teachers an A or B grade, but only 33 percent rated parents A or B for the way they raised their children (in another poll, 60 percent of teachers rated parents as fair or poor for the way they were "performing their roles" in the family, and in 1993 teachers said more help from parents was their number-one priority in improving education).[62]

Although citizens recognized that problems in schools resulted in large part from outside pathologies—violence, drugs, fragile families, poverty—the incessant din of criticism of schools profoundly discouraged educators. When teachers were asked why they became dissatisfied and left the profession, their top two grievances were "public attitudes toward schools" and "treatment of education by the media." In 1961 about 80 percent of public school teachers said that they "certainly" or "probably" would teach again. In 1981 teachers had more years of experience and substantially more professional preparation (half of them had masters' degrees) than their predecessors of twenty years before, but less than half indicated that they would have chosen to teach if they were starting over again.[63]

The public does not blame only educators or parents for the defects of public schools. Consider the percent of A and B ratings given in 1992 to national and state officials for their leadership in education:[64]

President Bush: 15

Congress: 7

Governors: 19

State legislators: 14

One reason people are cynical about national and state leaders is that they suspect that the goals these leaders have set are unrealistic, the sort of hyperbole they have come to expect from politicians.[65] The public trusts local institutions the most: 57 percent want district school boards to have more control of education (compared with 26 percent who want more federal control). One lesson for reformers is that decentralized approaches to change, drawing on local knowledge of problems and potential solutions, will be likely to capture public support. But this does not mean that citizens are interested only in their own backyard. In 1989, 57 percent of Gallup respondents said that they thought that inner-city schools had deteriorated, and 93 percent believed it important to improve them. That same year 83 percent said that extra funds should be allotted to schools in poorer communities.[66]

The Politics of Progress and Regress

In recent years, and particularly during the Reagan and Bush administrations, the older assumption that schools were growing better, generation by generation, has been replaced by a common assertion that public education is in decline. Indeed, the most influential call for school reform during the 1980s declared that the whole *nation* was "at risk" in international economic competition because of educational regress. "We have, in effect, been committing an act of unthinking, unilateral educational disarmament," the report declared. Many policymakers have narrowed the currency of educational success to one main measure—test scores—and reduced schooling to a means of economic competitiveness, both personal and national. *A Nation at Risk* was only one of many elite policy commissions of the 1980s that declared that faulty schooling was eroding the economy and that the remedy for both educational and economic decline was improving academic achievement.[67]

The historian Lawrence A. Cremin questions the assertion that bad schools are responsible for a deteriorating economy: "to contend that problems of international competitiveness can be solved by educational reform . . . is not merely utopian and millennialist, it is at best foolish and at worst a crass effort to direct attention away from those truly responsible for doing something about competitiveness and to lay the burden instead on the schools." We agree with his critique of this ideological smokescreen and think that much of the recent policy talk about schools has restricted discussion of educational purposes and obscured rather than clarified the most pressing problems, especially those of the schools that educate the quarter of American students who live in poverty. These children are indeed, in the phrase of the Carnegie Foundation for the Advancement of Teaching, "an imperiled generation."[68]

We believe that much of the evidence for alleged decline in public education is faulty. We raise doubts about the assertion that test scores have substantially declined, and that this, along with increasing "functional illiteracy" and "cultural illiteracy," proves that students are not learning as much as previous generations did. We think some uses of international test score comparisons are dubious. In questioning the validity of evidence and in denying the notion of a golden age in the past, we do not mean to urge complacency about the present state of academic achievement. Schools need thorough improvement, including better teaching of complex intellectual skills.

While federal officials were demonstrating on wall charts that test scores have been declining—a message that the media amplified and retailed to a public enamored of batting averages and statistical comparisons—a number of scholars questioned both the quality and the meaning of the evidence. Test results have varied, and some did indicate decline, especially during the late 1960s and early 1970s, but across the board they did not prove regress in academic achievement. Rather, the most valid measures for the purpose—the scores from the National Assessment of Educational Progress (NAEP)—attest to fairly level performance from 1970 to 1990.[69]

The most common and dramatic index of decline, and the one promi-
nently featured on the wall charts comparing the academic performance
of states, was the average score on the Scholastic Aptitude Test (SAT) of
the College Entrance Examination Board. The problems with using this
statistic are substantial: the SAT was designed to measure aptitude for
college, not achievement in general; it was not intended to be used to
compare states (the proportion of high school seniors sitting for the
voluntary test varied greatly by state, and the states having the largest
proportion of test takers not surprisingly scored the worst); and the
number of students taking the test has expanded greatly over the years
in question, especially among lower socioeconomic groups and minorities, whereas it had once been taken by small numbers of prosperous
students who ranked high academically. IQ scores, a more representative
measure of how "smart" students were than the voluntary SAT, rose in
the 1970s. On several of the College Board achievement tests, scores rose
between 1967 and 1976, the years of the largest reputed declines.[70]

Standardized achievement tests used by the schools are another kind
of evidence sometimes used to demonstrate decline. Carl F. Kaestle, an
expert on the history of literacy, estimates, however, that students performed about the same in reading in 1940 as in 1970 or 1983. To the
degree that there were test declines in the 1970s, they had bottomed out,
and test scores were on the rise in the early 1980s. Thus, Kaestle quips,
"instead of a 'rising tide of mediocrity,' [the National Commission on
Excellence in Education] should have proclaimed a rising tide of test
scores."[71]

In recent years critics have argued that the schools are turning out
illiterates in growing numbers. In 1982 Secretary of Education Terrell
Bell claimed that half the population was functionally illiterate. In 1993
a newspaper headline on a new report issued by the Department of
Education proclaimed, "Study Says Half of Adults in U.S. Can't Read or
Handle Arithmetic." On the tests used in this study, the prosperous did
far better than the poor, whites better than blacks, and those born in the
United States better than immigrants (the tests were in English). Clearly,
many people today lack the intellectual skills they need to cope with the
complex demands of modern economic and political life. Does this mean
that the long march to eradicate illiteracy has come to a standstill?[72]

The answer to that question depends on what is meant by literacy. In
1979 the Census reported that less than 1 percent of Americans regarded
themselves as illiterate. Such self-reports have been the traditional basis
of statistics on literacy, and these have indeed indicated steady progress.
When people speak of "functional literacy," however, they mean the

ability to meet educational requirements in adult life, and this definition is continually being racheted upward. Over time a literate person has been defined as a graduate of the third grade, or fifth grade, or even high school.[73]

In 1987 a best-selling author, E. D. Hirsch, Jr., popularized an even stricter version of literacy, the "cultural literacy" that specified what an educated person should know. Hirsch complained that "we cannot assume that young people today know things that were known in the past by almost every literate person in the culture."[74]

The idea of a decline from a golden age of common cultural knowledge appeals to many people, but when scholars summarize evidence on what students actually knew in the past—by trying to match test results in similar subjects across time and place—they typically discover little difference in students' knowledge—or "cultural literacy"—then and now. A *New York Times* quiz in American history given in the 1940s and repeated in 1976 found roughly the same (meager) results in both times.[75]

If studies of test scores and literacy over time cast doubt on the notions of a golden age and subsequent regress in the last generation, what about international comparisons of academic achievement? Doesn't everyone know that American students end up near the bottom on this score card? Not necessarily—American students scored second, after Finland, on a recent international reading test. It is true that American students have done worse than students of most other industrialized nations on many of the examinations, and that is a warning signal, but there are important defects in the score cards when they are used to compare nations.[76]

The most important problem is that the samples of people taking the tests have often been incomparable. In the early mathematics and science evaluations, notes analyst Iris C. Rotberg, the "assessments compared the average score of more than three-fourths of the age-group in the U.S. with the average of the top 9% of the students in West Germany, the top 13% in the Netherlands, and the top 45% in Sweden. It is not surprising that U.S. students did not do well in these comparisons." Another distortion comes from different patterns of curriculum in different countries; only a fifth of American students in twelfth-grade mathematics study calculus—which is on the examination—whereas in other nations almost all students do so. And finally, the motivation of the students taking the tests complicates comparisons; in some nations—Korea, for example—pupils are expected to uphold the national honor, whereas many U.S. youths regard the test as yet another boring set of blanks to pencil in on answer sheets.[77]

Most experts believe that the NAEP assessments provide the best current measures of stability or change over time in the academic achievement of pupils in American schools. These indicators offer a far more representative sampling than the SAT or international appraisals and test similar content over time. From 1970 to 1990 the NAEP tests showed some variation by age and subject, but overall the trend lines were fairly flat. Both minorities and children from impoverished families, however, improved their performance on the tests, significantly narrowing the gap between them and Caucasian and middle-class children and youth.[78]

Relatively stable results during those years can be interpreted in various ways, depending on the economic, political, or social context within which they are explained. One approach—favored by the Reagan and Bush administrations—juxtaposes rising per-pupil costs and "stagnant" NAEP achievement results (or worse, the dropping SAT scores) and concludes that Americans are not getting their money's worth from the public schools (especially in comparison with other nations). The logic of this contention can easily lead to the conclusion that public educators are lazy or incompetent, or both.[79]

Suppose, instead, that one juxtaposes relatively stable achievement, together with improving test scores among minorities and the poor, with changes from 1950 to the late 1980s in social conditions that could be expected to lower the academic performance of pupils: a tripling of the percentage of children living in single-parent families (which often means poverty for mothers and their children); an increase in teenage pregnancy; catastrophic rates of unemployment for young adult blacks; soaring arrest rates for youths under eighteen; and high rates of drug abuse and violence. We could go on to list many other challenges to educators: heavy TV watching, a sharp rise in the number of students with low proficiency in English, rising teenage part-time employment, the growing poverty of children, and gang activity in the schools.[80]

Would it not be reasonable to applaud the success of educators in holding learning steady in the face of so many impediments? David C. Berliner, an educational psychologist, argues that "the public school system of the United States has actually done remarkably well as it receives, instructs, and nurtures children who are poor, without health care, and from families and neighborhoods that barely function." For all their defects, schools may still be the most positive influence many children encounter, given the turbulence and dysfunction in many impoverished neighborhoods.[81]

Reflections

The ideologies of progress or regress in schooling are political constructs. Leaders have used them to mobilize and direct reform, persuading followers that they were joining a triumphal upward march to a utopian future or arresting a devastating backward slide. In both cases, people have held that their beliefs were supported by facts, but "progress" or "regress" in education lay much in the eye of the beholder. In periods both of supposed progress and supposed regress, the most severe problems were those in the bottom tier of schools that served the poor and people of color, yet these groups were all too often ignored.

The doctrines of progress and regress gave coherence and force to educational reform, though each imposed blinders on policymakers. The common school crusaders of the nineteenth century employed millennial rhetoric to persuade citizens to create a public system of schools. The administrative progressives were certain that their "scientific" plan for progress met the needs of all people. In both cases there were many people left behind by the apparent march of progress. When these outsiders mobilized in social movements to secure educational equality, they sometimes used a similar rhetoric of hope.

The prophets of regress, like the prophets of progress, have used hyperbole to motivate the public. Only if a complacent citizenry was aroused to danger would it act to rescue the schools and the economy. Those who were insistent about the regress of schooling often neglected the effect of talk of gloom and doom on the morale of teachers and on the commitment of parents to public education. The hyperbole of progress and decline more often obscured than illuminated the task of reform.

When critics say that schools have never been worse, advocates may be tempted to try to prove that they have never been better. We make neither claim. The public schools, for all their faults, remain one of our most stable and effective public institutions—indeed, given the increase in social pathologies in the society, educators have done far better in the last generation than might have been expected. At the same time, it is clear that the public schools need to do a better job of teaching students to think, not just in order to (supposedly) rescue an ailing economy but to serve broad civic purposes as well.[82]

As Cremin noted, the attempt in recent years to blame alleged educational decline for the nation's woes is irresponsible. The argument that poor schools produce poor workers and that improved schools would solve economic ills has two major defects: it scapegoats educators; and

38

it blurs understanding of a labor market in which the largest proportion of new jobs are relatively unskilled and millions of skilled workers are jobless.[83]

Robert Kuttner, a columnist for *Business Week,* observes that "improving the schools and reforming job training are . . . relatively easy. The hard part is improving the kinds of jobs that the economy offers." While business executives "bemoan the poor quality of applicants" for low-paying jobs, when they offer jobs at a decent wage, "qualified applicants line up at dawn. In circles where experts earnestly call for additional highly skilled workers, the dirty little secret is the scarcity of jobs that require more advanced skills." While "millions of college graduates are working at jobs that require only a high school diploma," he notes, the biggest demand for new workers arises in dead-end jobs like janitor, nurse's aide, and fast-food worker. The federal government has estimated that about half of the new jobs workers found in 1992 were part-time, temporary, and typically without good benefits. "The entire system has fragmented," observes Labor Secretary Robert B. Reich.[84]

It would take no great effort of the imagination to attribute U.S. economic ills to worldwide recession and to mismanagement on the part of business and government. Witness, for example, the effects of burgeoning deficits, deregulation of S&Ls that permitted a few knaves to squander billions of dollars of other people's savings, slowness to upgrade factories or to adopt new strategies of management, or undue attention to the short-term bottom line of profits. It may be convenient to blame the schools for lack of economic competitiveness, but this strategy distorts both educational and economic analysis. Good schools can play an important role in creating a just, prosperous, and democratic society, but they should not be scapegoats and are not panaceas.

The intensity of both optimism and pessimism about the state of schooling reflects a continuing conviction that good education is critical both for the individual and for the society. In recent years about four in five Americans have told pollsters that they think that schools are "extremely important" in shaping "one's future success." Likewise, almost nine in ten said that "developing the best educational system in the world" is "extremely important" to America's future. The issue at hand, then, is not to convince citizens that schooling is important; there is still a deep faith that better education is linked to societal progress. The key problem is to devise plausible policies for improvement of schooling that can command the support of a worried public and the commitment of the educators upon whom reform must rely.[85]

Thesis

39

2

Policy Cycles and

Institutional Trends

Two apparently contradictory notions about schools have persisted side by side over decades. One is the idea of steady educational evolution—seen usually as "progress"—that we examined in Chapter 1. The second is the claim that educational reforms have come in cycles, a repetitious process of "déjà vu all over again," in Yogi Berra's phrase. Can both notions be accurate, depending on what is meant in each case? We think so. If policy talk has cycled but institutional trends have not, then the two beliefs are consistent.[1]

It is plausible to interpret most major trends as a gradual and more or less linear evolution, not as a series of fitful bursts or cycling repetitions. Educators who argued that schooling was improving usually pointed to such trend lines to prove their case. The administrative progressives, for example, prided themselves on rising enrollment and graduation rates, longer school terms, larger school districts and school buildings, steadily growing per-pupil expenditures, and increasing differentiation of curriculum, programs, and school structures.

It is policy talk, we suggest, that cycles far more than practice in education. By *policy talk* we mean diagnoses of problems and advocacy of solutions. The next phase in educational reform, sometimes, is *policy action,* or the adoption of reforms—through state legislation, school board regulations, or decisions by other authorities. Actual *implementation* of planned change in schools, putting reforms into practice, is yet another stage, often much slower and more complex than the first two. Separating these stages in analysis helps in specifying just what is changing in what way and what remains relatively constant.[2]

Certain calls for change do seem to have recurred again and again in cyclical fashion, often within the lifetime of individual educators and sometimes at a dizzying pace, as in the last generation. Reformers, for example, have alternately proposed student-centered pedagogy or teacher-centered instruction, attention to academic or to practical knowledge, and centralized or decentralized governance of schools. In the early twentieth century, businessmen like Pierre S. DuPont were certain that centralization of control of urban schools and regulation by experts were the keys to school improvement, whereas today businessmen like Pete DuPont argue, to the contrary, that decentralization, deregulation, and choice will cure what is wrong with education.[3]

A common lament among veteran school people is that old reform proposals keep recycling as innovators reinvent them. Tired of what he regarded as a distracting merry-go-round of attempted changes in New York City, a skeptical teacher wrote a letter to the *New York Times* entitled "School Reform, Again? (Sigh)." Some reformers, in turn, fervently complain that rank-and-file educators sabotage innovation. Analysts wonder if it is true that nothing much actually changes in the schools. "The similarity between the current reform rhetoric and that of an earlier era is striking," write James W. Guthrie and Julia Koppich. "Is there educationally nothing new under the sun? Are reformers doomed repeatedly to reinvent the schooling wheel? When reform waves recede, do they leave behind them any structural or procedural residue upon which others can build?"[4]

The metaphor of the cycle induces a feeling of futility because the cycle returns to the same place, seemingly denying the possibility of progress. It also suggests irrationality: why can't people diagnose problems accurately and devise solutions that stick? We suggest that policy cycles and institutional trends need to be understood in relation to each other. Schools were changing all the time, as evidenced by trends, and this means that history did not strictly repeat itself. Each time that a familiar theme returned in reform discourse, the school context was different.[5]

We regard cycles of policy talk not as futile and irrational but as an inevitable result of conflicts of values and interests built into a democratic system of school governance and reflecting changing climates of public opinion. People are constantly criticizing and trying to improve public education. From time to time, worries about society and schooling so accumulate that widespread educational reform ensues. In such periods policy elites often take the lead in diagnosing problems and proposing educational solutions.[6]

Here we explore some connections between policy cycles and institutional trends. We examine the dynamics of policy talk, including the nature of reform periods; look at the high school as a case study of institutional trends in juxtaposition to curricular debate; and suggest some methods of tracking the uneven ways in which innovations were translated into institutional trends, asking why some reforms thrived and others faded.

Tracking Cycles of Policy Talk

What is one to make of cyclical policy talk about education? It would be a mistake to dismiss cycling discourse about school reform as "mere rhetoric" or as a cloak disguising reality (though sometimes talk about school reform has indeed deflected attention from more difficult and costly social and economic changes). It would be equally wrong to assume that policy talk gives an accurate portrayal of life in schools. Discourse and practice often sharply diverged. We treat the rhetoric of reform as a dramatic exchange in a persistent theater of aspiration and anxiety, for Americans have for over a century used debate over education as a potent means of defining the present and shaping the future. But the debates need constantly to be juxtaposed to the social and institutional history of schooling.[7]

Policy talk about schooling occurs all the time. It is not just the province of policy elites, though they have greater access to the media and government officials and tend to dominate discourse in periods of general reform. Conversations about the purposes and character of schooling take place in many contexts. Parents and children discuss education over the dinner table. Members of PTAs discuss how best to spend the funds they raise. A school board member drops by a coffee shop to discuss local school questions with the retired workers who gather there in the morning. After worship, members of a fundamentalist church discuss what to do about a program of sex education they dislike. Black activists gather to plan the formation of an all-male academy with an Afrocentric curriculum. School board members in a suburb facing fiscal cutbacks disagree about whether to cut advanced placement classes or special English classes for immigrant youth. In the school lounge, teachers debate tracking and the wisdom of mainstreaming children with special needs. Conversation about schools is one way that Americans make sense of their lives.[8]

Heavily influenced by their personal experience, aspirations, and anxieties, people have placed different weights on different purposes of education. Some degree of conflict over goals has been a constant, just as some degree of change in institutional practices has been a constant.

Americans have wanted schools to serve different and often contradictory purposes for their own children:

- to socialize them to be obedient, yet to teach them to be critical thinkers;

- to pass on the best academic knowledge that the past has to offer, yet also to teach marketable and practical skills;

- to cultivate cooperation, yet to teach students to compete with one another in school and later in life;

- to stress basic skills but also encourage creativity and higher-order thinking;

- to focus on the academic "basics" yet to permit a wide range of choice of courses.[9]

Citizens have also disagreed about the collective functions of schooling. They have wanted education to assimilate newcomers or to affirm ethnic diversity; to perpetuate traditional gender roles or to challenge them; to give equal opportunity to the poor or to preserve the advantages of a favored class. Advocates of one purpose or another work to influence—and often to balance—the different claims on the schools. Americans have a deep faith in educational remedies for societal ills but often disagree about what is wrong and how to fix it. This fuels policy talk about schools.

Under the decentralized system of governance in the United States, in which there is no national ministry of education to establish national agendas and adopt national policies, policy talk and policy action have taken place mostly at the state and local level. Periodically, however, public concern about public education has been so widespread and intense that it has become a national issue, publicized in the media, debated by politicians, and producing reform advocates who find mass audiences. Such eras have often been called reform periods. Usually some major societal change—typically called a "crisis"—triggers a burst of concern about schooling. These crises may be *domestic:* a dramatic rise in the immigration of people regarded as "strangers," different from those citizens already here; the "discovery" of poverty; the rise of protest movements such as civil rights; or a perceived mismatch between traditional values, such as the work ethic, and new conditions in the workplace. The perceived problems may also be *international:* the challenge of competition with other nations, military or economic or both. Often events trigger anxiety about the effectiveness of schooling—World War I and the fear of unassimilated immigrants, or Sputnik and the threat of Soviet military and technical supremacy in the Cold War.[10]

In such times of "crisis," when schools seem unable to accomplish the tasks thrust upon them, popular media focus attention on public education, and policy elites find bully pulpits for policy talk. Commentators in the media, muckrakers, leaders in business and unions, government officials, legislators, social reformers, activists in womens' associations, foundation officials, leaders of protest movements, and policymakers in education all starkly expose problems and confidently propose educational solutions. Then they pressure legislatures, school boards, and public school administrators to adopt their reforms. After that begins the slow and uncertain process of implementation. The journey from policy talk at the national and state levels to what occurs in schools and classrooms is long, often unpredictable, and complicated.[11]

Different concerns have driven reformers in these periods of educational reform. Does that mean that reform periods occurred in cycles that went from liberal to conservative and back again? Were they the products of contrasting political regimes?

Arthur M. Schlesinger, Jr., has developed an argument about recurring political cycles that can be easily applied to schooling. Schlesinger contends that in most democracies economic factors such as the level of unemployment and the amount of economic growth determine to a great degree who gets elected. Electoral changes produce public officials with conservative or liberal views concerning the role that government should play in the lives of citizens. Liberals are typically eager to use government to solve domestic social and economic problems, he argues, while conservatives are not.[12]

The rhetoric common in different periods of school reform might suggest parallels to Schlesinger's alternating conservative and liberal regimes in government. Watchwords shifted in different times from excellence to equality, efficiency to empathy, unity to pluralism—and then back again. In the politically conservative 1890s, 1950s, and 1980s, policy talk about schooling stressed a struggle for national survival in international competition—with the Germans (1890s), Soviets (1950s), and Japanese (1980s). In such periods, policy elites wanted to challenge the talented, stress the academic basics, and press for greater coherence and discipline in education. The editorials and articles on education in popular magazines of the 1950s, for example, might have been reprinted in the 1980s with scarcely any changes beyond changing the contestants from the Soviets to the Japanese. It is not surprising that conservative political climates favored a rhetoric of competition and quality, while liberal eras such as the 1930s and 1960s stressed an ideology of access and equality.[13]

It would simplify life for historians and make prediction easier for educational forecasters if in fact educational reform periods did simply cycle in accord with major political shifts. But the story is not so straightforward.

At any one time, the leaders of the Democratic and Republican parties have not differed very much in their views of education even if they had quite different policies in other domains. In this respect, American political parties have contrasted sharply with their counterparts in England and Germany, where Tories and Labourites, Social Democrats and Christian Democrats, have fought ideological and political battles over issues such as creating comprehensive high schools and attacking the class bias embedded in the structure of national systems of schooling. Neither the Democrats nor the Republicans proposed a new deal for public schools during the tumultuous Great Depression. Until the Reagan years—when philosophical conflicts in politics increased over social issues such as vouchers and school prayer—education planks in the platforms of the two parties were basically similar. In the United States, the educational policies of Republicans and Democrats have tended to move together in tandem over time, often following public opinion as much as leading it, the party lines on schooling rarely conflicting sharply in any one period.[14]

As for reforms in recent years, as Chester E. Finn, Jr., and Theodor Rebarber have observed, "it has been hard to discern many systematic philosophical differences between Democrats and Republicans with respect to schooling." Leaders in both parties have recently advocated decentralization of control while at the same time endorsing national standards. At Charlottesville, Virginia, in 1989, President George Bush and the fifty governors—Democrats and Republicans alike—called for national standards and decentralized decision making. At the state level in the 1980s, majorities in both parties endorsed tougher state graduation standards and assailed flabby curricula. Both have proposed laws to upgrade the qualifications of teachers and institute other means of professionalizing education. Both have approved "experimental schools" and lauded the attempt to identify the characteristics of "effective schools." Both claim to support equality of educational opportunity.[15]

During any one period of reform, then, both political parties have tended to agree about what is wrong with American public education and what to do about it. They may also have shared the same blinders

45

about what is *not* on the agenda for reform. This effort to achieve consensus in educational policy has a long history, going back to the common school crusaders of the nineteenth century and to the efforts of elite reformers of the Progressive era to "take the schools out of politics." Although there have sometimes been deep, even irreconcilable, conflicts between Americans over public education, the processes by which policy elites have sought to shape educational policy have stressed compromise.

The commissions on educational reform that stretch unbroken for over a century generally have pushed for unanimity, often achieved by common definitions of professional or public interest, horse-trading, avoidance of such intractable problems as racial discrimination, and agreement on what constituted the current "crisis." Although the content and recommendations of such commissions have varied widely over time, the pressure to conform at any one time to the contemporary conventional wisdom was constant. The same can generally be said of federal and state legislation on education that relied on compromise to achieve consensual goals. In a society that cherishes controlled conflict in economics, politics, religion, and sports, education has generally been a domain in which citizens should agree in principle at any one time on what was the common good.[16]

Although political processes and policy elites may have pressed for consensus, in every period of educational reform there were still underlying conflicts of value in the society. Thus it is difficult to cast any reform period as ideologically consistent. Historians dispute, for example, whether the so-called Progressive era was liberal or conservative in education. In the early twentieth century, reformers of different persuasions could agree that schooling had to be remodeled to deal with the results of industrialization, the growth of cities, and massive immigration. They could also agree about the defects of the school systems of the late nineteenth century. But they disagreed about vocational education— should educators sort out and train the "hand-minded" boys in separate schools or try to promote industrial democracy by infusing an understanding and appreciation of work in all pupils, as John Dewey urged? They saw immigration, too, in profoundly different ways—were all citizens "hyphenated Americans" in a pluralistic society, or should the newcomers be subjected to a hard-edged "Americanization"? Finally, there was—and is—disagreement about educational goals among reformers who span the spectrum of political philosophy. Radicals or liberals may favor a traditional academic curriculum as fervently as conservatives.[17]

There is another problem—the most serious one, in our view—with the proposition that there are alternating liberal and conservative cycles of school reform. Policy talk does cycle, but long-term trends follow their own different timetables, which do not necessarily correspond with what people are talking about.

There was far more actual racial desegregation in the South during the era of rhetorical "benign neglect" of race under President Richard Nixon, for example, than during the activist period that preceded his administration and set the agenda of racial justice. The timing of racial change did not neatly fit the election returns. It is asserted that "liberals like to throw money at educational problems," yet the percentage of per-pupil expenditures increased most sharply during the politically conservative decades of the 1920s and 1950s rather than in the liberal 1960s. A long-term institutional trend toward greater per-pupil expenditures counted for more than general shifts in political ideology.[18]

Another example of the delayed impact of reforms across periods is the implementation of innovative curricula in science and mathematics triggered in the Eisenhower years by the fear that the United States was falling behind the Soviet Union in training scientists and engineers. The heyday of curriculum development by leading scientists, retraining of teachers, and federal funding of these programs came in the early 1960s, an era when policy talk and public attention was shifting to assisting the "disadvantaged" and achieving social justice for dispossessed groups.[19]

Institutional developments in education may have an internal dynamic of their own only loosely connected with the periods of widespread and intense attention to schooling that we call periods of educational reform. Linking educational reform to reform periods may exaggerate the degree to which educational reform appears to be cyclical and underestimate the amount of gradual and evolutionary change. But policy talk does illuminate the concerns and hopes of policy elites and citizens as the schools and the society change. We turn now to a part of the educational system in which Americans took great pride and which they disputed about, incessantly: high schools.

The High School

Statistics on high schools over the last century reveal striking trends. The most salient of these—and the one that most sharply differentiates secondary schooling in the United States from that in other industrialized nations—is the rapid increase of students enrolled and graduating. In 1900 one in ten of those aged fourteen to seventeen was enrolled in high schools; in 1940 seven in ten were; and in 1980 nine in ten. There was also a sharp rise in the proportion of youth graduating from high school: in 1900 only 8 percent; 1920, 17 percent; 1940, 51 percent; 1960, 69 percent; and 1980, 71 percent.[20]

As the numbers of students have soared, high schools have grown steadily larger and more elaborate in structure and curriculum. In 1900, outside large cities, high schools were generally small; one-third of high school students had only one to three teachers, and two-thirds had one to ten teachers. Such small staffs could offer only a small set of courses. Sometimes what was called a "high school" was just another room added to a graded elementary school. By 1950 such modest institutions would have seemed as antique as the one-room country school. Over the years, as new functions appeared and became institutionalized, high schools grew much larger and more differentiated. They had administrative offices and secretaries, workshops and kitchens, nurses' rooms, gymnasiums, cafeterias, auditoriums, counseling offices, and athletic fields (where, in the eyes of many students, the most important work of the school took place).[21]

Such enlarged secondary schools offered a constantly expanding range of courses aimed at different groups of students. These courses were typically grouped into tracks, most commonly called college, commercial, vocational, and general. The percent of students taking academic subjects dropped in certain fields, such as Latin, German, foreign languages, algebra, and physics. Likewise, students in noncollege tracks were often offered watered-down "general mathematics" and "general science" instead of traditional academic courses. Schools added new fields, physical education in particular, required for all students. Enrollments rose sharply in the newer practical subjects, such as typing, industrial arts, and home economics. Especially during the 1960s, schools created large numbers of electives that substituted for regular sequences in fields such as English and social studies. Most statistics on enrollments actually underestimate the degree of differentiation, for the labels used are somewhat arbitrary and do not include a wide range of subjects. In 1890 the federal government gathered statistics on secondary course enrollments under just 9 headings, but in 1928 it listed 47. In 1973 high school principals reported over 2,100 names for courses, including such tempting subjects as "terminal mathematics."[22]

Why did American high schools come to enroll such a high proportion of the age group? A number of broad societal trends—economic, demographic, and attitudinal—sketch part of the answer. High schools cost a great deal, and the rapidly rising gross national product created resources needed to expand them. Increasing urbanization and consolidation of rural districts produced the concentration of population required for larger and more differentiated high schools. Demographic changes helped as well: a dropping birth rate (until the baby boom following World War II) made it easier for parents to support their children for more years in school and to defer their earnings. A high ratio of adults to children eased the general tax burden. Labor market demand for teenagers as full-time employees dropped, and the combination of child labor laws and compulsory attendance legislation pushed and pulled working-class youth into school. Increasingly, parents and teenagers came to believe that secondary schooling counted in getting a good job. In 1972 George Gallup asked parents an open-ended question about why they wanted their children to be educated. The top-ranked reply was "to get better jobs," and the third-ranked response was "to make more money."[23]

Within the context of these broad institutional and societal trend lines, a variety of policymakers and reformers debated the functions and character of the high school. People who have worked in high schools have never lacked advice about how to do their job better, both from professional experts and from lay people. Although the major trends of expanding access for students and increasing differentiation of programs and courses continued unabated, policy talk about what these developments meant varied sharply from period to period. When Americans repeatedly turned to secondary education to solve profound economic, social, and political problems, they differed in their diagnoses and their solutions.[24]

By the 1890s the schools had a new world on their doorstep. America was becoming the most powerful industrial nation on earth and aware of its rivalry with the fast-rising economy of Germany. Vast corporations were gaining power undreamed of only a decade or two earlier. Violent strikes were erupting. The cities were drawing millions of new recruits from the farms and immigrants from abroad. Social philosophers were wondering if institutions such as the family could continue their traditional functions of socializing the young.[25]

In 1893 the authors of the first major national report on the high school, the Committee of Ten, led by President Charles William Eliot of Harvard, wrote as if these transformations were largely irrelevant to their task. For the most part, the members of the Committee of Ten were college presidents and professors who wanted to bring some order to the hodgepodge of the high school curriculum and to standardize preparation for higher education. In the 1890s, David K. Cohen observes, "the high school curriculum had begun to resemble a species of academic jungle creeper, spreading thickly and quickly in many directions at once."[26]

The colleges lacked students, especially well-trained students. For their part, high school officials were confused and angered by the highly diverse admissions requirements of the colleges. The problem, then, was to devise sequences of courses in academic subjects that would provide coherent intellectual training. The members had no doubts about their qualifications for the task, for they were experts in education, which meant the imparting of knowledge and the development of intellectual powers.[27]

Eliot saw high schools as a chaotic nonsystem that taught a mishmash of academic fields and vocational subjects like bookkeeping. Most public high schools were in cities, which meant that the rural three-quarters of the student population had little opportunity to attend them. Even the city schools served only a tiny fraction of teenagers; only 3.5 percent of seventeen-year-olds graduated. Cities, eager to attract the children of the prosperous to public education, built high schools that often looked like Renaissance palaces or fortresses. Mezzotint pictures of the Appian Way and characters from the novels of Sir Walter Scott lined the walls, reminders that the "people's colleges" were a world apart from everyday life.[28]

Eliot and his colleagues recognized that high schools were mostly serving academically talented students whose parents could subsidize their secondary education. Even so, only a minority of graduates would go on to college, but Eliot and his colleagues believed that all secondary students would be best served by a rigorous academic training, one that offered them some choices of classical or modern subjects. The Committee of Ten saw the high school as an agency for honing intelligence for its own sake but also as an institution for preparing students for careers in a complex and interdependent society. In the next generation, however, secondary education would begin to become a mass institution with a significantly broader mission.[29]

A quarter-century later, in 1917, another group of reformers—mostly specialists in the new field of education—wrote a strikingly different position paper on the high school entitled *Cardinal Principles of Education.* Even in the 1890s, alternative conceptions of the high school had emerged to challenge the Committee of Ten. In 1895 John Dewey had observed that the high school "must, on the one hand, serve as a connecting link between the lower grades and the college, and it must, on the other, serve not as a steppingstone, but as a final stage" for those directly entering the life of the society. It was with this second group of students that the authors of the *Cardinal Principles* were chiefly concerned. In fact, from 1910 to 1950, policy talk about high schools was riveted on the question of how to teach the increasing numbers of students, many of whom were weary of school and many of whom, allegedly, were incapable of learning the traditional academic curriculum.[30]

Many educators welcomed the *Cardinal Principles* as an enthusiastic rationale and blueprint for "social efficiency," the broad socialization of youth for work, family life, good health, citizenship, ethical character, and worthy use of leisure. They believed that schools could and should sort out and prepare students differently for their various destinies in life as adults. This led naturally to the use of intelligence tests and tracking as a form of social engineering. Like Dewey, the advocates of social efficiency were concerned about the effects of industrialism on democracy, but they generally lacked Dewey's profound and subtle understanding of the processes that made democracy real both in the school and in the larger society.[31]

The *Cardinal Principles* reflected both the generalized anxieties of the Progressive era of the early twentieth century and the extraordinary faith of reformers that schooling could ameliorate social ills. They pointed to major changes in the larger society: the development of the factory system, which subdivided labor and eroded the apprentice system; the presumed atrophy of traditional socialization of children by parents in urban settings, where families no longer lived and worked in the same place; and the arrival of masses of immigrants unfamiliar with American institutions.

But high schools could solve these problems only if pupils stayed in school. Worried about the high drop-out rate of students, educators believed that the high school should offer different training for pupils of "widely varying capacities, aptitudes, social heredity, and destinies in life." The report stressed "activities," "democracy," and "efficiency," and seemed to relegate traditional academic subjects and pedagogy to the scrap heap. It provided an influential rationale for an expanded and differentiated curriculum that was supposedly adapted to the "new students" of the day.[32]

The reformers' starting point was not the academic disciplines—indeed, they did not even mention academic skills and knowledge in their first draft—but rather their analysis of the transformation of society, the changing character of the enlarged student body, scientific theories of education, and a new social role for the school. Underlying much of their program for change, as David K. Cohen has pointed out, was an assump-

51

tion that most of the new students entering high schools were uninterested in academic subjects and probably incapable of thriving in the traditional curriculum. The reformers multiplied courses and tracks, trying to provide something sufficiently practical and engaging to persuade adolescents to remain in school. This enthusiastic watering down of the curriculum culminated in the similar "life adjustment" program of the 1940s and became, Cohen quips, "a democracy of anti-intellectualism."[33]

Through all this planning for a socially engineered new society, educational leaders showed little appreciation of ethnic differences, for they were convinced of the appropriateness of their middle-class "American" values and unconscious of the bias in their supposedly universal science of education. Their confidence about that science, their optimism about the power of education to correct social ills, and their search for professional autonomy led them to intervene, with an arrogance that was typically unwitting, in the lives of people different from themselves. The facts of racism, of poverty, of gender bias, of alienating relationships in the new mass-production industries—these realities undermined the aspiration of making the high school an efficient engine of social progress.[34]

In the 1950s a new set of reformers echoed the Committee of Ten's call for an academically challenging curriculum. This group of critics—key spokespeople were academics, business executives, and even an admiral—reviled what they regarded as the lackluster and anti-academic character of the high schools of the 1950s. They blamed the progressive philosophy and practices of the *Cardinal Principles* and its ilk for the erosion of intellect and the trivialization of culture they saw as endemic in high schools. These critics decried a watered-down curriculum, poor discipline, incompetent teachers, neglect for the gifted, and a takeover of the schools by educationists who had no business being there, for they were not teaching anything.[35]

The attack grew more shrill with the deepening of the Cold War, as fears of external security in an unstable world intensified with the launching of Sputnik by the Soviets in 1957. The solution, these reformers contended, was to place much more emphasis on science, mathematics, foreign languages, and the other traditional liberal arts. They wanted rigor, a demanding adult world of discipline, and high cognitive expectations for the mostly dull and disorderly young of the nation. Turning back from "life adjustment" to the earlier goal of mental training, critics demanded a revamping of curricula, tougher selection and training of teachers, greater regimentation in the classroom, attention to patriotism, and fewer "frills." This attack put progressive educators on the defensive and fueled concern for the academic basics, but the high school remained an institution that continued to provide a highly differentiated course of study to its rapidly growing body of students.[36]

In the 1960s and early 1970s reforms came fast and furiously from many quarters as the high school became an arena for achieving new forms of equality, participation, ethnic self-determination, and liberation from bureaucratic controls. This was a time of massive change in society as well as in education. Blacks, Hispanics, women, the handicapped, and other groups too long ignored in educational policy demanded a say in shaping secondary education. Activists turned to the courts and to legislatures to bring about changes in school finance, in student rights, in segregated schooling, in rights for linguistic minorities, in entitlements for the handicapped, and in a host of other matters previously left to the professionals and their elite allies.[37]

The curriculum of the high school, responsive to new demands of activists and the needs of students who had once been outsiders, became much more heterogeneous. New courses in ethnic studies, bilingual and English as a second language programs for immigrant students, remedial courses for the "disadvantaged," storefront schools, and other innovations flourished for a time. As more actors with divergent views entered the fray of school politics, the older idea of governance by experts seemed anachronistic; everyone, and no one, was in charge.

In the late 1970s and 1980s most policy talk and policy action in education once again proceeded as a conscious reaction to the period that preceded it. As in the 1950s, reformers attacked the "mediocrity" of academic performance, the proliferation of elective courses, poor discipline, and lax teachers. Dozens of commissions, the most influential of which produced *A Nation at Risk,* focused on the "basics," hard work, and competition.[38]

Enormous changes have taken place over the past century in the American political economy, in the scope and purposes of the high school, in the clientele it has served, in the complexity of its bureaucratic structure, and in its relation to opportunity in adult life. Over that span of time numerous reformers have sought to interpret the educational implications of such changes in the society and the schools. At times such policy talk has seemed to cycle, but the institutional and social context was different in each case as a result of gradual but powerful institutional trends that were far more steady than the discourse that punctuated reform periods.

Despite the apparent cycling of discourse about the high school, underlying the disputes of each period, David Labaree has suggested, was a continuing tension between two competing elements of American ideology, one that "elevates liberty and promotes free markets" and the other that "elevates equality and promotes participatory politics." This dialectic between capitalistic markets and democratic politics generated two basic alternative prescriptions in policy, one stressing open access and adaptation of schooling to the students, the other stressing competition for favored place and selection for adult roles. The enduring but unsatisfactory compromise represented in school trends, he writes, was "a simple exchange—open access in return for differentiated instruction."[39]

The Relation of Policy Talk to Implementation

Assessing the actual impact on schools of proposals for reform requires careful detective work. The implementation of particular reforms takes time and moves in mysterious ways, more like a Slinky Toy than like a piston, as Susan Moore Johnson puts it. The connections between policy talk and institutional trends have been ambiguous and complicated.[40]

Major changes have sometimes taken place in relative silence. Minor changes, deliberate at first, have often become so common as to be taken for granted and not perceived as reforms. Some reforms have been heralded as panaceas but implemented only in token, symbolic ways. When some reformers have spoken, few heard or acted. By contrast, other policymakers have proposed changes that took hold rapidly, as in the case of vocational education in the 1920s or special education in the 1970s.

The widespread adoption of coeducation in the first half of the nineteenth century illustrates a major transformation that took place without much debate or even notice—in effect, a silent revolution. Only when most boys and girls were already learning together did the subject of coeducation become a hotly disputed topic, but by then the torrent of critical commentary had little effect on practice.[41]

Other innovations, once deliberate reforms, became so pervasive that they were no longer seen as reforms and thus disappeared from the scoreboard of successful changes. Indoor plumbing, central heating, and blackboards are examples. They may seem trivial, hardly worth the label of "reforms," yet not long ago they were high on the agenda of necessary innovations. Complaints about outdoor privies once peppered the reports of state superintendents; they ranked separate outhouses for boys and girls high on their agenda for reform. In their diaries, teachers lamented green firewood and inefficient fireplaces and longed for decent stoves. Today no one counts indoor toilets, separated by sex, and central heating as successful reforms, though they are all but universal. Blackboards, likewise, were once effusively praised as a magical new technology of learning. Today, having turned green, chalkboards exist in almost every classroom, but hardly anyone considers them to be what they are: highly successful innovations.[42]

Sometimes grandiose policy talk led to minimal, but symbolically important, implementation. Reformers with social agendas often approached the schools carrying blueprints for social salvation, ambitious plans to set society straight. Advocates of home economics claimed that it would lower the divorce rate and strengthen the family. Public health officials sought to combat venereal disease by sex education. Educators often complied with such outside demands to solve social problems by adopting the reform but then relegating it to the periphery of the school. School leaders could then say that they were doing their part to save the family and squelch sin and disease, but they did so without much modifying the core activities of the school.[43]

Three features of reform complicate tracking how policy talk became translated into institutional trends: the *time lag* between advocacy and implementation; the *uneven penetration of reforms* in the different sectors of public education; and the *different impact* of reforms on various social groups.

Reformers are often impatient about the time lag in educational reform because they operate on a schedule driven by election deadlines, career opportunities, the timing of foundation grants, the shifting attention of the public, or the desire of media people for the dramatic photo opportunity or sound bite. People with problems look for educational solutions; people with solutions look for problems; but implementation does not follow smoothly from the pairing of problems and solutions.

Once a reform is actually put into practice, people may have redefined what they want or may have agreed to ignore the problem the reform was designed to solve. Policy talk may follow the short cycles of politics or media attention, but implementation has a momentum and schedule of its own. The time lag in implementation of reforms helps to explain a phenomenon we discuss in Chapter 3, the goal displacements that occur when reforms such as the junior high school or kindergarten slowly find their way into school districts. By the time a reform becomes widespread, practitioners may have forgotten or altered its original purposes and promises.

American public schools have been and are extremely diverse. This helps explain the uneven penetration of reforms, though policy talk about educational reform sometimes conveniently neglects variability. The enthusiasts who pushed the panacea of instruction by films and radio in the 1930s, for example, did not bother to note that tens of thousands of rural schools had no electricity. Reforms have moved in and out of different school systems at different times and rates depending on the region of the country, the urban or rural character of the school, the wealth of the district, or the demographics of the community. Innovations in public education have flowed like the tides in San Francisco Bay, moving at different rates, still filling the long deep deltas while they are ebbing from shallow quadrants.[44]

Paul Mort found that different school systems installed new practices at quite different rates (rich suburban districts are substantially more innovative than poor rural ones). Some school systems—they are often called "lighthouse" districts—stand out as leaders in adopting new ideas. Others adopt reforms only when they have fallen out of fashion elsewhere. A few never even hear of the innovations.[45]

American educators may have used similar professional language and may have aspired to run modern schools, but the districts they staffed and the communities they served spanned an enormous spectrum of privilege and poverty. The gulf between rich and poor districts was even greater in the past, before federal aid and state finance equalization, than it is today. During the Great Depression the African American children in the dilapidated Dine Hollow School in the Deep South had no desks or books and went home to shacks and a bit of cornpone; the well-fed and well-dressed pupils in Shaker Heights, a suburb of Cleveland, left their prosperous families to attend an elegant high school that had a cafeteria, a swimming pool, a well-equipped medical facility, and a library of twelve thousand books. They might have been living in different countries.[46]

Even within the same communities, educational reforms influenced different groups in different ways, especially blacks and whites in the South. The peaks and nadirs of educational reform for blacks are quite different from those for whites. After the Civil War, Reconstruction was a period of great progress for blacks, whereas reform in the Progressive era in the South was designed primarily for whites, who disenfranchised blacks and systematically denied them an equal education. One group's progress underscored another's comparative disadvantage, as when southern counties found funds to bus whites to their segregated schools but not blacks to theirs. Even where such explicit discrimination did not occur, reforms have often been aimed at particular groups: advanced placement classes for the academic elite, bilingual programs for immigrants, special classes for the disabled, special classes for pupils who posed discipline problems, vocational training for the "hand-minded." Educational reforms bore many faces and reached different groups in different ways.[47]

Were any kinds of reforms implemented smoothly? What kinds lasted long enough to register as institutional trends?

Reforms that were *structural add-ons* generally did not disturb the standard operating procedures of schools, and this noninterference enhanced their chances of lasting. As accretions to the central core of instruction, they did not demand fundamental change in the behavior of teachers. If educators added a wing to the high school where students learned typing or mechanical drawing or built a gym for physical education, these innovations did not disturb what happened in English or mathematics classes. Indeed, as a result of the power of pedagogical custom, teaching in new subjects such as commercial education frequently came to resemble instruction in traditional fields.[48]

The add-on reforms that were adopted and lasted tended to be *noncontroversial* to the lay people on school boards or in legislatures. They did not exceed the pedagogical speed limit by directly challenging the public's notions of what a "real school" ought to be doing (an issue we pursue further in Chapter 4). And in most communities educators sought to adapt change to local circumstances and values.

Programs were likely to persist if they produced *influential constituencies* interested in seeing them continue. Partly this was a matter of jobs. People employed in new programs—teachers of driver education or vocational classes, counselors, school nurses, workers in school cafeterias—often campaigned to have their programs retained and expanded. Some programs won constituents outside the schools; for example, insurance companies and car dealers supported driver education, and some business people lobbied for vocational training.[49]

Reforms also tended to persist if they were *required by law and easily monitored*. A legal mandate did not guarantee implementation, of course—many laws were discreetly ignored. But laws and regulations often contained provisions for enforcement and sometimes allocated new money to pay for new programs. In vocational education, for example, both federal and state agencies issued quite specific rules and checked on compliance before re-funding programs. As the most effective school lobby in state capitols, educators often were able to persuade legislators or state officials to freeze favored reforms into law or state regulations.[50]

Reforms proposed and implemented by school administrators and teachers themselves to make their work easier or more efficient or to improve their professional status were likely to stick better than innovations pushed by outsiders. Teachers generally supported increased certification requirements, for example, because they supposedly upgraded the status and pay of the profession by restricting entry into the occupation. Educational leaders sought to eliminate one-room schools because they believed small rural schools were inefficient and unprofessional workplaces. Superintendents trained in the new university administration programs prided themselves on expanding school systems according to an up-to-date professional model. Such administrators made reputations by becoming specialists in improving the "school plant" or introducing standardized testing programs or spreading other reforms. Once established as part of the structure of schooling, innovations might be criticized, as were certification and graded classrooms and standardized testing, but rarely were they abolished.[51]

Whether policy talk led to implementation depended much on who was talking. Many reformers went unheard—especially outsiders without clout. But when recognized leaders inside education—such as the professors and superintendents who used to be called the "educational trust"—spoke about policy, other professionals were apt to listen and to adopt the reforms they proposed. These insider elites developed whole templates of "scientific" reforms as the blueprint for "progress," as we discussed in Chapter 1. Their policy talk shaped a broad professional agenda for reform. Up-to-date leaders could thus ride trends of pedagogical fashion while attacking as old fogies the educators who bucked them. In the 1920s, for example, hype about the virtues of intelligence tests and tracking of students into differentiated courses of study led to rapid adoption of these practices.[52]

Reflections

We see the history of public school reform neither as an ineluctable evolution—progressive or otherwise—nor as a set of fitful repetitions. Rather, we see it as an interaction of long-term institutional trends, transitions in society, and policy talk. Proposals to change schools, and through them society, do appear to cycle, sometimes with new labels but basically with recurrent messages. The feeling of déjà vu in school reform is so common—and so annoying to many school veterans and frustrating to disillusioned innovators—that it should not be dismissed as illusory.

As we understand cycles of policy talk, they are not futile or irrational, even though they may seem so to teachers inundated by frequent waves of reform or to people who believe that they have the definitive answer to school problems. Cycles of reform talk and action result, we believe, from the conflicts of values and interests that are intrinsic to public schooling. The rhetoric of reform has reflected the tensions between democratic politics, with its insistence on access and equality, and the structuring of opportunity in a competitive market economy.

The compromises reached in successive periods of educational reform have often papered over those basic conflicts in an effort to reach consensus. Policy elites have tried to persuade the public that their definition of problems and proposed solutions were authoritative. Significant segments of the democratic polity have not been heard in the process, and sometimes even teachers were barely consulted about the changes that they were expected to bring about. What was not on the agenda of reform was often as important as what was debated.

Policy elites have often dominated discussion of reform, especially when concern about education grew intense and widespread at the national level. But conversation about the purposes and character of schooling is not—and should not be—a matter for experts or visible leaders only. It is an essential way for citizens to exercise their trusteeship in preserving what is valuable in a common institution and correcting what is not.

3

How Schools

Change Reforms

How will schools change the anti-bullying bill? How will the logistics play or not play out? Do schools have to authorize its implementation? alter its

People usually ask: how do reforms change schools? Here we examine the reverse: how schools change reforms. Some innovations seem to die on contact with the institutional reality of the school. It is the rare reform that performs and persists precisely according to plan. Even long-lasting reforms are not static but evolve in ways often not foreseen by their proponents.[1]

Although policymakers may lament that their plans become transformed in practice, another view is equally plausible. Goals and plans might be construed as hypotheses; alterations of policies in practice might then be expected as institutional facts of life. If policymakers anticipate and encourage adaptations of their plans, they can design reforms to produce hybrids that are blends of the new and the old, the cosmopolitan and the local.[2]

When reforms do not work out in practice as planned, people tend to give different explanations. Some blame educators. Technocrats may assume that their policies are fine but believe that educators lack the competence—or, more politely, capacity—to implement plans as they were intended. Some social reformers eager to use schools to ameliorate society accuse educators of coopting the reforms, distorting them, or turning them to their own benefit. This kind of goal displacement suggests corruption of a noble dream by bureaucrats who consult narrow institutional interests, or their own self-interest, rather than the public good.[3]

Not surprisingly, practitioners typically arrive at a quite different interpretation: elite policymakers rarely know what schools really need and propose reforms that could never work as planned. Hence the best way

Is this anti-bullying bill what we really need?

to live with new mandates from distant legislators and administrative agencies is to adapt innovations to local circumstance, or comply in minimal ways, or sabotage unwanted reforms. And skeptical educators suspect that some reforms were never intended to work. Symbolic gestures, and the overpromising that accompanies them, have at times interested policymakers more than substance.[4]

Producing sonorous rhetoric about solving social problems through education is easier than carrying out fundamental social change through schooling. Some advocates of home economics, as we mentioned, argued that it would halt the rise in divorce, buttress the family, and attract women back to traditional roles. In practice, young women learned to make white sauce and stitch seams, while divorce continued to increase, family patterns to change, and women to enter the public sphere. Often reforms as implemented only chipped away at the obdurate problems they were expected to solve.[5]

Since schools have almost always changed reforms, it is useful to ask what people mean when they talk of "success" or "failure" in school reform. Consider three criteria: fidelity to the original design; effectiveness in meeting preset outcomes; and longevity.

In one model of rational decision making in school reform, experts analyze problems, devise solutions, and then see if the reform is carried out according to plan. Does implementation get high marks for fidelity? The answer may be "yes," yet the benefit of the reform may be questionable. An illustration is one of James Bryant Conant's major prescriptions in 1959 for a good high school. Believing that there were too many small high schools, Conant called for graduating classes of at least one hundred students. In the 1960s educational leaders and state legislators worked hard to consolidate small rural secondary schools and to build large high schools in suburbs and cities. They succeeded in weeding out most very small high schools. Was this, then, a "successful" reform? In terms of Conant's plan, yes. But a generation after Conant's report, close observers of secondary education were complaining that large high schools produced feelings of alienation and anonymity among students and isolation among staff. Fidelity to plan without continuing attention to unintended by-products masks mistakes.[6]

A second measure of "success" is effectiveness in meeting preset outcomes. Accountability in terms of improved test scores has been common during the last generation. When reforms fail to produce predicted results, pessimism often ensues. In the 1970s two scholars surveyed a varied set of educational experiments designed to reveal which innovations had achieved superior predetermined goals. When they

61

found that none had, they subtitled their book *Should We Give Up or Try Harder?* A problem with defining "success" as meeting predetermined goals—say, raising the IQs of little children through Head Start—is that some of the most significant dimensions of actual programs, both positive and negative, may not be captured by the measured outcomes.[7]

If reformers attend only to fidelity to plan and to achievement of predetermined goals, they may ignore unintended consequences. Such unforeseen results are typically thought to be perverse. Albert O. Hirschman points out that "'unintended' easily slides over to 'undesired' and from there to 'undesirable.'" A shorthand way to express this notion of perverse results, he writes, is "*everything backfires.*" In the 1980s, for example, state laws mandating minimum competency testing put pressure on teachers to teach students to take the test and to stress the "basics" by using "drill-and-kill" rote methods. An unintended result was inattention to complex thinking skills and to the challenge of fitting the curriculum to the cultural backgrounds of the students.[8]

But not all unforeseen consequences are unfortunate. Legislators passed laws in the 1980s requiring all students—boys and girls alike—to take more courses in mathematics and science. Policymakers were seeking to strengthen the academic basics; the laws did not explicitly promote gender equity. But a positive unintended consequence was that girls took fewer traditionally "female" electives and became better prepared to enter scientific and technical fields if they so chose. Previously, lack of such a background had narrowed career options for many young women.[9]

How useful is longevity as a criterion of "success" in school reform? Assessing how long a reform lasted turns out to be a difficult task. An innovation may have changed so much over time that it bears little resemblance to the initial reform, even though it continues to have the same name and hence to be thought of as having a long life. One example is the "continuation school," which once was a part-time institution for employed youth, but which became a school of last resort for students unsuccessful or disruptive in regular high schools. By contrast, some reforms have faded to the point where few people even recognize their names, but some of their key practices became embedded in schools. The Dalton Plan of individualized study, discussed in the next chapter, illustrates this pattern of longevity.[10]

In addition, longevity does not necessarily equate with benefits to students. Some long-lived reforms created new problems. The graded school, with its annual assessments for promotion, generated new opportunities for failure not present in the nongraded schools that preceded them, such as the rural one-room school. Likewise, IQ testing and ability grouping have met the test of longevity, but critics argue that these reforms have fostered discrimination against students from poor families. By contrast, some acclaimed reforms, such as those sponsored by the Progressive Education Association in the Eight-Year Study in the 1930s, had a short (but happy) life before curriculum and pedagogy returned to traditional patterns. Even though such reforms may have faded over time, at their peak they energized both teachers and students.[11]

As the difficulty of judging the "success" of a reform illustrates, the story of how schools have changed reforms is very complex. We find it useful to think of reform plans not as clearly mandated policies but as concepts to be evaluated on the basis of their practical effects, positive and negative, and then reframed accordingly. This is what the pragmatist philosopher John Dewey proposed and practiced. When he found that progressive educators who purported to be his "disciples" were downplaying the importance of coherent subject matter and condoning ill-mannered behavior of students, he reformulated his progressive principles. Aims and practices, he thought, should be in continuous interaction.[12]

In this chapter we use case studies to explore how schools have changed reforms. First, we look at the history of two major structural and pedagogical reforms, the kindergarten and the junior high school. Here we examine the reformers' goals and the ways in which the two reforms, originally intended to be distinctive educational niches, came under institutional pressure to adapt to the rest of the system. In part, the kindergarten and junior high school did become assimilated to established practices, but they also helped to introduce new ways of thinking and new practices.

Next, we look at interactions of reforms with each other. For the most part, reforms tend to accumulate, one on top of another, adding to rather than simply replacing what went before. Reformers in New York City, for example, have sought in successive periods to improve education by changing the governance of the schools. But whether they wanted to centralize or decentralize control, reformers could not start with a clean political and institutional slate. Each governance reform built on layers of previous changes going back more than a century. Under such circumstances, the complexity of running a vast system makes "school governance" sound like an oxymoron.

We also discuss what happens when different kinds of instructional reforms interact in rapid succession, as has occurred in the last decade. Practitioners have faced a surge of new laws, regulations, and reform ideas coming on top of a system of curriculum and instruction that was already many layers deep in partially assimilated innovations. Often the messages sent by policy elites in any one year's laws or regulations have conflicted with what went before or came after, creating inconsistency and confusion.

If the aims of reforms seem vague, contradictory, or unattainable, educators often respond by turning reforms into something they have already learned how to do. Policy means often are inconsistent with policy goals. The talk this year may be about "excellence," but if teachers respond by coaching students for minimum competency tests—a tactic they used to satisfy last year's critics—the results are counterproductive.[13]

Finally, agreeing with Lee Shulman that teachers have their own "wisdom of practice," we explore ways in which pride of place in shaping school reform need not go mostly to policy elites. Instead, we suggest, reforms can be deliberately designed to be hybridized to fit local circumstances. In this way, educators can adapt innovations to the ongoing lives of their schools and seek to create coherence where it counts the most—in classroom instruction.[14]

Interactions of Reforms with Schools

The reformers who created kindergartens and junior high schools believed that they should be distinctive institutions, antidotes to the faults of public schools rather than simply new rungs on the existing ladder of grades in elementary and high schools. At the same time, however, these institutional innovations were lodged in public school systems whose practices slowly altered the original designs. Not surprisingly, both the kindergarten and the junior high school came to resemble and serve the primary grades and the high school into which their graduates moved. Influences did not move in one direction only, however; both kindergartens and junior high schools also shaped philosophy and practice in the school systems that surrounded them.

The Kindergarten

As Barbara Beatty observes, nineteenth-century pioneers in the kindergarten movement "were highly critical of the traditional school curriculum." Elizabeth Peabody, an advocate of the "children's garden," believed that the graded public school treated students as automata, learning machines, rather than as spontaneous, curious, active, impressionable children. She urged kindergartners (the term then used to

64

describe teachers, not students) to treat their pupils as "children in society . . . a commonwealth or republic of children," to be contrasted "in every particular, with the old-fashioned school, which is an absolute monarchy." Children, she believed, achieved social and intellectual development through organized games, music, gardening, art work, socialized play, and gymnastics—not by sitting silently at bolted-down desks until called on to do rote recitations.[15]

Reformers expected the kindergarten to be a cure for urban social evils as well as a model of education for young children. German refugees from the Revolution of 1848 had founded the early American kindergartens (based on the theories of Friedrich Froebel). Peabody started the first English-speaking kindergarten in Boston in 1860. In the next two decades private kindergartens serving the middle and upper classes spread rapidly across the East and Midwest. Philanthropists soon concluded that the institution would also benefit the children of the urban poor as a kind of "preventive charity" to counteract the pauperism and vice that awaited them otherwise.[16]

Elite women in large cities across the nation embraced kindergarten work as a social mission of child saving. In private kindergartens in slum neighborhoods the teachers went beyond the standard Froebelian curriculum and fed the pupils breakfast, washed them, and attended to their health. They reached out to create a bridge between home and school. Often the middle-class, native-born teachers in these charity, or "free," kindergartens spent their afternoons visiting mothers in crowded tenements to instruct them in the ABCs of cleanliness, citizenship, and proper child-raising. An elementary school teacher in San Francisco wrote her superintendent in 1892 about the wonderful results of kindergarten training. As the children pour into kindergartens from crowded tenements, she said, "I hear no more . . . the wild phrases of the Barbary Coast or the mule-drivers' oaths. The little ones are clean, self-respecting, eager for knowledge." They learn "to respect older people, to be honest, and to tell the truth. It is a rare thing now to find a child that does not know it is wrong to steal. If you meet one, you may be sure that he has never been to kindergarten."[17]

Kindergartens proved to be popular with parents, social reformers, settlement house workers, women's groups, unions, foundations, experts in "child study," and philanthropists. When it became apparent that private charity schools could not keep up with the demand from parents, these groups lobbied to include kindergartens as a regular part of the public school systems (especially in large cities). Already hard pressed to provide enough elementary classrooms for the onrush of immigrant children, school boards and school administrators were often ambivalent about the expense of adding a new level of schooling.[18]

Some public educators were enthusiastic about what kindergartens could do for the public schools and for American society. As superintendent of the St. Louis public schools in the 1870s, William T. Harris persuaded his board to support kindergartens under the leadership of Susan Blow. In 1903, as U.S. Commissioner of Education, he wrote that "the kindergarten is really essential for the salvation of the children of the slums, that is to say, the children of the three weakling classes of society." The offspring of these "weaklings"—the thriftless, the immoral, and the unintelligent—can be redeemed by the "powerful system of nurture" of the kindergarten that teaches self-respect, perseverance, moral ideals, and industry. In this version, the kindergarten provided compensatory socialization.[19]

In 1900 only about 7 percent of five-year-olds were enrolled in kindergartens, in 1920, 20 percent, in 1950, 38 percent, and by 1970, 60 percent. The public "child garden," then, was no modest experiment. Reformers claimed that it could rescue children and their parents from poverty and crime, turn immigrants into Americans, solve "the race problem," and tame the unruly cities. But more: some educators also believed that the kindergarten, with its aim of adapting education to children rather than children to schooling, would soften, even melt, the hard-edged uniform curriculum and instruction that had become standard in the graded elementary school.[20]

As kindergartens became incorporated into the system, what happened to their initial goals, what alterations appeared both in the kindergartens and the primary grades? When public sponsorship took the place of private, an early casualty was the outreach program that sent kindergarten teachers into the homes of the pupils. In the charity schools, teachers typically taught during the morning and had the afternoons free to visit mothers. In the public schools, they typically had to teach double sessions, one in the morning and one in the afternoon, mostly because of large enrollments and the high cost of half-day, small classes (recall the common complaint of school superintendents that kindergartens cost too much). Kindergarten teachers still tried to link home and school for the children, in part by providing a quasi-motherly and homelike atmosphere in school, but the new schedule made it virtually impossible to spend much time in the homes of their pupils. Even so, one kindergarten teacher said that "the home and the kindergarten are sometimes felt to be more closely united than the kindergarten and the next grade of the school."[21]

As Marvin Lazerson has shown, the adaptation of the kindergarten to the primary grades became a controversial issue: was it to remain distinctive in philosophy and pedagogy, a world unto itself, or was it to have as its main task the preparation of five-year-olds for the first grade? Once the kindergarten had been folded into the public school system, educators had a range of options in the mutual adjustment of the newcomer and the existing system: to preserve the kindergarten as a somewhat exotic niche; to remake the primary grades to resemble the kindergarten; to pattern the kindergarten more on the tasks and philosophy of the grades and to merge the supervision and standards of training of the teachers in kindergartens and grades 1–3; to create a connecting class between kindergarten and first grade—a boot camp of sorts—to prepare children for the rigors of first grade; or some combination of these. In fact, all these adaptations occurred in practice as kindergartens became assimilated into the institutional structure of public education.[22]

In a number of cities, public schools took over the old charity kindergartens and retained their supervisors and teachers, providing some continuity with previous practice, at least in the early years of public control and support. The supervisors treasured the special character of the kindergarten. In hiring teachers, they said, they sought "sympathy, understanding, seeing from the child's standpoint," and "play spirit," whereas they wanted elementary teachers who were "trained to consider and deal with the child as a *learning* being, and not primarily as a feeling, doing individual." To some degree the "child gardeners" stressed intrinsic more than instrumental values, play more than drill, individual creativity more than group socialization. But they were also concerned with shaping regular habits, sharpening skills, and reforming society by improving the character of the young—goals that were also prominent in primary school education.[23]

What did first-grade teachers think about the effects of the kindergarten on their pupils? Surveys reported mixed opinions. Some respondents said that kindergarten graduates were "more alert and observant" than those who did not attend kindergarten, and found that they "have learned to be punctual and regular in attendance, to follow directions, to wait on themselves in the dressing rooms and lavatories," and that they "have been taught to play fairly and to be conscientious and helpful in the schoolroom." Others complained that the kindergarten gave children wrong ideas about what school was all about: pupils didn't know how to pay attention, to be silent, and to work steadily. They were too dependent and expected more help than primary school teachers could provide in their crowded classrooms. One summed up the problem as "the flabby kindergarten intellect of the kindergarten child." This mix of praise and blame about kindergarten-trained children entering elementary school revealed deep differences in teachers' beliefs about how to educate children.[24]

City superintendents and school boards, eager to create more systematic bureaucracies, sought ways to align the kindergarten with the primary grades. One strategy was to integrate the supervision of the kindergartens and the primary grades by placing both under the direction of elementary principals and a general supervisor of primary grades. This move eliminated the practice, common in the first generation when private schools were folded into the public system, of retaining the former private directors as supervisors who reported directly to the superintendent. Second, school districts began to construct written curricula that tied together kindergarten and first grade by providing for more silent, independent work and reading readiness in the kindergarten. Partly as a result, observers found that teacher-centered instruction was the dominant pattern in both kindergartens and primary grades. Third, school districts began to require kindergarten teachers to obtain training and certification comparable to that of elementary school teachers. Accordingly, many kindergarten and primary teachers were exposed to similar ideas in their education classes, and some taught alternately in the primary grades and kindergarten.[25]

Influenced by the newly emerging science of psychology, kindergarten leaders began to encourage teachers to treat the grades K–3 as a continuous developmental sequence. This approach downplayed the symbolism and specific pedagogical techniques of the German philosopher Froebel. From the psychologist G. Stanley Hall kindergarten leaders borrowed methods of systematic observation of children, and they heeded John Dewey's advice to stress active learning in social groups. They used the terminology and concepts of behavioral psychology in constructing a "conduct curriculum" (they talked of good "habits" rather than "character," but the resemblance to nineteenth-century moral training was still strong). They gave IQ and readiness tests to kindergarten children to sort them into ability groups and to determine if they were prepared to enter the first grade. Studies showed that kindergarten graduates progressed faster in the grades and won higher scores on standardized mental and achievement tests than nonkindergarten children, and this seemed clear proof of the success of the reform. The National Society for the Study of Education devoted two yearbooks to the correlation of the kindergarten and the elementary school, showing that the issue was of general interest among scholars in education.[26]

In many ways, then, both in theory and in practice, public school kindergartens became assimilated to the primary grades, a departure from the earlier praise of the kindergarten as an antidote to the traditional school. When the kindergarten became institutionalized, the original claim of reformers—that it would redeem society through compensatory socialization of the misfits—was diluted if not forgotten. A much more modest bureaucratic rationale became central: that the kindergarten would prepare five-year-olds for first grade in a scientifically determined developmental way. Some of the features that had made the kindergarten exotic were slowly trimmed away or changed to fit the institutional character of the elementary school.[27]

But as progressive education spread to more and more public elementary schools in the twentieth century, the primary grades came more and more to resemble kindergartens. Observers found many elementary schools where bolted-down desks were being replaced by small movable tables and chairs, teachers were using group games and play as an adjunct to learning, children were building with blocks or hammering or sewing, art and music were becoming more central in the curriculum, instruction was relying more on concrete objects and less on abstractions, and pupils were freer to move about the classroom and to talk to each other. Institutional hybrids, kindergartens preserved much that had once made them distinctive and in addition helped to reshape the primary grades. The child's garden influenced the environment in which it grew.[28]

The Junior High School

Like the kindergarten pioneers, the founders of junior high schools were profoundly critical of the public school system. The advocates of junior high schools considered young adolescents to be a group at risk. So defective was education in the upper grades of the urban elementary schools that a new institution must be created for that age group.

In 1900 most large school districts had eight elementary grades and four high school grades. The attrition of pupils was horrendous. In 1909 a researcher reported that "the general tendency of American cities is to carry all of their children through the fifth grade, to take one-half of them to the eighth grade and one in ten through high school." Something must be terribly wrong, thought reformers, if half the students don't even reach the eighth grade and if the high school remains an elitist institution.[29]

The rigidity and narrow academic emphasis of the educational structure was a major cause of this problem, reformers asserted. All children were expected to ascend the ladder of the graded classrooms, studying the same subjects in the same ways and taking exams for promotion from rung to rung. Many were left behind each year. "Retarded" pupils aged ten to fifteen years, many of them poor and from immigrant families, crowded the upper grades of elementary schools, shamed and bored as individuals and collectively producing what educators called "waste"—a social sin in an age that glorified "social efficiency." When young people dropped out or were pushed out, those who did find work usually ended up in repetitive, mind-numbing, dead-end jobs. Academically talented students experienced another kind of "waste" as they marked time academically in the standard pace of the grades until they qualified for entrance to high school.[30]

Educational reformers—supported by social investigators, developmental psychologists, and foes of child labor—designed the junior high school as a structural and pedagogical solution to the problems of attrition and "waste." There should be only six elementary grades, they believed, and a new kind of school, the junior high school, should be inserted in place of grades seven to eight or nine. In some cases the junior high school was housed in a separate building; in others it was added to a reorganized secondary school comprising grades seven to twelve. Such an institution would give new hope and appropriate curricular choices in a new setting to discouraged young people. It would prevent them from dropping out and offer them chances to explore their vocational opportunities in a setting adapted to the particular needs of adolescents. In addition, it would challenge academically capable students. Advocates claimed that the junior high school might become a model for the regeneration of the whole school system, a lever for broad curricular reform.[31]

The junior high school appealed to people who analyzed educational problems from three different angles of vision. One set of reformers was primarily concerned about drop-outs and preparing the young for work. Some of these wanted to train potential drop-outs directly for specific jobs, but most wanted the junior high school to provide students with attractive opportunities to discover their vocational aptitudes and interests. A second group were interested in transforming the curriculum of the entire educational system, beginning in the junior high school. These reformers wanted to chip away at the rigidities of the graded classroom and to introduce new subjects and forms of pedagogy. Charles H. Judd, a leader among the administrative progressives, asserted that "reorganization of the three intermediate grades . . . in reality means reorganization of the entire public school system." A third group, influenced by

70

the "discovery of adolescence" by psychologists like G. Stanley Hall, wanted to tailor the work of the school to the particular stage of development of young teenagers. Students of that age were distinct from grade school youngsters and high school students, these reformers argued. Intellectual, emotional, and physical spurts made these years unpredictable; individual differences multiplied as physical growth accelerated; tensions between youth and adults increased; and interest in adult life and work expanded. A scientifically valid plan for schooling must take note of these psychological changes.[32]

The very ambiguity of purpose and comprehensiveness of these aims made the junior high school a reform to conjure with during the second decade of the twentieth century. Each organization, group, and individual reformer could see in the junior high school a reflection of different worries and hopes. A speaker at the National Education Association declared in 1916 that "the junior high school movement is sweeping the country." People everywhere, he said, are climbing aboard the bandwagon: the Department of Superintendence of the NEA, the U.S. Bureau of Education, state departments of education, large cities, and experts in university schools of education. "Textbook houses, with expected enterprise, are announcing a new junior high school series of textbooks. . . . There is a literature, a terminology, a lingo, a cult."[33]

By the end of the second decade of the twentieth century educators were talking a lot about junior high schools, but the actual number of junior high schools in operation was quite small. In 1920, 94 percent of secondary schools still followed the traditional pattern of four years on top of eight years of elementary school, only 0.4 percent were free-standing junior high schools, and the rest were combined junior-senior high schools. Almost two decades later about two-thirds of secondary schools were still traditional four-year institutions, a quarter were combined junior-senior high schools, and less than one in ten were separate junior high schools. Only after World War II—a time of rapid expansion of secondary enrollment and construction of new schools, including junior highs—did traditional four-year high schools become a minority of secondary schools. By then about 80 percent of pupils who entered fifth grade continued on to tenth grade in high school, making drop-outs primarily a problem in senior high schools rather than in elementary or junior high schools.[34]

The most rapid increases in school retention rates and declines in child labor occurred in the 1920s and 1930s, decades when the junior high school was taking root only slowly and when the dominant form of secondary school organization was the still the traditional 8–4 pattern.

71

Thus it is questionable whether the junior high school was itself a major factor in lowering the drop-out rate, especially given the strong influence of compulsory attendance laws, child labor legislation, technology that eroded the need for youthful labor, and the scarcity of jobs during the Great Depression. In addition, in the late 1920s and 1930s more and more districts shifted to a policy of "social promotion" of students by age rather than promotion through examinations or assessments by teachers, further lowering the percentage of pupils who were overaged for their grades. As teenagers increasingly entered senior high school, the focus on drop-outs and vocational training shifted to that level (all along, federal funds for vocational education under the Smith-Hughes Act of 1917 went only to senior high schools).[35]

Reflecting these developments, policy talk about the junior high school shifted away from the early emphasis on retention of students and vocational exploration to the other two major arguments: that the school should meet the special psychological needs of the early adolescent age group; and that it should be a seed ground for developing new forms of curriculum and instruction that one day might transform the entire educational system.

Amid the chorus of praise for junior high schools in the early years, some educators voiced the fear that the new institution could be a curricular and psychological Potemkin village, a fine façade with little inside. In 1922 Thomas Briggs, a professor at Teachers College, Columbia, said that "unfortunately, it must be recorded, there are some who . . . loudly proclaim the establishment of junior high schools when, in truth, they have changed but little the traditional organization and work of the school." He warned: "The junior high school is an opportunity, not a specific [remedy]; and unless you have a definite program for the reform of the curricula, of the courses of study, of the methods of teaching, and of the social administration of your intermediate grades, I strongly urge you to defer the organization of the junior high schools to your successors."[36]

Briggs's warnings were prophetic. The junior high school did not prove to be a panacea. In fact, repeated studies, decade after decade, detailed similar criticisms. Aubrey Douglass, an early advocate of the innovation, wrote in 1945 that the "persistent problems" were excessive departmentalization into an academic curriculum modeled on the high school; teachers who were inadequately trained to understand or guide young adolescents; and tracking of students by ability.[37]

In other words, junior high schools mirrored what progressives considered to be the defects of senior high schools. In 1977 a comprehensive study by Kenneth Tye of twelve junior high schools in quite different communities disclosed patterns quite similar to those described by Douglass. In 1989 a task force of the Carnegie Council on Adolescent Development warned that

> a volatile mismatch exists between the organization and curriculum of middle grade schools and the intellectual, emotional, and inter-personal needs of young adolescents. For most young adolescents, the shift from elementary to junior high or middle school means moving from a small, neighborhood school and the stability of one primary classroom to a much larger, more impersonal institution, typically at a greater distance from home. In this new setting, teachers and classmates will change as many as six or seven times a day. This constant shifting creates formidable barriers to the forma-tion of stable peer groups and close, supportive relationships with caring adults. The chances that young people will feel lost are enormous. Today, as young adolescents move from elementary to middle or junior high schools, their involvement with learning di-minishes and their rates of alienation, drug abuse, absenteeism, and dropping out begin to rise. The warning signals are there to see.[38]

Despite the advice of pioneers like Briggs that educators should com-prehensively plan junior high schools as unique institutions before they built them, few did. Instead of providing a new model for the rest of the system, junior high schools appear to have been patterned on high schools. Why?

It is easier to copy another institution than to invent one from the ground up. Would-be innovative schools often come to resemble tradi-tional ones. The initial goals of the junior high school were ambiguous and the means of achieving them uncertain. Since the public provided tax dollars and children, educators were understandably concerned that the public—parents, school boards, students, as well as educators—per-ceive junior high schools as legitimate institutions. And what was the model of legitimacy, the jewel in the crown of American public educa-tion? The high school.[39]

Given their pedagogical goals, junior high educators might have pat-terned reforms on progressively-minded elementary school teachers, who prided themselves on correlating different subjects, guiding individuals sensitively, and adapting instruction to stages of psychological develop-ment. It is rare, however, for policymakers to emulate less prestigious models, and elementary school teachers typically had less education and lower social standing than high school teachers. Gender bias may also have played a part. The urban elementary school was a woman's world— too much so, thought many male educators, who argued that a feminized curriculum alienated the boys. To the men who dominated school district administration, the high school, with its male principal and mixed staff of men and women teachers, was a more authoritative model for the junior high school than was the grade school.[40]

Practical organizational considerations also help explain why junior high schools came to resemble high schools. Until 1970 most junior high schools shared a building and teachers with the senior high school. To provide sharply different schedules, curriculum and teaching methods, programs of guidance, and extracurricular activities for the junior and senior high students would have been costly and impractical. Most of these junior-senior high schools were small, even after students from the upper elementary grades flowed into the lower division of the junior-senior high school.

Although junior high schools may have had some distinctive hallmarks, like courses giving vocational and personal guidance, for the most part they followed the standard procedures of the high schools. The experience of a seventh-grade boy in the Hamilton, Massachusetts, junior-senior high school in 1942 illustrates common practices at that time. He was required to take a course in "occupations" and dutifully wrote a report on making a career in the navy. But the academic courses were simpler versions of what the high school students studied. Since the school was small—about 180 students—all of his teachers also taught senior high courses in the subjects the seventh-graders pursued: English, science, social studies, mathematics, manual training, and gym. Extracurricular life also mixed the junior and senior high students. He and his seventh-grade classmates went with high school students to varsity baseball and basketball games, attended assemblies and dances, and participated in clubs. After having been the giants of the elementary school as sixth-graders, they were downgraded to the status of midgets in the high school, but they were at last part of the adolescent culture in the high school. Townspeople agreed that a "real school" for teenagers was one that had the emblems, ceremonies, and patterns of instruction of a high school.[41]

Most junior high schools did not turn out to be basically different from high schools, as advocates had originally hoped. Reformers did identify, however, some problems with which educators are still contending. One is how to smooth the educational transition for students as they move between two quite different institutional environments: from the self-contained primary classroom in a small school to a multitude of different classes and teachers in a relatively large high school. Another is how to take a developmental approach to teaching and learning academic subjects and how to adapt the school to the social, vocational, ethical, and health needs of young adolescents. While reformers have lamented the gap between the goals and the practices of junior high schools (and their close cousins now called middle schools), they have nonetheless focused attention on these problems and encouraged educators to find solutions.[42]

Some of the changes pioneered in progressive junior high schools did spread both to other middle grade schools and upward and downward in the system. One reason for this diffusion was that many teachers began their secondary careers in junior high schools and imported practices such as team teaching and cross-disciplinary curriculum into the high school. The notion that teachers should offer more guidance to help adolescent students through times of turmoil—a key tenet of junior high schools—spread to high schools across the country. Changes moved downward in the system as well; elementary schools came to employ more specialist teachers for students in the upper grades.

Although the junior high school did not become distinctly different from the high school, and although it came to be seen as a particularly troubled part of the American educational system, it did sponsor changes that became hybridized in various ways. Today, junior high and middle schools are the site for numerous reforms that may also become more widely diffused: attempting to create "small communities for learning"; correlating instruction in different subjects; delegating more decision making to teams of teachers; and paying more attention to the emotional and physical health of students.[43]

The pioneer kindergarten leaders and the founders of the junior high school shared some common convictions as reformers. They were sharply, even passionately, critical of the rigidity of the existing public school system and claimed that it laid waste young lives. They focused on a specific age group. They believed that the regular schools were so poor, and the two age groups so in need of special attention, that it was essential to create new educational institutions, not simply to remodel the old system. At the same time, they were not isolationist; they hoped that their reforms would over time transform the rest of schooling. Through a process of institutional assimilation, the kindergarten and the junior high school ended up resembling the primary and high school grades above them. The advocates of kindergartens and junior high schools did not transform the system, but they did focus attention on serious problems and experimented with practices that rippled through corners of the traditional pattern of schooling.

Interactions of Reforms with Reforms

Educational reformers may have wanted to wipe the institutional slate clean and start again, but that has rarely happened. Instead, reforms have tended to layer, one on top of another. The evolution of schools is in part the story of the interactions between these layers of change, whether they are deposited at lengthy intervals or accumulate in rapid succession. To ask what prior reforms do to reforms suggests another way of thinking about what schools do to reforms. Sometimes new reforms have merged well with past reforms; sometimes they have been incompatible. To explore the interactions between reforms, we look at two cases: the long history of attempts to transform the governance of schools in New York City and in the last decade the staccato beat of reforms designed to raise academic achievement.[44]

Governing New York Schools

New Yorkers have a long history of trying to reform their schools by reshaping the system of governance. Some have been convinced that centralization offered the one best system, others that the path of progress led to decentralization. But each time that they attempted to change governance, they confronted layers of institutional experience and vested interests left by previous reforms.[45]

Elite reformers in the 1890s thought governance was entirely too decentralized. They had a simple formula: centralization and expert management. Impressed by the consolidation of control in business and the increasing influence accorded to experts in most professions, they wanted to rid the city of ward school committees, create a small and businesslike central board, and delegate the running of the schools to experts. With centralization and specialization of functions, in theory, would come accountability—one could pin down the responsibility for success or failure. The organizational chart showed who was in charge of what.[46]

In 1896 the mayor signed a bill that abolished the decentralized ward school committees. This did not bring about managerial Nirvana, however. The old school politicians on the large central board proved resilient. They reappointed as superintendent John Jasper, who had held the position since 1879 and who was regarded as an incompetent "common man" by the elite reformers. Jasper, in turn, appointed fifteen of his cronies to key positions as assistant superintendents and supervisors; most of them had opposed centralization. When the five New York boroughs were united in 1898, the next superintendent, William Maxwell, who had cut his teeth on Brooklyn school politics, proved to be an adroit manipulator of the large central board. With the ward boards out of the way, he managed to concentrate power in a large central bureaucracy which he then dominated.[47]

When a new charter reduced the central board from forty-six to seven members in 1917, the school district was already on the way to being one of the largest centralized public bureaucracies in the world. By the 1960s the district employed more administrators than all of France. Few observers of this vast system would argue that centralization really brought, as advertised, accountability through specialization. Rather, the very complexity of the bureaucracy frustrated the plans of the elite reformers and provided staff with the familiar excuse, "It's not my department." In centrally controlled schools, complained one critic, when you have a problem, the local administrator says "'I'm sorry, but that matter is completely out of my hands; you will have to go to headquarters.' But you never can get close enough to the man at headquarters who makes the decisions, and you give up."[48]

In the 1960s came a frontal assault on the centralized management of the New York schools. Angered by the glacial pace of racial integration and convinced that blacks deserved the chance to direct their own education, activists called for community control of schools. What resulted was not the local control they wanted but thirty-two "decentralized" districts, each as big as a medium-sized city. Community control was a basic challenge to the existing form of governance and was opposed by the newly powerful teachers' union as well as by incumbents at headquarters. The political compromise of thirty-two enormous districts satisfied few people. Critics complained that the new district boards and sets of administrators simply added a new layer of bureaucracy to an already top-heavy system. Many advocates of local participatory democracy thought the plan was a fraud. Within a few years, citizens rarely bothered to vote for these new school boards.[49]

Alongside the home-grown layers of control and bureaucracy have sprung up new positions spawned by dozens of new programs and mandates created by the federal government and New York state. These produced still more mid-level administrators at the 110 Livingston Street headquarters to supervise, coordinate, or obscure the inconsistencies in these programs aimed at different categories of students. Accounting to state and federal officials became a bureaucratic art form.[50]

When a new chancellor, Joseph A. Fernandez, arrived in New York in 1990 to administer the school district, he found it was not clear who was in charge, if anyone. His office windows were dirty, so he called an engineer to clean them. Sorry, he learned, by contract the engineers cleaned windows only once a year. When he asked his secretary to order highlighting pens, he was informed that delivery would take four weeks. It was unclear just what were the prerogatives of the thirty-two decentralized school boards. Only by negotiating with the principals' union could he change a policy that gave principals, in effect, a tenured fiefdom in a particular building.[51]

The interactions of attempted reforms in governance in New York City produced a complexity in decision making that only Rube Goldberg could appreciate. Far from being either an efficiently centralized system or a fully decentralized one, the New York district illustrates how successive reforms over time have produced the "fragmented centralization" found in many districts today.[52]

Raising Academic Achievement

The complexity of governance in the New York City schools is in part the product of a century of interactions of reforms. In the decade from 1983 to 1993, a much shorter time span, reformers adopted various strategies to increase the academic achievement of students. When one approach to reform did not appear to work, innovators quickly turned to alternatives but generally left the original reform laws and layers of rules and regulations in place. As a result, exhortations for change and mandated practices often worked at cross-purposes. "We are asked to reinvent schools, to break the mold," complained a central office administrator, "and they put a moat of mandates around us. It's like putting on handcuffs and leg irons and saying climb Mt. Everest." Confronted with contrary reform demands, practitioners sought refuge through strategies of accommodation, resistance, and hybridization. In the process, schools changed reforms quite as much as reforms changed schools.[53]

In the mid-1980s, responding to the "crisis" announced by *A Nation at Risk,* the states promulgated more educational laws and regulations than they had generated in the previous twenty years. The major goal of the legislation was to promote educational "excellence," and the target was lazy students and incompetent teachers. The remedy was *More:* more days and hours of schooling, more academic courses, more attention to "basics," more discriminating standards for evaluating and compensating teachers, more standardized testing of pupil achievement, more elaborate reporting of test results by local districts to state officials. The state-mandated model of reform in the 1980s, Richard F. Elmore wrote, relied on "standardization, central bureaucratic control, and externally imposed rules as a means of controlling the performance of schools."[54]

To the degree that these 1980s state reforms sought an *intensification* of what already existed, practitioners found compliance relatively straightforward. From the middle 1970s onward, teachers had been under pressure to teach the "basics" and to raise students' scores on standardized tests. They already were familiar with drills and other rote methods of teaching the discrete skills and facts measured by minimum competency examinations. Years of stress on the so-called basics gave teachers a kit of tools to use to comply with the new state mandates.[55]

But many teachers were ambivalent or hostile toward required statewide testing, as the Carnegie Foundation for the Advancement of Teaching found in its survey of 13,500 teachers. Indeed, two scholars who investigated the local impact of such programs called their study "Statewide Testing and Local Improvement: An Oxymoron?" The teachers they interviewed generally believed that the tests "offered few benefits for students, particularly in terms of providing additional information . . . to determine which students could be better served." In a state where the tests carried high stakes for students and public opinion, districts showed "a single-minded devotion to specific, almost 'gamelike' ways to increase the test scores." Teachers reported "a decreased reliance on their professional judgment in instructional matters, increased time demands, more staff reassignments, greater pressure, more paperwork, and heightened concern about liability"—but not better results for students as a result of all the stress.[56]

When educators view reform demands as inappropriate, they are skilled in finding ways to temper or evade their effects. They may exclude low-achieving pupils from the state examination. They may respond to a longer school day by extending the time between classes. They may raise grades for students in danger of violating the no-pass, no-play rule in athletics. They may put new labels on old courses to appear to comply with new academic requirements. When it becomes apparent that enormous numbers of students may be failing promotional or graduation examinations, thus increasing the likelihood of even more drop-outs, educators may adjust the cut-off points on the tests.[57]

Although mandating stiffer state standards to create "excellence" gen-

erated defensive organizational maneuvers of this sort, studies of implementation did show at least routine compliance with the strategy of
intensifying existing practices in academic instruction. The results of this
approach, sometimes called "the first wave of reform" of the 1980s,
proved generally disappointing, however. The Secretary of Education's
wall charts comparing the performances of the states and the achieve-
ments of the United States with those of other nations seemed to show
that top-down mandates were not producing the dramatic changes reformers sought.[58]

Could the state mandate educational excellence by top-down regulations? In their study of the implementation of state reforms in the 1980s,
Thomas B. Timar and David L. Kirp say no; excellence cannot be
coerced. At best, laws and rules might create some necessary but not
sufficient conditions under which competent and caring teachers and
intellectually curious students might flourish. But legal mandates can
have negative unintended consequences as well: they compel responses,
yet the result may be compliance of a kind that actually dampens excellence.[59]

As faith in top-down state mandates to raise academic achievement
waned among policy elites, a new catchword became fashionable in
educational reform: "restructuring." It is by no means clear what the
term means, though its currency among business people active in school
reform may reflect their own experience in "restructuring" corporations.
A colleague who discusses education reform with business executives
says that when she describes the everyday realities of life in classrooms,
their eyes glaze over, but when she mentions "restructuring," they come
alive.[60]

It is no accident that a *vague* word has also become a *vogue* word.
Elmore writes that "the theme of restructuring schools can accommodate
a variety of conceptions about what is problematical about American
education, as well as a variety of solutions." People regard restructuring
as a synonym for the market mechanism of choice, or teacher profession-
alization and empowerment, or decentralization and school site management, or increased involvement of the parents in their children's
education, or national standards in curriculum with tests to match, or
deregulation, or new forms of accountability, or basic changes in curriculum and instruction, or some or all of these in combination. But underlying most conceptions of restructuring is the goal of raising academic
achievement.[61]

Proposals for restructuring go every which way. In 1989 when President Bush and the fifty governors assembled at Charlottesville pro-

claimed the need for "clear, national performance goals" and "detailed strategies" for reaching those targets, they were recommending a policy that would previously have been anathema—a national curriculum (it was not so long ago that over a hundred members of Congress voted to call the U.S. Commissioner of Education the Commissar of Education). One wonders how that ardent states rights advocate Thomas Jefferson might have reacted when they called their statement "A Jeffersonian Compact." With President Bush declaring that "the American people are ready for *radical* reforms," the President and governors also called for "decentralization of authority and decision-making responsibility to the school site, so that educators are empowered to determine the means for accomplishing the goals and to be held accountable for accomplishing them."[62]

So *national* goals and curriculum standards, presumably to be followed by some form of national assessments, are to be coupled with school site management of the learning process. Teachers are to be told what to teach but not how to teach it, and they are responsible for achieving those goals. Under the new conventional wisdom in school governance, school district administrators and school board members, once considered a bastion of local control, have become suspect to many modern reformers, part of the problem and not part of the solution. It is not clear what role school districts should play in the combined top-down and bottom-up version of "restructuring" or what has become known, alternatively, as "systemic reform."[63]

As diagnoses of problems and proposed solutions have piled on top of each other during the decade from 1983 to 1993, most of them emanating from policy elites, educators have been caught in the middle of interactions between reforms. Many policymakers have lost faith in the power of state mandates to improve teaching and learning, but the laws and regulations mostly remain on the books and along with them a continuing concern about audits and noncompliance.[64]

Elmore sees a fundamental inconsistency in the notion that "system-wide change will occur by lodging greater responsibility with people who work in schools." It appears contradictory, he observes, "to argue that all schools will or should change in the same way as a result of school restructuring, since to do so, schools would all have to arrive spontaneously at more or less the same solutions to highly complex problems of content, pedagogy, technology, organization, and governance."[65]

Some educators worry about keeping their jobs when they hear the word "restructuring," an understandable concern to anyone familiar with layoffs reported in the business pages of newspapers. But some reform-minded teachers understand the word "restructuring" to mean greater autonomy and new ways to teach for deeper understanding. That interpretation of the concept contains the seeds of a social movement among scholars and teachers to spread what many call "constructivist" (or neo-progressive) pedagogy. This strategy to improve academic achievement has the potential of actually changing instruction in ways that teachers themselves can adapt to their own pedagogical histories and to their own circumstances.[66]

The implementation of a constructivist program of "teaching for understanding" in mathematics in California illustrates that teachers do not start from scratch in putting pedagogical reforms into practice. Such efforts, David K. Cohen and Deborah Loewenberg Ball point out, always take place within a context framed by previous reforms: "the new California math framework is part of an infatuation with higher order thinking and teaching for understanding that began to grip Americans in the late 1980s. But between the mid-1970s and the mid-1980s Americans had been flailing schools for flabby teaching and sagging Standardized Aptitude Test (SAT) scores." For a time, policy and practice focused on direct teaching methods designed to raise students' scores on standardized tests; they stressed "accuracy and convergent thinking" that would lead to the right answer. The new framework, by contrast, encouraged divergent thinking and understanding "big mathematical ideas." Was the stage set for confusion and conflict for the teachers expected to carry out the new math?[67]

Although Cohen and Ball "thought that there was a real conflict here" between the didactic and constructivist approaches, they discovered that in practice teachers found ways to blend the new and the old, perceiving the demand for understanding and cooperative work "through the lens of older policies that stressed learning skills and facts." "Initially it seemed odd," they comment, "but upon reflection it made sense . . . teachers are busy and engaged actors, who must make their classrooms work: To do so, they must balance all sorts of contrary tendencies." Policymakers may "ignore the pedagogical past," but teachers and students cannot.[68]

Reflections

Reformers who adopt a rational planning mode of educational reform sometimes expect that they will improve schools if they design their policies correctly. They may measure success by fidelity to plan, by whether predetermined goals are met, and by longevity. Such a technocratic and top-down approach, however, slights the many ways in which schools shape reforms and teachers employ their "wisdom of practice" to produce pedagogical hybrids. Innovations never enter educational institutions with the previous slate wiped clean. The business leaders who today advocate restructuring and decentralization are trying to undo the defects of the centralized systems endorsed by business leaders almost a century ago. Rational planners may have plans for schools, and may blame practitioners if they think that the plans are not properly implemented, but schools are not wax to be imprinted.

For the most part, reforms have become assimilated to previous patterns of schooling, even though they may, like the kindergarten and junior high school, have inserted alternative practices into the work of schools. Reforms have rarely replaced what is there; more commonly, they have added complexity. When reforms have come in staccato succession, they often have brought incoherence or uncomfortable tensions. They have unsettled the balance between different forms of decision making. They have introduced progressive notions of meeting the developmental needs of each individual student in a system geared to batch-processing. They have made new demands of time and effort on heavily burdened teachers.

Since schools do change reforms, often in unforeseen ways, what might be a sensible strategy for people who want to improve education where it counts the most, in classroom instruction? We have suggested treating policies as hypotheses and encouraging practitioners to create hybrids suited to their context. Instead of being ready-made plans, reform policies could be stated as principles, general aims, to be modified in the light of experience, and embodied in practices that vary by school or even by classroom.

There are potential problems here. Is accountability lessened if policies are hypotheses? Is there a danger of producing eclectic, almost random hybrids? If reform were an atomistic process occurring in solitary classrooms, the answer could be yes in both cases. But if teachers work collaboratively with each other and with policy advocates, sharing goals and tactics, supporting each other in assessing progress and surmounting obstacles, then such an approach to school improvement could work better than mandates from above. It could produce what Milbrey W. McLaughlin and Joan E. Talbert call an "integrated reform strategy [of] seeking policy coherence at the classroom core, in the everyday interactions of students and teachers around content."[69]

This strategy for change is, of course, not new. It stems in part from Dewey's pragmatic conception of constantly reassessing goals and results in the light of experience. Movements to improve learning have often been based on shared general principles and flexible implementation. But it would be unwise to underestimate the force of the "pedagogical past" and the difficulty of changing basic institutional forms, the grammar that organizes the central work of the school: instruction.

4

Why the Grammar of
Schooling Persists

The basic grammar of schooling, like the shape of classrooms, has remained remarkably stable over the decades. Little has changed in the ways that schools divide time and space, classify students and allocate them to classrooms, splinter knowledge into "subjects," and award grades and "credits" as evidence of learning. In 1902 John Dewey warned against dismissing the way schools are organized "as something comparatively external and indifferent to educational purposes and ideals." In fact, he declared, "the manner in which the machinery of instruction bears upon the child . . . really controls the whole system."[1]

Continuity in the grammar of instruction has puzzled and frustrated generations of reformers who have sought to change these standardized organizational forms. In this chapter we ask how this grammar came about, why it was so tenacious, and why even vigorous and imaginative challenges to it tended to fade, leaving behind a few new practices here and there but not fundamentally altering the way schools are organized for instruction.

Practices such as age-graded classrooms structure schools in a manner analogous to the way grammar organizes meaning in verbal communication. Neither the grammar of schooling nor the grammar of speech needs to be consciously understood to operate smoothly. Indeed, much of the grammar of schooling has become taken for granted as just the way schools are. It is the *departure* from customary school practice that attracts attention (as when schools decide not to issue student report cards).[2]

People are accustomed to elementary schools that are divided into self-contained classrooms called "grades." In these rooms individual teachers instruct pupils of about the same age in a variety of subjects. High schools are organized quite differently. Every hour, students shift from one subject to another, one teacher to another. Teachers belong to specialized departments and instruct about one hundred and fifty pupils a day—in five classes of perhaps thirty each—in their particular fields. When students complete these courses, they are rewarded with Carnegie units. In secondary schools, but generally not in elementary classes, students have some degree of choice of what to study.

Under these institutional arrangements, teachers have been expected to monitor and control students, assign tasks to them, and ensure that they have accomplished the work. Over the past century there has been a good deal of continuity in how teachers taught. We attend here, however, not so much to what happens in classrooms as to the organizational framework that shapes how teachers do their work.[3]

The grammar of schooling is a product of history, not some primordial creation. It results from the efforts of groups that mobilize to win support for their definitions of problems and their proposed solutions. The more powerful and prestigious the groups, the more likely it is that they will be able to buttress their reforms with laws, regulations, and accreditation requirements. The timing of innovations also has much to do with their implementation. Reforms that enter on the ground floor of major institutional changes, such as the rapid expansion of elementary education in the nineteenth century or the differentiation of secondary schools in the twentieth, have a good chance of becoming part of the standard institutional template.[4]

Once established, the grammar of schooling persisted in part because it enabled teachers to discharge their duties in a predictable fashion and to cope with the everyday tasks that school boards, principals, and parents expected them to perform: controlling student behavior, instructing heterogeneous pupils, and sorting people for future roles in school and later life. Habitual institutional patterns can be labor-saving devices, ways to organize complex duties. Teachers and students socialized to such routines often find it difficult to adapt to different structures and rules. Established institutional forms come to be understood by educators, students, and the public as necessary features of a "real school." They become fixed in place by everyday custom in schools and by outside forces, both legal mandates and cultural beliefs, until they are barely noticed. They become just the way schools are.[5]

Periodically, innovators have challenged the structures and rules that constitute the grammar of schooling, perceiving them not as the reforms they once were but as straitjackets preventing the schools from providing students with the best possible education. Over the years, innovators have often tried:

to create ungraded, not graded, schools;

to use time, space, and numbers of students as flexible resources and to diversify uniform class periods, same-sized rooms, and standard class sizes;

to merge specialized subjects into core courses in junior and senior high schools or, alternatively, to introduce departmental specialization into the elementary school;

and to encourage teachers to work in teams rather than to function as isolated individuals in separate classrooms.[6]

In the 1960s, for example, reforms in the grammar of schooling sprang up nationwide. Inspired by a vision of high schools of the future, reformers experimented with flexible scheduling and class sizes, variable-space classrooms, team teaching, independent study, and core courses. In earlier times, as well, innovators assaulted standard organizational arrangements, as in the Dalton Plan of individualized instruction or the progressive experiments of the Eight-Year Study. These reforms swept through educators' journals and conferences, seizing the attention of superintendents, teachers, school boards, parents, and professors.

Reformers who opposed the familiar grammar of schooling insisted that it was irrational, narrow in aim, antiquated in design, and harsh in effect. They found allies in foundations, associations of progressive educators, and cadres of enthusiastic teachers and principals. Various innovators blamed different groups for the persistence of the traditional grammar: administrators with perverse notions of efficiency, college officials who tried to dictate practice to high schools, or mossbacked teachers unwilling to try the new. Whatever the character of the "establishment" that supposedly inhibited changes in the grammar, confident reformers asserted that the logic and persuasiveness of their attack would undermine the foundations of the old order and provide the blueprint for a new order in the schools.[7]

But this did not happen. The standard grammar of schooling has proven remarkably durable. When new departures survived more or less intact, they typically took hold on the periphery of the system in specialized niches: industrial education, continuation schools, or special education for gifted or handicapped students—groups of pupils who did not fit the requirements for standard instruction. Here and there, teachers selectively incorporated some reform practices in regular classrooms, hybridizing the new with the old.

We start our exploration of the stability of the grammar of schooling by examining how two practices, the graded school and the Carnegie unit, became institutionalized. We then ask how the grammar survived three vigorous challenges: the Dalton Plan, the Eight-Year Study, and the new-model flexible high school of the late 1960s and 1970s. And in our reflections on these case studies, we suggest that the "establishment" that has held the grammar in place is not so much a conscious conservatism as it is unexamined institutional habits and widespread cultural beliefs about what constitutes a "real school."

The Creation of Enduring Institutional Forms

The graded elementary school—in which the curriculum is divided into year-long batches, students are sorted according to academic proficiency and age, and individual teachers instruct them in self-contained classrooms—is now so familiar that it is hard to imagine a time when it did not exist or to conceive of alternatives. But once it was a deliberate invention that spread rapidly across the urban landscape and that promised to make schools efficient, equitable, and easily replicable.

Efficiency and standardization were also goals of an academic accounting system called the Carnegie unit. The reform had unlikely and now largely forgotten origins, but it rapidly became an established part of the grammar of schooling, influencing three fundamental resources in secondary education: instructional time, specialized subjects, and academic credits.

The Graded School

The one-room country school was nongraded, a place where students of different ages learned together and often taught each other. Its schedule was flexible and adapted to individual differences among pupils. Parents and school trustees often came to the classroom to see what the children had learned, and they frequently took an active part in making decisions about education.

Today many people regard such practices as desirable, but during most of the twentieth century, reformers in universities and state departments of education have done their best to eliminate the one-room school. They wanted to replace it by a larger, multigrade school because they regarded the one-room school as inefficient, unprofessional, meager in curriculum, and subordinated to lay control, the teacher being too much under the eye and thumb of the community. Most rural residents, however, wanted to keep their local schools and resisted their consolidation into graded schools. Well into the twentieth century, one-room schools numbered over a hundred thousand and sometimes existed in towns as well as in rural areas. Now, as we noted in Chapter 1, they have been consolidated and legislated practically out of existence, all in the name of progress.[8]

Before the Civil War, another type of classroom was common in cities. It mixed together masses of pupils of differing ages and academic attainment—often two hundred or more—under the direction of a "master" who was responsible, sometimes along with one or two assistant teachers, for hearing all children recite their lessons. Reformers like Henry Barnard thought this a pedagogical monstrosity, for the masters had to move quickly from child to child, each at different levels of achievement, while maintaining draconian discipline.[9]

Many advocates of the graded school, prominent among them city and state superintendents and school board leaders, were impressed with the division of labor and hierarchical supervision common in factories. Why could this tidy system not be adapted to public education? they asked. They did not question the age-old assumption that a classroom is a self-contained place where one teacher sets tasks for a group of students and evaluates their performance. But they did seek greater efficiency by concentrating the work of a teacher on one grade in which students could be grouped by academic proficiency and could learn a uniform curriculum. One teacher could then teach all children in the classroom the same subjects, in the same way, and at the same pace. A school thus "graded" seemed egalitarian to the reformers, for schooling was thus supposedly the same for everyone, boys and girls, rich and poor, immigrant and native-born. Administrators, most of them male, divided the traditional curriculum—reading, spelling, arithmetic, writing, and the rest—into required yearly sequences and supervised the teachers, mostly female, to make sure that they were following the courses of study. At the end of the year, the pupils took tests to determine whether they were ready to move to the next level: success meant moving up to the next grade; failure meant staying in place.[10]

By 1860 the graded school, with its prescribed curriculum, was common in large cities, and by 1870 it had spread almost everywhere there were enough pupils to classify into grades. In addition to its claims of pedagogical efficiency, the graded school had the virtue of being easily reproduced as the population of children mushroomed in cities, no small consideration in the chronically overcrowded urban systems. It mirrored as well the hierarchical, differentiated organizations in which urban dwellers increasingly conducted their business, both public and private.[11]

Beginning in the 1870s, the urban graded school had its critics both inside and outside the educational profession. The strict curriculum and system of promotional examinations meant that the "normal" student was one who progressed at the regular pace demanded by the imperatives of the graded school. Batch-processing of pupils created a category of organizational deviant: the "retarded," or slow, student who was not promoted. In the nongraded informal one-room school, by contrast, students could progress more at their own pace, making "failure" less visible and less absolute, especially since there were many ways to learn and achieve in rural communities. Even the pedagogical conservative William T. Harris worried that too rigid a plan of age-grading and testing would lead to "premature withdrawal from school," or what a later generation would call drop-outs. A state superintendent warned that teachers might "groove" their instruction to the annual tests for promotion to the next grade. Lay reformers believed that the system had grown too rigid and that overwork and pressure in schools led to stress and illness.[12]

Early in the twentieth century careful studies showed that a very large minority of students in city schools—perhaps one-third—were denied promotion (the "retarded" pupils). The result was that many urban students were lumped in the lower grades of the system, and the held-back pupils were considered to be "overaged." People began to recognize that the graded school might have been efficient for the majority of students whose culture matched its requirements, but for the poor and immigrants the system seemed geared to produce failure. And failure, to the efficiency-minded educators of the Progressive era, was waste.[13]

Rather than abandoning the graded school, however, most reformers fine-tuned it. Some proposed that tests be given semiannually so that lagging students would not have to repeat a whole year's work. Some urged the development of different curricular tracks or niches with different standards for promotion (the development of IQ testing fueled this alternative, for disparities in scores were interpreted as indicating genetic differences, both between individuals and between ethnic groups). Where schools had sufficient pupils, educators sometimes sorted them into separate classes by IQ scores. More common was instructional grouping of students by "ability" within individual classes. By the 1930s and 1940s, districts had increasingly begun to practice "social promotion," or automatic advancement by age cohorts.[14]

Here and there educators experimented with more sweeping alternatives to the year-by-year system of grading, as in a "nongraded" primary system that treated the K–3 years not as separate grades but as a pedagogical continuum. For the most part, however, school districts made incremental rather than fundamental changes in the graded school. The graded school became firmly ensconced as part of the grammar of schooling, for it seemed to solve key organizational problems. Over the years, the public came to regard distinct grades as emblematic of a "real school."[15]

The Carnegie Unit

Like the graded school, the Carnegie unit rapidly became part of the grammar of schooling. In 1906 the president of the Carnegie Foundation for the Advancement of Teaching, Henry S. Pritchett, defined a "unit" as "a course of five periods weekly throughout an academic year" in secondary school subjects (by common custom, these "periods" came to be about fifty to fifty-five minutes long). So firmly has this academic accounting device—quickly labeled the Carnegie unit—been established in the operating routines of high schools that successive attempts to dislodge it have been unsuccessful, except in peripheral parts of the system, such as vocational training programs or continuation schools for potential drop-outs.[16]

In 1905 Andrew Carnegie established the foundation with an endowment of ten million dollars for the purpose of providing pensions for retired college professors. What connection could this possibly have had with the time allotted to subjects in high schools? From the first, the leaders of the foundation, and especially Pritchett, were not content simply to distribute money to retired professors. The trustees who gathered at Carnegie's mansion in New York on November 15, 1905, were a stellar cast of university presidents, including such luminaries as Charles William Eliot of Harvard, Woodrow Wilson of Princeton, Arthur Hadley of Yale, and David Starr Jordan of Stanford. These elite educators, confident that they had the answers to improving American education, were determined to reform from the top down, beginning with the colleges, a system of schooling that they regarded as chaotic and ineffective. They saw Carnegie's grant as an opportunity to raise standards in American secondary and higher education through unifying and centralizing academic practice. They had no doubt that what was good for the elite colleges was also good for the country. The prestige of the presidents ensured that their proposals would carry weight.[17]

First the trustees had to decide what a college was, no easy task in a country in which over six hundred institutions of "higher education" ranged in character and quality from struggling small academies (sometimes bearing the title of "university") to major research institutions like Columbia, Cornell, and Chicago. How could they distinguish work that was genuinely of college grade from teaching that was barely on a secondary level? "To be ranked as a college," the trustees agreed, an institution must have at least six full-time professors, offer "a course of four full years in the liberal arts and sciences," and require for admission "not less than the usual four years of academic or high school preparation." The foundation also decided not to include sectarian or state institutions. They judged that only fifty-two colleges met their criteria.[18]

It was not enough simply to prescribe four years of secondary instruction, Pritchett warned. They should also develop a standard measurement of time and credit for each subject—the Carnegie unit—and demand that a college require at least fourteen of these units. The foundation officials did not stop there: they also wrote eight pages specifying in great detail the content of units in subjects such as English, mathematics, Latin, Greek, foreign languages, history, and science. Thus they not only standardized time and credits but also gave pride of place to traditional academic disciplines. In addition, they put the weight of their influence behind the departmentalization of high school subjects, based partly on practice in higher education. The creation of departments became another key element in the grammar of secondary schooling.[19]

Pritchett and his colleagues in the foundation did not invent from whole cloth either the Carnegie unit system of academic credits or the specifics of academic courses. The latter they largely copied from the curriculum advocated by the College Education Examination Board. The unit system had slowly evolved from the work of two college-dominated committees of the National Education Association in the 1890s, the Committee of Ten and the Committee on College Entrance Requirements. What the foundation did do, however, was to give a more precise definition to the unit as an accounting device and to put its prestige behind the notion that a "standard" high school was one that organized time and subjects in Carnegie units.[20]

Pritchett regarded the educational system as a pyramid in which those on the top—the experts in the universities—should set the standards for those below. He agreed with Eliot of Harvard that secondary education was a mishmash. The best way to reform it—and to solve the problem of preparing students better for rapidly expanding colleges—was to use the most prestigious schools as the template for the rest. "The better high schools," he wrote in 1907, "require pupils to recite . . . studies daily five times a week." If that practice was good for the "better" schools, it must be good for all.[21]

Pritchett and the Carnegie trustees were seeking to impose a reform that was feasible at that time in only a minority of high schools. The colleges wanted what the run-of-the-mill secondary school could not provide. In cities with populations under eight thousand, the average high school had fifty-two pupils and two teachers in 1902. In such a school there was no way that students could study all the college pre-paratory subjects by reciting in standard-sized classes for an hour a day to gain the required fourteen Carnegie units. There were neither enough students to form classes in the necessary subjects nor enough teachers to teach them, yet the basic calculus of the Carnegie unit was hours spent in class recitation.[22]

Increasingly, regional associations of colleges and secondary schools required the use of Carnegie units for accreditation of high schools. High schools sought this seal of approval because their graduates could thereby be admitted to college by certificate and usually without exami-nation. The North Central Association of Colleges and Secondary Schools, for example, demanded in the 1920s that schools require fifteen Carnegie units for graduation, class periods of at least forty minutes, and a school year of at least thirty-six weeks. State laws also built the Carnegie unit system of credits into the template of the "standard" high school. Although originally intended to improve preparation for college, the Carnegie unit system of accounting and the division of teachers into separate departments also provided a tidy framework for the differentia-tion of curriculum as the high school expanded.[23]

A system of academic bookkeeping that originally was patterned on "the better high schools" and designed to upgrade preparation for col-lege admissions and to standardize the credit system eventually became part of the grammar of schooling in nearly all high schools, thus affecting students in non-college-bound tracks as well as those headed for higher education. Critics of the Carnegie unit argued that it had frozen sched-ules, separated knowledge into discrete boxes, and created an accounting mentality better suited to a bank than to a school. Learning was becom-ing institutionally defined as serving seat time, progressives claimed, while the reward at the end of the rigid progression was merely a "credit." It was time, thought some reformers, to end what they saw as the domination of the high school by the colleges.

Challenges to the Standard Grammar of Schooling

Although the graded school and the Carnegie unit rapidly became standard practice in moderate- to large-sized school districts, were incorporated into state school standards and accreditation requirements, and increasingly became part of the cultural definition of a "real school," they did not go unchallenged. The major critics of the standard grammar of schooling, like the originators of that system, were influential educators who worked through their associations and reform networks to bring about change. It proved far harder to alter that entrenched system, however, than to create it.

In the Dalton Plan, advocates of individualized instruction assaulted what they regarded as lockstep instruction in high schools. In the Eight-Year Study, sponsored by the Progressive Education Association and foundations, innovators challenged the sort of top-down domination of secondary education represented by Pritchett and his colleagues in colleges and universities. And in the 1960s, individual reformers, activists in the National Association of Secondary School Principals, and foundation officials questioned the conventions governing space, time, grouping, and the self-contained classroom with its one teacher of departmentalized subjects.

The Dalton Plan

Helen Parkhurst developed the Dalton Plan in the early 1920s (it was named after the Massachusetts town where the innovation was first introduced in the high school). A teacher, trainer of teachers, and founder of a private school, Parkhurst challenged essential components of the graded school in which teachers sought to instruct pupils en masse in a prescribed curriculum.[24]

Heavily influenced by child-centered progressives and Maria Montessori, Parkhurst was aware of earlier attempts to break the standardized movement of students in graded classrooms. Superintendent Preston Search in Pueblo, Colorado, and Frederick Burk in the San Francisco Normal School had pioneered methods of tailoring instruction to individual students and small groups rather than the whole class (Parkhurst visited Burk's model school and adapted some of his ideas, as did Carleton Washburne, who designed a system similar to Parkhurst's in the Winnetka, Illinois, public schools). The Dalton Plan was only one episode in a long series of efforts to correct the defects of the graded school.[25]

94

Parkhurst wanted to organize secondary schools in ways that would revolutionize teaching and learning by eliminating self-contained classes, whole-class recitations, fifty- to fifty-five-minute periods, and annual promotions and retentions. She deplored the graded class and the batch-processing of intrinsically different individuals as irrational relics of the past and violations of the best educational thought. She emphasized the individual student's freedom and responsibility, cooperation with other students and adults, and time-budgeting to complete assigned tasks. The revolution was only partial, however: Parkhurst basically retained the traditional curriculum and textbook-based instruction.[26]

Central to Parkhurst's reforms were monthly contracts that teachers negotiated with students. These laid out both the minimum tasks the students had to complete and additional choices if students wanted to go beyond the basic content and skills. The more tasks students chose to do and the better they did the work—as measured by written reports—the higher were their grades. Students were expected to revise unsatisfactory work until they mastered the content and completed the terms of the contract. Large charts recorded the progress of individual students. All students had to study certain required subjects, but it was their responsibility to decide the pace of the work, to select other students to work with, and to elect whether to do supplementary study.[27]

Students moved at their own pace through academic courses in the mornings and then spent afternoons on other subjects such as art, music, or physical education. For each field of study they went to a room, renamed a laboratory, where the teacher and materials were located. When pupils completed the activities they had agreed to undertake for a given period of time, they moved to another laboratory. The plan encouraged students to work individually but also promoted group projects. No fifty-minute periods. No bells. No teachers lecturing or listening to students reciting lessons in large classes.[28]

Teachers were expected to negotiate the contracts, stock the laboratory with learning materials needed to fulfil the contracts, coach students when they ran into problems, counsel when necessary, and monitor the progress of each student. Parkhurst believed that any student could learn if given enough time, and her plan abolished, in theory at least, the draconian judgment of nonpromotion.

Word spread quickly about the Dalton Plan both in the United States and abroad. Popular magazines such as *Colliers* and the *Saturday Evening Post* profiled Dalton Plan schools. Educators learned about the reform through books, journals, conferences, and word of mouth. Recognizing that the plan required dramatic changes in school organization, only a few schools adopted Parkhurst's reforms wholesale. Many more adopted features piecemeal. By 1930, 162 (2 percent) of 8,600 secondary schools surveyed in a national study reported that they had completely reorganized their schools to conform with the Dalton Plan. Another 486 (6 percent) of the secondary schools reported that they had introduced a modified version of the plan in their buildings.[29]

If the 162 secondary schools really did institute the whole Dalton Plan, they would have made drastic alterations in business as usual. In the 486 secondary schools that adopted some features of the plan, it is difficult to verify to what degree classrooms were converted into laboratories, fifty-minute periods had been eliminated, promotion practices altered, and contracts and progress charts used. Not counted in the survey of secondary schools were the many elementary schools that also incorporated portions of the Dalton Plan into their upper grades.

However appealing the Dalton Plan may have been in theory and successful in practice when carried out by skilled and energetic educators, it influenced policy talk far more than practice. By 1949 a researcher could find only one school that continued to follow the Dalton Plan—the private school Parkhurst herself had founded in New York City. At Dalton High School itself, the plan lasted only one year in unmodified form and then was dropped entirely after a decade. It did leave at least a modest legacy, said the Dalton superintendent two decades later: "even in this conservative New England town we are privileged to try little experiments in educational procedure."[30]

From attempted revolution in education to a few "little experiments in educational procedure" might be regarded as a considerable comedown. Habituated to the traditional organizational practices and either taking them for granted or seeing them as institutionally and socially functional, educators, school boards, and parents resisted fundamental change. The hold of the standard grammar of schooling was tenacious.

Resistance came from several quarters. Many teachers objected to the massive amount of paperwork and time for individualization that the plan required. Parents and educators protested that motivation and discipline of pupils deteriorated under the Dalton Plan; it was too easy to cheat or goof off, they said. Pupils sometimes complained that fulfilling solitary contracts was more boring than regular classwork. Some educators criticized the plan for not giving students enough social stimulus and training. A New York teacher saw it as yet another example of the method mania in public schools: "Last year it was the socialized recitation, or the Gary Plan, or dramatization or correlation; this year it is motivation, silent reading, or the Dalton Plan. Each is taken up in turn, indiscriminately adopted, presently elbowed out to make room for the next newcomer; and yet we are not saved. The old problems remain."[31]

Individual teachers, however, did "try little experiments in educational procedure" by using certain features of the reform in their self-contained classrooms. The Dalton Plan gave teachers optional strategies that they could adapt to classrooms organized in traditional ways. Components of the Dalton Plan also continued to appear in programs catering to potential drop-outs, low achievers in need of remedial work, disabled students, or creative pupils unmotivated by traditional instruction. Self-paced materials, contracts, flexibility in the amount of time students take to complete their work, periodic checks to determine whether content and skills have been mastered, and the use of teachers as coaches—these practices are common in such programs. Some vocational classes incorporated parts of the Dalton Plan and divided time in segments different from the traditional Carnegie unit. The notion of "laboratories" has reappeared from time to time as learning centers in progressive elementary classrooms.[32]

Convinced that the traditional grammar of schooling made no sense, Parkhurst wanted high schools to embrace her plan all at once in all of its details. This rarely happened, for it would have fundamentally changed the standard grammar of secondary schools and required school boards, parents, educators, and pupils to alter their cultural beliefs about the character of a "real school." But many of her ideas reappeared as hybrids in an evolving system of public education.

The Eight-Year Study

Other challenges to the standard grammar of schooling cropped up across the country. Innovative educators sought to blend subjects and to experiment with curricula, time, space, and numbers of students. They regarded departmental specialization, the Carnegie unit, and the graded school as straitjackets.

Time after time, teachers have experimented with merging high school subjects into core programs—fusing, say, American history and American literature—to permit greater intellectual integration and flexible use of time and class sizes. In the 1930s in the Canton, Mississippi, High School three teachers created what they called "the integrated work program" in which they and a group of first-year pupils spent five periods a day studying such topics as "Ethiopia, Her Friends and Enemies." They used social science, English, and mathematics to answer the questions generated by the students.[33]

One of the most famous and long-lasting attempts to revise curriculum and instruction along progressive lines occurred in Denver. It persisted through the tenure of four superintendents during the 1920s and 1930s. Jesse Newlon, who began his superintendency in 1920, was committed to Deweyan principles of relating the school to everyday life and involving teachers actively and continuously in devising curriculum and pedagogy. When a group of teachers work together over a period of time on a plan for instruction, he said, when that group "has carried on a series of investigations, has debated the issues pro and con in departmental meetings, in committee, and in faculty meetings . . . that group of teachers will teach better and with more understanding and sympathy than they could ever otherwise teach." Compared with the staff in similar cities, the teachers in Denver were highly educated. Between 1920 and 1930, over seven hundred teachers and principals worked on thirty-seven committees to revise thirty-five courses of study. Teachers chaired the committees, were given time during the day to work together, and had the assistance of university curriculum specialists. Committees revised syllabuses and test items based on the comments of the classroom teachers who field-tested the courses. In the process, Denver gained a reputation as a national leader in implementing progressive instruction.[34]

In Denver and elsewhere, progressive educators resented what they called domination by colleges of the secondary school program. "The reason for the nearly complete failure of the secondary schools to respond to the progressive stimulus," wrote a critic, "seems to lie in the college-entrance requirements, which effectively determine the major part of the secondary curriculum" and freeze the "curriculum in 16 admittedly artificial Carnegie units." To subordinate youth to an antiquated system of academic accounting in order to satisfy the demands of the colleges was artificial and anti-educational, reformers declared. The battle lines were drawn: progressives versus traditionalists.[35]

Out of this concern to adapt schooling to students—to what they needed to learn, in the way they learned best—instead of perpetuating institutional patterns dictated by the colleges, arose a major attempt to reform secondary education, the Eight-Year Study (1933–1941). The Progressive Education Association (PEA) sponsored the study, and the General Education Board and other foundations gave the participants over a million dollars (an immense sum at the time) to carry it out. The PEA's Commission on the Relation of School and College persuaded over two hundred colleges to admit highly qualified students on the recommendation of the principals of the schools selected to participate in the experiment. It was not difficult to enlist the colleges, for they were having trouble attracting students in the Great Depression and the twenty-nine schools were chosen as "institutions of the highest character and excellence and established reputation" from over two hundred nominated for the project. Among these model schools were ten innovative public high schools, including all the high schools in Denver, six model high schools in universities, and thirteen prestigious independent schools.[36]

Freed from such college requirements as Carnegie units in specific subjects, the schools came up with highly individual responses. Philosophically, the commission was determined not to tell local schools what to do with their newfound freedom, but it did provide curriculum consultants and a sophisticated group of evaluators to help them plan and appraise their programs. Often local reformers chose to experiment in mini-schools within a larger secondary school, which was the case in Denver.[37]

As time went by, reforms in the schools settled into certain common patterns. Teachers developed core programs that crossed departmental boundaries and varied the time periods and sizes of their classes. Students spent less time on mainline academic subjects and more on art, music, and drama. The distinction between the formal and informal curriculum began to dissolve as students participated in community service, artistic productions, publications, and decision making in school affairs. Teachers spent much time with each other and students in planning these activities. In short, the grammar of instruction became more individualized and student-centered, deemphasizing batch-processing.[38]

When evaluators compared the college grades of graduates of the twenty-nine schools in the Eight-Year Study with a matched set of graduates of more traditional secondary schools, they discovered that the former performed about as well as the latter in their courses and were more active in collegiate social, artistic, and political life. They also found that the graduates of the most progressive schools did the best in college. Given the high social-class background of most of the students and the quality of the selected schools, the success in college of the graduates of the twenty-nine schools does not seem surprising. The chief message of the experiment, said Frederick L. Redefer, the director of the PEA at the time of the study, "was that there is no single course of preparation for success in college." In theory, then, the high schools should have been free to alter the traditional departmentalization of subjects and other features of the grammar of schooling.[39]

If any schools should have been able to break the mold, to install a lasting new set of institutional practices, these should have been. They had originally been selected because they appeared to be outstanding schools, well financed and with staffs hospitable to reform. For the most part, they served prosperous student bodies. The sponsorship of the PEA, the enormous foundation grants, the curriculum consultants and evaluators, the summer workshops for planning, the favorable professional and popular publicity given to the project—these were assets not available to the average reformers of the time.

In 1950 Redefer and twenty-nine other participants in the Eight-Year Study—including representatives of fifteen of the private and public schools—gathered to assess the results of the study eight years after the official sponsorship ended. It is likely that these participants were more committed to the reforms than the average staff member. Redefer asked the group what was happening to the educational experiments as they aged: "Do they effect any permanent change in education? Do they leave any appreciable residue the year after?. . . Five years later? . . . Ten? How does educational change take place? Is education a carousel with widely heralded experiments slowly fading from the educational scene as some new attraction takes the spotlight and the music goes round and round?"[40]

The participants mostly agreed that the reforms had faded, and this judgment was confirmed when Redefer later visited sixteen schools. One of the participants at the conference captured the consensus of his colleagues when he said "the strong breeze of the Eight-Year Study has passed and now we are getting back to fundamentals. Our students write fewer articles in English and social science but they are better spellers." Core courses had dropped away, the Carnegie unit with its uniform periods had reappeared, and departments had reasserted their control of the curriculum. Students spent less time on the arts and extracurricular activities and more on conventional college preparatory subjects. Most schools had returned to the old grammar of schooling, though some evidence of the experiments remained.[41]

Redefer asked why this was the case. The participants pinpointed a number of external reasons: World War II and the Cold War produced a "concern for security [that] tended to strengthen conservatism and authoritarianism" in the school as well as in the society; in such times "everything connected with 'progressive education' was under fire" (some at the meeting suggested dropping the name "progressive"). Having more applicants, the colleges could be more selective than in the

1930s or early 1940s and either did not know about or disagreed with the finding that progressive programs produced good results. The experiment had been "too intramural," said one, and failed to anticipate resistance from parents and trustees.[42]

Internally, the experiment faded in part because the committed teachers became "exhausted by the demands made on them, [since] challenges' came too thick and fast for the faculty to digest them." Collaborative progressive teaching was highly labor-intensive and potentially unstable because of turnover of teachers. In many schools, traditionalists had opposed the reforms from the start and were happy to reassert the authority of the departments, standard schedules, and the academic disciplines when a more conservative climate reappeared. In some cases, as Redefer found when he visited individual sites, the "model schools" had not been progressive to begin with and had been more interested in the prestige of belonging to the elect than in experimenting. High turnover of teachers and administrators frustrated continuity. Where reforms stuck, typically the schools had been progressive even before the study and had continued to experiment afterward.[43]

The story of the Eight-Year Study and its aftermath reveals that substantial changes in the grammar of secondary schools were possible under highly favorable conditions. Colleges were eager to attract students and thus willing to suspend some requirements (as for Carnegie units in traditional subjects). Liberal ideologies attracted both teachers and families. Powerful support came from foundations and professional associations.

But when conditions changed—when elite colleges changed their tune in admissions, when the political and pedagogical climate turned conservative, and when the initial energy and enthusiasm for change dissipated—most of the schools reverted to the traditional grammar of instruction, understood by most parents and teachers as standard features of a "real school." Progressives were often only a fraction of the total faculties of the participating schools, and the changes they introduced probably penetrated their institutions only to a limited extent. In some schools, the traditional grammar of schooling was challenged only in experimental classes within the larger institution, and a decade later traditional forms of organization reasserted themselves even in these interstices of innovation. The familiar division of subjects into departments typically reemerged where core courses had thrived for a time. Herbert M. Kliebard observes that "if the success of the 65-year effort to reform the American curriculum is to be judged by the extent to which

English, mathematics, science, history, geography and the like simply survived the assault against them, then the effort must be counted a failure."[44]

In retrospect, the participants in the Eight-Year Study did not regard the experiment as a waste of time. They agreed that the effort "had been eminently worthwhile." It had energized both teachers and students. As a reform, the Eight-Year Study had a short, and largely happy, life. Teachers learned to plan together. "Much of the camaraderie developed between administrators and classroom teachers has continued . . . The part of the Study that has persisted is that which grows out of the thinking and philosophy of individuals." The major influence of the Eight-Year Study came not from creating a durable new grammar of schooling but from its impact—then and later—on participants who engaged in building a new pedagogical order.[45]

High Schools of Tomorrow

In the 1960s, years of innovation when rebels were questioning the conventional wisdom in education, reformers proposed another rethinking of time, subjects, space, and class size. They believed that they could and should change institutional forms when they no longer served humane goals. Typically they regarded the old grammar of schooling as rigid, hierarchical, and based on a constricted view of human nature. Students, the old system implicitly announced, were young workers who needed to be compelled to learn a desiccated curriculum by their supervisors—teachers—in standardized classes. Instead, the young should be seem as active, intellectually curious, and capable of taking charge of their own learning. Starting from that premise, reformers argued, the existing grammar of schooling made no sense.[46]

Reinventing the Rousseauean notion that people are born free but are everywhere in chains, some radical reformers rejected the institutional form of the public school outright, advocating "free schools" and "schools without walls" to take the place of conventional classrooms, preset curricula, and traditional teacher roles. A few followed the lead of Ivan Illich in calling for the "deschooling" of society. Although "free schools" briefly became a hot topic in the popular media and won influential advocates, they flourished for only a short time. Adventurous "schools without walls," where students became actively engaged in their communities, were tamed in practice into more traditional off-campus activities such as vocational programs offering academic credit to students working as salespeople in stores.[47]

Other reformers, more moderate in outlook and aspiration than the free schoolers or the deschoolers, proposed major organizational changes within the walls of the public schools. They called for ungraded and "open" elementary schools. They developed blueprints of high schools in which

time was a flexible resource (a system often called "modular scheduling");

year-long courses in established fields were often chopped into "mini-courses" to match the current interests of students and teachers;

teachers worked in teams rather than alone and taught students in large, medium-sized, and small classes;

classrooms were transformed into resource centers for independent study, split into rooms of different size for different teaching styles, and made into social centers where students could meet during time "modules" when they did not have a class.

Architectural and pedagogical forms should follow new functions, they argued, and new conceptions of education demanded a new grammar of instruction as well as open buildings.[48]

In the 1960s a coalition of influential organizations and individuals agreed that it was time to overthrow the Carnegie unit, the eggcrate classroom, the teacher-dominated traditional curriculum, passive styles of learning, and the isolation of teachers from each other. Beginning in 1961, the Ford Foundation poured millions of dollars into "lighthouse" high schools to demonstrate the value of comprehensive attacks on the pedagogical status quo. In 1968 the Danforth Foundation gave a grant of more than a million dollars to the National Association of Secondary School Principals (NASSP) for a Model Schools Project designed to create the "Schools of Tomorrow" incorporating these new ideas. Universities entered the reform partnership, developing computerized scheduling programs and training teachers and administrators for the new system.[49]

The experiment took place under favorable auspices, then, just like the Eight-Year Study. The decade of the 1960s was a time of optimism and urgency when innovation was the watchword among the enterprising principals in the NASSP. Foundations and the federal government (under Title III of the Elementary and Secondary Education Act of 1965) provided large amounts of seed money for schools deemed most likely to succeed. And changes did come rapidly. In Oregon, to which the Ford Foundation gave a statewide grant of $3.5 million in 1962, many educators decided to transform their high schools.[50]

At Marshall High School in Portland, Oregon, the principal and staff shifted to a flexible schedule, altered the building to house resource centers and classes of different sizes, and created teams of teachers assisted by aides who worked in the resource centers and performed other tasks. When the new plan started in September 1963, students no longer faced the familiar routine of six periods a day with the same teacher in the same subject at the same hour. The two thousand students met in eleven hundred separate class sessions, some in large groups, some medium-sized, and some small discussion groups of fifteen people. One-third of a student's time was unscheduled and free for conferences with teachers, working in the library or resource room, or lounging in the cafeteria. By holding the content of the curriculum more or less constant—preserving the departmental system and more or less traditional subject matter—Marshall High School avoided reinventing the entire program from scratch. For the motivated pupil the system worked well; it helped to individualize instruction and gave breathing space. But the unmotivated or alienated student tended to fall through the cracks or to cause disruption. "We still have discipline problems at Marshall," said the vice principal, "but we are trying to find ways to interest students who are convinced they hate school."[51]

Such students were a major concern of the team of educators who established John Adams High School in Portland in 1970. Because of their "frustrations . . . in their previous teaching in public schools," said the head of the instructional division at Adams, the team was "generally sympathetic to the view of human nature and human learning espoused by such contemporary educators as John Holt, Paul Goodman, and Herbert Kohl. We took it as a matter of faith that all students learn best in a free, unstructured setting where comparative evaluation and other extrinsic pressures are kept to a minimum." The school had most of the flexible organizational forms of Marshall, but the staff were also determined to alter the curriculum and the mode of governance. They replaced departmentalized academic courses with a team-taught interdisciplinary "general education program" that focused on social problems, basing it on the conviction that the course "should be a means to learn about a society in flux, one in which the only constant is change." They struggled to create a participatory mode of decision making in which not only administrators and teachers collaborated but students as well.[52]

Again, for some students—especially those who were "highly individualistic and creative"—the new form of schooling worked well. Many who had learned to succeed in a more directive environment, however, became frustrated when teachers did not tell "the student what he is to do, what he is to learn, nor how." A third group—alienated students "who had been damaged by previous failure" and lacked basic skills—cut classes, roamed the halls, and ended up without the help they needed "to survive in the world of work." And as for the teachers, getting used to new schedules and groupings of students, inventing the multidisciplinary curriculum, being responsive to students, and sharing in decision making left the staff "in a state of near exhaustion."[53]

The self-critical and adventurous educators who had planned the high school recognized that they faced a clash between their goals as reformers and the values embedded in the community they served. Although writers in the popular media and in the educational profession praised the school as a model for reforming secondary schooling, many local people in the lower-middle-class neighborhood surrounding the school were outraged at Adams's departure from what they knew to be a proper school. Two months into the first year of the Adams experiment, some parents formed a critical group called Citizens for a Better Adams. One parent complained: "Adams High does not teach respect for authority, discipline, basic scholarship, or orderly use of time. The school teaches gross egotism, extreme self-centeredness, myopic self-delusion, and general anarchy."[54]

By coupling fundamental changes in curriculum and governance with flexibility in the use of time and space and other challenges to the familiar grammar of instruction, Adams High School went well beyond reforms in most other innovative high schools of the era. Was it in fact easier to try to change everything at once? Probably not.

Few high school reformers went so far as to base learning on the libertarian philosophies of Holt and Goodman. But in a period when the bulge of youth from the baby boom began entering secondary schools, when the civil rights and feminist movements were attacking the educational status quo, when activists were protesting the war in Vietnam, and students were questioning traditional norms in unprecedented ways, educators in many high schools were seeking to individualize education, to stress inquiry and social betterment, and to give pupils more choice and initiative in their own learning.[55]

In the innovative schools, many students appreciated the new forms of flexibility, such as modular scheduling, electives, classes of different sizes, and free time during the school day. Reactions of teachers tended to be mixed. Some applauded the opportunity to work together, to hold large or small classes for different periods of time, and to revise the curriculum and create electives. But other teachers felt that they lived in a goldfish bowl as visitors poured in to see the schools of tomorrow (or, alternatively, that they worked in a "zoo"—a favorite epithet used by conservatives). High turnover among principals in the Model Schools Project hurt continuity in reform, especially since administrators had been catalysts for change in most schools.[56]

Many communities grew tired of the reforms and instead wanted the comfort of the familiar grammar of schooling. Most of the high schools of tomorrow gradually reverted to the familiar grammar of schooling. A substantial proportion of the parents and other community members criticized the way students used their free time. When principals in flexible high schools were asked to identify problems encountered, 94 percent said that low-achieving students had trouble budgeting time, 84 percent claimed that more students cut classes, 78 percent found that teachers had fewer individual conferences with students than expected, 84 percent observed that teachers continued to dominate discussion even in small classes, and 72 percent said that parents of children who were not performing well in school tended to blame the modular schedule.[57]

An evaluator of the projects supported by the Ford Foundation observed that "without exception, questions of student autonomy and discipline were raised by granting free time. This, along with the perceived erosion of academic standards, resulted in pressure from the communities as well as within schools to revert to more traditional patterns of organization." He found that over half the schools had dropped modular scheduling by 1970, and others had substantially modified it (recall that these were specially selected schools that had received grants and technical assistance as well). Policy talk about the virtues of flexible scheduling rose sharply in the 1960s and then dropped just as abruptly in the 1970s when the troubles in the high schools of tomorrow became more evident.[58]

By the 1970s, people had begun to think that high schools were in decline and that the institutional innovations of the previous decade were partly to blame. Gallup polls revealed that Americans were concerned about lax discipline and lower academic standards. In this new policy outlook, flexibility was a fault, not a virtue. Students should be in a regular class for a regular period, supervised by their teachers. They should have fewer curricular choices, not more. Students need a "real school." Go back to the good old days was the theme of much criticism, summed up by a California legislator who said the purpose of new school laws was to make "the little buggers work harder." Although they would have used more decorous language, the urban educators of the nineteenth century would have approved the sentiment. The aim of schooling, wrote an advocate of the graded school in 1885, "is the imposition of tasks; if the pupil likes it, well; if not, the obligation is the same."[59]

A bold yet fragile challenge to the grammar of schooling, the "High Schools of Tomorrow" of the 1960s and early 1970s ebbed as "back to basics" and "excellence" became mottoes of the next wave of reform. The experiment left behind here and there some new forms of flexibility and the memory that the grammar of schooling was mutable. But in most districts, the Carnegie unit, not the flexible schedule, remained the normal pattern.

Reflections

We have suggested a variety of interlocking reasons why some reforms become so institutionalized that they became the grammar of schooling. Political support for innovations like the graded school and the Carnegie unit came from powerful sponsors adept at persuading local school boards, state legislatures, state departments of education, and accrediting agencies to freeze their reforms into regulations and laws. The timing of these reforms was also crucial; the graded school arrived at the start of the rapid expansion of elementary education and the Carnegie unit on the threshold of a massive differentiation of the high school. The graded school and the departmentalized high school became building blocks in an interlocking and interdependent system; to change one part—say the accounting device of the Carnegie unit—disrupted familiar external controls such as standards for college admissions or accreditation.

Inside the schools, the grammar of schooling offered a standardized way to process large numbers of people. The grammar was easily replicable. The institutional design of graded schools produced a cookie-cutter sameness. The departmentalized high school had a greater variety of offerings but a uniform system of accounting, the Carnegie unit. Administrators, teachers, and students learned how to work in this system; indeed, the grammar of schooling became simply the way schools worked. Over time, the public, schooled in the system, came to assume that the grammar embodied the necessary features of a "real school."

Although laws, institutional custom, and cultural beliefs worked together to hold the grammar of schooling in place, from time to time reformers have argued that this grammar—itself a product of history—ill serves its purpose of educating students. Let us build instead, they have said, a new system based on sounder educational principles. Although the challengers have conducted energetic experiments, for the most part their reforms did not last long. Trying to create major change in one part of the system—a classroom, a school within a school, or even a whole school or district—proved difficult in a broader interdependent system based on the standard grammar. If the reformers attracted funds and professional attention, jealousies from more traditional peers intruded. Turnover of administrators and teachers undermined complex innovations that depended on commitment and special talents.[60]

Two serious problems recurred in the challenges we have examined. One was that the reforms were "too intramural." Lawrence A. Cremin has observed that progressive education declined in part because leaders lost some of their political savvy and lost touch with the opinions of citizens who were not educators. Concentrating on convincing their professional peers, they did not cultivate the kind of broader social movement that might nourish educational and social change. Failure to enlist the support and ideas of the community was especially harmful to fundamental reforms that violated the public's notions of a "real school," as was apparent, for example, in public reactions against the "high schools of tomorrow" in the late 1960s. In the face of such opposition, particularly when the climate of opinion was conservative, it was difficult to retain the resources and enthusiasm that sustained change.[61]

A second common problem was burnout among educational reformers. Changing basic organizational patterns created overload for teachers, for it did not simply add new tasks to familiar routines but required teachers to replace old behavior with new and to persuade pupils, colleagues, and parents and school boards to accept the new patterns as normal and desirable. Since evidence on outcomes of major structural reforms has been ambiguous, the practitioner "contemplating a change in classroom organization," Milbrey W. McLaughlin writes, "might be confronting a complicated innovation that shows no clear advantage over existing practices—at least in the ways that often matter most to school boards, voters, and anxious parents."[62]

Despite the problems faced by those who challenged the standard grammar of instruction, reform episodes such as the Eight-Year Study or the revisions of instruction in Denver were hardly a zero-sum game. Even if the reforms gradually faded, participants questioned in basic ways what they were doing and were energized by collaboration with colleagues.

What they learned still remained part of their potential teaching repertoire when their schools returned to more conventional patterns.

What does the historical experience suggest about attempts today to refashion the grammar of schooling? Should one conclude that it is impossible to improve schooling in basic ways? We think not, though the task is much harder than many people suspect. We suggest that actual changes in schools will be more gradual and piecemeal than the usual either-or rhetoric of innovation might indicate. Almost any blueprint for basic reform will be altered during implementation, so powerful is the hold of the public's cultural construction of what constitutes a "real school" and so common is the teachers' habit of hybridizing reforms to fit local circumstances and public expectations.

One reason that changing the grammar is difficult is that reforms in one classroom or mini-school or school or district take place within a larger interdependent system. Teachers in an experimental school may agree that they should combine subjects and teach for depth of understanding, believing that "less is more," yet college admissions officers may want applicants to have Carnegie units in specific academic subjects. State and district regulations and standard time schedules often impede change. Gaining the freedom to experiment demands political and organizational savvy and collective action.

Both in the past and in the present, reformers who have challenged the grammar of instruction have banded together for support and have often felt that they were part of a broad educational movement. They have embraced common goals, formed organizations to mobilize people, ideas, and funds, and worked collaboratively to lessen a sense of isolation and burnout and to encourage risk-taking and staff development. In this way, they have sought a middle course between the top-down mode of reform of the administrative progressives and the random approach of letting a thousand flowers bloom.[63]

Lest they, like their predecessors, become "too intramural" and thereby neglect public understanding and participation, reformers who want to change the grammar of schooling today need to enlist the support of parents, school boards, and the community more generally. Participation of the public in school decision making can, of course, lead to conflict and seem to threaten professional autonomy. But in a democracy, fundamental reforms that seek to alter the cultural constructions of a "real school" cannot succeed without lengthy and searching public dialogue about the ends and means of schooling.

5

Reinventing Schooling

"Imagine a new generation of American schools that are light years beyond those of today." This was the utopian goal that the New American Schools Development Corporation (NASDC) posed for educational reformers in the early 1990s. Chartered as part of President George Bush's "America 2000" education strategy, NASDC was formed to "unleash America's creative genius to invent . . . the best schools in the world . . . to achieve a quantum leap in learning." Don't be content with incremental change, said NASDC, but "assume that the schools we have inherited do not exist." This was no ordinary task, said President Bush; the redemption of society was at stake: "Think about every problem, every challenge we face. The solution to each starts with education. For the sake of the future—of our children and the nation—we must transform America's schools."[1]

In a mission with such high stakes, many leaders thought it time to bypass traditional educators and to ask business executives to take the lead in transforming education. The original board of directors of NASDC was composed almost entirely of the chief executive officers of large corporations, including the Commissioner of the National Football League. When the businessman Christopher Whittle decided to create a network of hundreds of for-profit schools, his original design team included only one experienced public educator. He was confident, however, that his high-technology, market-sensitive schools would provide a template of reform for all elementary and secondary education. He called his business venture the Edison Project because he claimed that his schools would be as superior to the average public school as a lightbulb is to a candle.[2]

Seventy years ago Thomas Alva Edison had similar dreams of transforming instruction. "I believe," he said, "that the motion picture is destined to revolutionize our educational system and that in a few years it will supplant largely, if not entirely, the use of textbooks." Maybe replace the teacher, too. Here is how one teacher of that time, Virginia Woodson Church, responded to this new dispensation:

Mr. Edison says
That the radio will supplant the teacher.
Already one may learn languages
   by means of Victrola records.
The moving picture will visualize
What the radio fails to get across.
Teachers will be relegated to the
Backwoods
With firehorses
And long-haired women.
Or perhaps shown in museums.
Education will become a matter
   of pressing the button.
Perhaps I can get a position
   at the switchboard.

Faith in electronic pedagogy has returned again and again.[3]

The radio did not quite supplant the teacher, and both NASDC and Whittle's break-the-mold schools may also fade. Such attempts to reinvent schooling have reappeared from time to time and attracted fresh attention, for many Americans revere inventors and entrepreneurs and persist in hoping that efficient management or novel technologies will solve intractable educational problems. For over a century, ambitious reformers have promised to create sleek, efficient school machines "light years" ahead of the fusty schools of their times. But in practice their reforms have often resembled shooting stars that spurted across the pedagogical heavens, leaving a meteoric trail in the media but burning up and disappearing in the everyday atmosphere of the schools.[4]

Innovators proposing or supporting start-from-scratch reforms have usually been people outside the public schools—technocrats, university professors, salespeople with products to push, politicians intent on rapid results before the next election, foundation officers, and business leaders. Impatient with the glacial pace of incremental reform, free of institutional memories of past shooting star reforms, and sometimes hoping for quick profits as well as a quick fix, they promised to reinvent education. When corporations decided to sign contracts with school districts to teach basic skills to potential drop-outs, their salespeople were counseled to employ "maximum plausible optimism" in convincing the public (this term was borrowed from the pitch of aerospace contractors to the Pentagon).[5]

Some of these innovators held the educational "establishment" in low regard as mossbacks. Major changes were really not that complicated, they said. Progress required that new reformers, sleeves rolled up, step in to set things right. NASDC, for example, "was cloaked in the image of American business taking swift, no-nonsense action," comments James A. Mecklinburger. "At the request of President Bush, business would fund and manage a you-ain't-seen-nothin'-yet competition." The first stage in reform was to convince citizens that the present system of schooling was inefficient, anachronistic, and irrational. The second stage was to claim sure-fire solutions. This has long been a strategy of utopians who condemned existing arrangements in order to persuade others to adopt their blueprint for a transformed future.[6]

During recent decades innovators who wanted to reinvent the public schools often turned to other social sectors for inspiration or support for the models of change they advocated—to business, the federal policy establishment, higher education, or foundations. They invoked the ideologies and practices of technology, business management, behavioral engineering, and new organizational forms to convince the public. Advocates of technology sometimes promised "teacher-proof" instruction (as if machines and software were free-standing mini-schools rather than one pedagogical tool among many). Business-oriented reformers adopted economic terms when they discussed schools, using words like "productivity," "market," "customers," "restructuring," "payoff," "rollout," and "Total Quality Management." The terms have changed over the years, but not the impulse to emulate business and to impress business elites, who dominated many school boards and policy forums.[7]

Like the board of the NASDC, past reformers believed that if they could create new-model schooling—lighthouse schools—their ideas would spread quickly across the educational landscape. This was an act of faith, for rarely did the advocates of new-model schools consult either history or practitioners. History was a source of problems more than of insight.[8]

And as for practitioners, why should policy analysts and entrepreneurs consult the very people who created the mediocrity of public education in the first place? But whether educators agreed or not with the break-the-mold innovators, the publicity given to the shooting star reforms made it difficult to disregard them entirely. At least it was prudent for practitioners to *seem* to respond lest they simply confirm the fusty image of educators. In the aftermath of Sputnik, for example, when some reformers sought technological solutions to educational problems, a panel of flashing lights in the high school physics classroom was reassuring on parents' night (even though teachers might find dry-cell batteries more useful for students' experiments than finicky electronic gadgets).

In this chapter we explore some examples of how outsiders tried to reinvent schooling

by importing into schools complex new techniques of management and budgeting developed by business and government during the 1960s and early 1970s;

by contracting instruction to innovators who claimed that private corporations could do a better job of teaching the basics than the public schools—and make a profit in the process;[9]

by employing technology to transform instruction;

and by basing incentives and career paths in teaching on competition and hierarchy.

The results of these attempts differed by reforms, but in the main, they had little lasting impact on public schools.

It is easy to trace the early trajectory of shooting star reforms, for there is a rich paper trail of such reforms in the advocacy stage, when people make grandiose claims for them. It is harder to discover why reforms fade, for when they do, strategic silence often ensues. Since success is often equated with survival, few people have bothered to chronicle transitory innovations. The volume of articles in the popular and professional press on transitory break-the-mold reforms has risen rapidly, then fallen as precipitously.[10]

Why were the start-from-scratch innovations proposed by outsiders mostly short-lived? Innovators outside the schools who wanted to reinvent education were often skilled in publicity and the politics of promising and claimed to use the latest models of rational planning. But they rarely factored into their plans a sophisticated understanding of the school as an institution or insight into the culture of teachers. They tended to treat "schools as though they were made of silly putty," easily molded, whereas good schools are more like healthy plants, needing good soil and careful tending over long periods of time. Outsiders who

113

tried to reinvent schooling rarely understood the everyday lives of teachers, their practices, beliefs, and sources of frustration and satisfaction. The hope that a few demonstration lighthouse schools would become models to transform entire school systems rarely became reality; instead, they were more likely to become boutique schools isolated from the mainstream.[11]

The Business of Schooling

Like their predecessors in the Progressive era, the business-oriented reformers of the 1960s and 1970s had ready-made technocratic solutions to educational problems. Sometimes they had products in search of markets. Many of them thought the current administrators of schools were incompetent as planners and unaccountable for results. One approach to reform was to transform the management of schools by adopting new managing and budgeting techniques such as Management by Objectives, the Program Planning and Budgeting System, and Zero Based Budgeting. Another was to treat public schools as a marketplace of instructional services in which corporations could compete in teaching children by using the latest technologies of instruction and behavioral engineering, such as teaching machines and extrinsic rewards for learning. Business methods of planning and budgeting, competition, and incentives, aided by new technologies—these could transform antiquated public schools into centers of efficient learning.[12]

Managing Education

In the early decades of the twentieth century, as we said in Chapter 1, business and professional elites increasingly controlled the school boards of cities. In their attempt to counter criticisms that the schools were inefficient, superintendents and university education experts rushed to borrow language and concepts from business, and "businesslike" became almost synonymous with "scientific."[13]

Ellwood P. Cubberley, for example, liked to propose the board of directors of a bank as the template for an effective school committee and the expert business manager as a model for the "scientific" superintendent of schools. He spoke of schools as "factories in which the raw materials (children) are to be shaped and fashioned into products to meet the various demands of life." Aware of criticisms that schools wasted the public's taxes, city school chiefs avidly calculated the cost effectiveness of everything from a lesson in Latin to the purchase of school desks. They

114

wrote detailed educational "objectives" and blueprints for instruction. Like efficiency experts in industry—the time-and-motion folk—they thought it possible for managers to plan tasks while workers (teachers, students) did the work.[14]

The language and imagery of business efficiency proved useful to superintendents who needed to please local elites, but much emulation of business was rhetorical and did not directly translate into classroom practices. Schools were not factories, and children were not passive raw materials. Like their students, teachers were active agents, not docile workers on a pedagogical assembly line. Once the schoolroom door was shut, most teachers retained considerable autonomy to instruct the children as they saw fit. The governance of education was not identical to the management of business, and school boards continued to be political agencies, however much they claimed to be "above politics." When business leaders fell out of favor during the Great Depression, for a time so did much of the impulse to emulate the rhetoric of business.[15]

A demand for accountability and cost-effective management in public schools revived the cult of efficiency in education during the 1960s and 1970s. Reformers urged educators to reinvent educational management and budgeting by adopting techniques developed by corporations, the military-industrial complex, university budgeting experts, and government agencies. These technocratic reformers had ready-made rational solutions in search of problems, and educational system seemed to them ripe for experiment.[16]

One such technique, Management by Objectives (MBO), stemmed from efforts to streamline business and industrial organizations. G. S. Odiorne defined MBO as "a system in which the first step of management is the clarification of corporate objectives and the breaking down of all subordinate activity into logical subdivisions that contribute to the major objectives." The Program Planning and Budgeting System (PPBS) also had its origins in industry. It proposed collecting and analyzing data in such a way that the costs of programs—or their alternatives—could be linked to short- and long-term plans and goals. Secretary of Defense Robert McNamara adapted PPBS to program planning and budgeting in the Pentagon in 1961, and in 1965 President Lyndon B. Johnson extended it to all government departments. Jimmy Carter discovered that Texas Instruments had developed Zero Based Budgeting (ZBB) as a way of forcing each unit to justify its budget in terms of company objectives— starting from zero. Carter then used ZBB in governmental budgeting as governor of Georgia and President of the United States. In each case, the goals were to increase the rationality of planning, to relate budgeting and management to specific organizational objectives, and to use data in the service of control (though such power was supposedly exercised in a "neutral" way). All three techniques of management and budgeting were applied to education, but the most prevalent was PPBS.[17]

Scholars disagree about how effective these systems were even in businesses where there was a clear objective—profit—or in a government agency, the Department of Defense, that used it to procure weapons. Aaron Wildavsky called PPBS "tremendously inefficient," saying the "inputs were huge and its policy output is tiny." In 1971 the federal Office of Management and Budget dropped PPBS. President Carter's first ZBB budget, in 1979, resulted in fewer program cuts than previous budgets in the 1970s, and the system met its demise when he was defeated in 1980. PPBS and ZBB cost a great deal of time and money, created new layers of bureaucracy, and heaped up piles of paper.[18]

Vulnerable to pressure from federal and state governments to become more accountable—especially when funding from those levels increased—school systems in many parts of the nation adopted PPBS. By 1970 about three-fourths of the states either had mandated or were considering requiring school districts to report in a program budget format. Their experience illustrates the problems of importing elaborate systems of accounting into educational governance and finance. In comparison with objectives at the Ford Motor Company or the Department of Defense, educational goals are often diffuse, and organizing them is like herding cats. One district ended up with fifty-eight separate objectives just for mathematics in the primary grades. "Results" were hard to measure and quantify, and the methods of achieving these objectives were frequently unclear.[19]

Many public school districts lacked staff with the analytic skills to gather and interpret the data used in PPBS. In any case, educators questioned whether such an expenditure of time, money, and paper was worthwhile, for it was unclear how it might improve instruction. While recognizing the need to demonstrate that children were learning and that money was well spent, teachers complained that "Mickey Mouse in triplicate"—their rendering of PPBS—was not the way to become accountable. In his ethnographic study of the implementation of PPBS in Oregon, Harry Wolcott argues that teachers regarded it as obtrusive and meaningless make-work rather than as a help in planning and accounting for their work.[20]

In 1966 California took its first steps to implement PPBS. Clothed in the trappings of expertise, PPBS appeared on the surface to be neutral and nonpolitical, but like Progressive era reforms, it centralized decision making. In California as elsewhere, education is intrinsically a value-laden and political enterprise. Many stake-holders who had traditionally negotiated and compromised in making school budgets felt excluded. Various citizens' groups, on the right as well as the left, attacked PPBS because they correctly perceived that planning involved basic moral and civic questions obscured by technocratic jargon. Thus it is not surprising that in 1972, responding to powerful opposition from both educators and lay citizens, the California State Board of Education dropped PPBS. PPBS manuals that had cost millions to create sat gathering dust in the state archives. Other states followed California's example, and before long PPBS and its kin dropped from sight.[21]

Contracting for Performance

In the late 1960s and early 1970s, many policymakers outside the schools and some educators inside them believed that business corporations could revolutionize the performance of low-achieving students. A number of large firms, several of them defense contractors, saw in the schools a vast potential market to cultivate as spending on the Vietnam War was decreasing. The federal government was adding about a billion dollars to state and local school budgets, and as former U.S. Commissioner of Education Francis Keppel quipped, "a billion dollars looking for a good, new way to be spent does not ordinarily turn the American businessman into a shrinking violet." For a time it seemed that the way to raise the achievement of low-achieving students was to contract out the teaching of basic skills to business corporations. This would assure efficiency and accountability.[22]

In Texarkana, Arkansas, in the fall of 1969, over a hundred pupils identified as potential drop-outs entered "Rapid Learning Centers" set up by Dorsett Educational Systems. In carpeted, newly painted rooms they went to pick up folders in which the teacher—called the "instructional manager"—had put the day's assignment and a record and filmstrip for each child. Then students plugged the software into a Dorsett teaching machine, put on the headset, and logged their time onto punch cards that were used to plan the next day's assignment. When they had correctly answered all the questions on the programmed lesson, they received ten Green Stamps. If they advanced a grade-level in reading or mathematics, they earned a transistor radio. The child who made the most progress for the year on achievement tests won the grand prize: a portable TV set. Diagnosis, prescription, achievement, reward—it was a *learning system* coupled with extrinsic rewards. The goal: to accelerate

117

the learning of children who were falling behind in school—and to make a profit for Dorsett, which had created the system.[23]

Texarkana represented the dawn of a bright new day, some thought, when for-profit businesses would contract with school districts to use technology and scientific management of learning, well-laced with extrinsic incentives, to produce *Results:* higher student achievement in the basic subjects. No results, no pay. The Behavioral Research Laboratories (BRL) took charge of a public school in Gary, Indiana, the Banneker School, in 1971. When a systems analyst with experience at Lockheed took over as "center manager" at Banneker, he asserted that there was basically no difference between schools and industry. "I view things analytically," he said. "Keep out emotions . . . You don't have to love the guy next to you on the assembly line to make the product. He puts in the bolts, you put in the nuts, and the product comes out." A Gary teacher retorted: "There's no way a man with that attitude can succeed in a school. No way."[24]

The worlds of the technocrats and the teachers were, indeed, miles apart. BRL had developed programmed books and materials to teach reading and saw the chance to run its own learning system in a Gary public school as a way to shake up what the chairman of BRL's board called the "mindless, inefficient, hideously mismanaged" public school system. There were, in name at least, no "teachers" at the Banneker School; instead, it employed a center manager, a learning director, five curriculum managers, fifteen assistant curriculum managers, and twenty learning supervisors in a hierarchy of responsibility and pay (the word "teacher" apparently had bad connotations for BRL). Just as students had done decades before in Gary's "platoon system," the students in the BRL school circulated from room to room—or rather from curriculum center to curriculum center—to work on different academic subjects and in fields such as art, music, and physical education.[25]

Some leaders of teachers' organizations and educational policymakers protested that in Texarkana, Gary, and elsewhere the systems people had radically restricted the goals of schooling to drill and practice on the basic skills and performance on standardized tests. The tests themselves, some argued, were faulty measures of achievement. Gains in test scores might be only temporary results of the "Hawthorne effect" (the positive impact of attention), the fanfare about the project, and carpeted and air-conditioned rooms. Many teachers considered extrinsic rewards to be inappropriate bribery for learning and questioned the effectiveness of "contingency management." One teacher in Texarkana said, "I wonder if the children are *really* learning or just storing a little knowledge for long enough to get the reward." Teachers complained that the prepackaging of learning robbed them of the chance to exercise their own professional knowledge and discretion, and some feared that "curriculum managers" and machines might threaten their jobs. But the most fundamental criticism, and one that led people to legally challenge the BRL-run school in Gary and to close it down, was that public districts were abdicating their role in shaping public policy in education when they delegated instruction to private agencies.[26]

Dorsett and BRL were only two of dozens of corporations, large and small, that regarded performance contracts as a way to make profit by teaching children who were lagging in academic achievement. These companies saw schooling as a vast new market that might take up the slack in defense contracts that were winding down along with the Vietnam War. Many school board members, government officials, and educational entrepreneurs were eager to give businesses a chance to raise levels of academic performance among these students. In 1970 President Nixon's Office of Economic Opportunity (OEO) sponsored a performance-contracting experiment in which thirty-one companies competed for performance contracts in eighteen selected school districts (this coincided with another OEO experiment with markets in education, a voucher plan).[27]

The six companies that won the contracts agreed to receive no payment if pupils did not make a year's gain on standardized tests but stood to make a good profit if they did. In 1970 the federal government also subsidized twenty other performance contracts. In most cases, the companies relied on teaching machines and/or programmed materials, individual diagnosis and prescription of learning, and extrinsic incentives. The resulting trend, said two observers, was "not so much toward educational reform under the initiative of the public sector as it is . . . toward marketing and sales with the private sector setting the terms. The public may find that in the majority of cases it is simply paying a higher price to put last year's product in this year's favorite package." The chair of the House Education Subcommittee, Representative Edith Green, worried about the funds flowing to defense contractors that were entering the education business: "It is accurate to say that anyone with a brainstorm can come to Washington and get financing from the Office of Education or the Office of Economic Opportunity."[28]

Although Dorsett's instructional system in Texarkana became the model for most other performance contracts, in one respect it became a scandal to be avoided. One day the district's project director was visiting its Rapid Learning Centers to monitor the year-end test that would determine how well Dorsett had done its job. A boy mentioned to him that he had already seen one of the test items; it was about a visit to a submarine. The cat was out of the bag. It turned out that in their daily lessons just before the big examination the students had been studying items taken from the test. The centers were not just teaching *to* the test; they were teaching the test. The person responsible explained that Texarkana had assigned too many low-IQ students to the program and that the standard curriculum did not work well with them. Under pressure to show results and to make a profit for the company, she wove test items into the daily lessons.[29]

The Texarkana scandal moderated but did not halt enthusiasm for performance contracting. It made government agencies such as OEO and local districts more careful about getting independent audits, however, and these reports deflated the claims of the promoters. A study by the Rand Corporation in December 1971 reported that the experiment did speed up instructional change but that it focused narrowly on basic skills and introduced tricky problems of measurement and legal responsibility. The Rand researchers found a very mixed picture of test gains. The Battelle Memorial Institute, the agency charged with evaluating the OEO experiment, presented its findings in 1972. In comparing the experimental classes taught by the companies with similar groups taught in the traditional manner, Battelle discovered that twice as many traditional classes scored better than the experimental classes in math and nine control classes did better in reading compared with six of the performance contracting groups. Overall, there was no significant difference between the experimental and control groups. The OEO discontinued its funding. By 1975, after further negative studies, *Education Daily* declared that "performance contracting has been pronounced dead."[30]

As Myron Lieberman pointed out, the brief "experiment" was flawed as a scientific and practical enterprise. Thus it is not clear precisely what was being measured: performance contracting, incentive plans, differentiated staffing, new instructional technology, or what? But it did become clear that effective teaching of educationally disadvantaged children was no simple matter to be solved by business expertise, extrinsic incentives, and programmed instruction. And it was equally obvious that even with federal subsidies there were few rich lodes of profits for companies to mine in the serried hills of American public education. The hope for easy solutions to educational problems and profits from pedagogy did not disappear, however. New reformers, salespeople, and political allies would come again to promise that the private sector could succeed where the public "establishment" had allegedly failed.[31]

Teaching by Machine

Many Americans relish technological solutions to the problems of learning. It has long been so. Hear the rhetoric of another era: "The inventor or introducer of the system deserves to be ranked among the best contributors to learning and science, if not among the greatest benefactors of mankind." The time was 1841. The "system" was the blackboard, which another salesman forty years later described as "the MIRROR reflecting the workings, character and quality of the individual mind." And so it went, as advocates of educational radio, film, television, and programmed learning predicted pedagogical Nirvanas that never materialized.[32]

Worry as well as hope has fueled waves of enthusiasm for educational technology. Reformers have turned to machines when they were concerned about the competence of teachers, or the high cost of schooling, or some external threat to American security or prosperity that gave special urgency to education.

The people who promised educational moonshots through technology were an assorted lot. Not surprisingly, many were business people who wanted to market their wares to the schools. Some were scholars and academic entrepreneurs—psychologists, for example, who thought that programmed instruction would streamline pedagogy. Foundation officials seeking a quick impact on schooling sometimes saw the new media as a way around the briar patch impeding educational change. Some educational administrators who wanted their schools to be up to date embraced new technologies. A new specialist who had a vested interest as well as a faith in technology appeared in colleges, state departments of education, and school districts: the audiovisual expert.[33]

In the top-down process of advocating and implementing technology, teachers were rarely consulted, though it was mainly their job to make it work in the classroom. A small minority of teachers welcomed media such as radio and films, believing that they would motivate their reluctant students and make their own instruction easier and more effective. Most, however, used the new devices minimally or not at all. As new forms of pedagogy by machine appeared, a familiar cycle of reform recurred: hyperbolic claims about how a new invention would transform education; then research showing that the technology was generally no more effective than traditional instruction and sometimes less; and finally, disappointment as reports came back from classrooms about the imperfections of the reform and as surveys showed that few teachers were using the tool.[34]

Whom to blame? The obvious scapegoat was the teacher unwilling to climb onto the new bandwagon. Whatever the audiovisual reformers might have hoped, behind the classroom door teachers remained the key influence on instruction. By and large, they used the technologies that fit familiar routines and classroom procedures—in other words, that helped them solve their problems of instruction. The rest they mostly ignored.[35]

Many technical inventions have in fact made their way into classrooms and are now so familiar that few people even notice them. Consider these: the blackboard, of course; cheap paper, which replaced slates; books for each child made possible by sharp drops in production costs; paperbacks, which supplemented hardcover textbooks; globes and maps; ballpoint pens, which replaced the steel-nib pens that had replaced quill pens; and, though they were controversial, cheap hand-held calculators. More complex technologies have had much less impact on everyday teaching than the simple, durable, reliable improvements like the chalkboard that enhanced what teachers were already doing. Teachers have regularly used technologies to enhance their regular instruction but rarely to transform their teaching.[36]

Advocates of film as a mode of instruction saw it as the very emblem of progressive pedagogy, for it promised to breathe visual reality into the spoken and printed word. But again the companies that wanted to sell technical solutions and the educators enjoined to use them tended to live in different worlds. One advocate of films reported that teachers "failed to make their problems articulate to the commercial producers," while business people "failed to grasp or to study the nature of instruction and the complexity of educational institutions." Many of the early "free" films were thinly disguised commercials for products and resented as such by teachers. Especially to blame for the cool reception teachers gave film was "the stupidity which has characterized the advertising, propaganda, and sales methods of companies" that claimed that moving pictures might supplant textbooks and even teachers.[37]

The early projectors were expensive and required constant maintenance, and films themselves were costly and needed to be shared by many teachers. For these reasons, film was first used in large cities and wealthy suburbs. Most districts had no projectors; rural schools often lacked electricity. In 1936, after a decade of florid claims about educational motion pictures, a survey of 21,000 districts (9,000 replied) found that across the nation there were only about 6,074 silent-film projectors and 458 sound-film projectors (it did not say how many of these were in good repair and actually in use). By 1954, when equipment was cheaper and more reliable, the National Education Association estimated that schools had one projector for every 415 students.[38]

But even when districts had the necessary equipment and films, teachers used educational films sparingly, except for a small cadre of enthusiasts. A study of 175 elementary teachers in New Haven, Connecticut, discovered that teachers ordered about fifteen hundred films in one year, but two-thirds of the orders came from twenty-five mediaphiles. When researchers investigated obstacles to the use of moving pictures, they pinpointed the teachers' lack of skills, the cost of purchase and upkeep of the equipment, and the inability to find the right fit between films and class lessons.[39]

On its face, radio was a simpler medium to use than film. But again, lack of equipment originally limited diffusion of the reform. In the mid-1930s superintendents reported only about one radio per district. An expert on educational radio estimated in 1945 that only 5 percent of children heard radio regularly in their classrooms. When principals in Ohio were asked what were the blocks to greater use of radio, they listed lack of radios (50 percent), poor equipment or reception (30 percent), and lack of coordination of radio programs with the curriculum. But advocates of radio education instead blamed teachers' "indifference and lethargy, even antagonism, toward this revolutionary means of communication."[40]

Television was going to be different, said reformers. In the 1950s, when the Ford Foundation entered the arena of electronic teaching with its subsidies and publicity, the campaign for instructional television gained momentum. Soon an airplane was circling over the Midwest beaming down programs to six states. Hagerstown, Maryland, developed a model system of closed-circuit television that promised a richer curriculum at less cost. By 1961 the Ford Foundation had spent $20 million for classroom television, and the next year Congress appropriated another $32 million for that purpose.[41]

Despite unprecedented public attention and enthusiastic promotion, instructional television made slow headway. A survey of public schools in 1961 found only 1.65 TV sets per district. In the mid-1960s, as federal dollars flowed into the schools, districts that had been too poor to buy adequate audiovisual equipment were able for the first time to acquire television sets along with many other kinds of machines and software. But the machines often sat idle in closets. In the 1970s teachers reported that they showed TV programs only 2 to 4 percent of classroom time. A decade after classroom television was introduced with a flourish, a fervent advocate lamented: "If something happened tomorrow to wipe out all instructional television, America's schools and colleges would hardly know it was gone."[42]

The history of film, radio, and television in the public schools shows a common pattern. Initially, nonteachers who pushed teaching by machine made extravagant claims. When a minority of teachers responded enthusiastically, technophiles were pleased. But this rarely happened, for electronic learning was marginal to most instruction in classrooms. How might this historically dominant pattern be interpreted?

Explanations abound. Disappointed reformers complained that teachers were laggard and fearful if not incompetent. Teachers gave other reasons. They pointed to problems with hardware: there was not enough, or it was broken or complicated, or it took too much time to arrange for its use. They criticized the content of the films or television and radio programs as inappropriate to the curriculum, as not fitting the class schedule, or as of poor quality. Top-down implementation provoked many teachers to dig in their heels or simply to put technology in the closet.[43]

But perhaps the most fundamental block to transforming schooling through machines has been the nature of the classroom as a work setting and the ways in which teachers define their tasks. We have suggested that the regularities of institutional structure and of teacher-centered pedagogy and discipline are the result of generations of teachers' experience in responding to the imperatives of their occupation: maintaining order and seeing that students learn the standard curriculum. Teachers have been willing, even eager, to adopt innovations such as chalkboards or overhead projectors that help them do their regular work more efficiently and that are simple, durable, flexible, and responsive to the way they define their tasks. But they have often regarded teaching by machines as extraneous to their central mission.[44]

Will teaching and learning by personal computers suffer the same fate of hyperbolic claims by advocates and then marginalization in schools? Certainly there has been plenty of hyperbole about the educational uses of computers, but computers are different in important ways from the other machines and media we have examined.

Computers are tools that are sweeping across workplaces as diverse as offices, stores, airlines, steel plants, hospitals, and the military. Increasingly, families use computers at home for a variety of tasks. Citizens have put pressure on schools to familiarize the young with the uses of this powerful new tool, believing that if they do not, the next generation will be handicapped in getting jobs in an age of information. No public urgency compelled such attention to the media previously used in schools.

As a result of this public concern, computers have spread far more rapidly in schools than did any earlier forms of electronic hardware. From 1984 to 1992 over a billion dollars was spent on equipping schools with computers. A few statistics suggest the broad outlines of a rapidly changing picture:

In 1981, only 18 percent of schools had computers, but by 1993, 99 percent had them.

In 1981, only 16 percent of schools used computers for instructional purposes. By 1993, 98 percent reported that they did so.

The number of students per computer decreased from 125 in 1981 to 14 in 1993.[45]

Although substantial progress has been made in installing computers in schools and in convincing the public that facility in using them is vital to students' success in school and jobs, there are serious social inequalities in the use of computers in schools. Students from high-income families have far more access to computers and to sophisticated uses of them than do students from low-income families. Black students use them less than whites, females less than males, and pupils whose native language is not English less than those who are proficient in English. Charles Pillar, who investigated use of computers in schools for the magazine *Macworld,* lamented "the creation of the technological underclass in America's public schools." He observed that "computer-based education in poor schools is in deep trouble. Inner-city and rural school districts rarely have the skills or funds to maintain their machines. These districts lack the training and social support to use computers effectively. In most cases, computers simply perpetuate a two-tier system of education for rich and poor."[46]

Simply having access to computers and learning to use them as tools is only part of the story of the educational use of computers. To what degree are they actually employed as sophisticated teachers' aides and integrated into instruction? A study reveals that when students do use computers (and not all do), they spend only a little more than an hour per week on the machines. What students do on computers varies greatly. Eleventh-grade students, for example, mostly go to computer laboratories to learn about computers and seldom use them in their academic subjects. Low-income students are more likely to do drill and practice on computers than to use them for problem solving and complex thinking. Excellent software for classroom learning is scarce; typically it lags far behind the capacity of the hardware. Computers can communicate efficiently and enhance learning, but often what humans place in them is pedestrian.[47]

A significant minority of teachers have welcomed computers as an aid to learning and incorporated them in imaginative ways in their classrooms. These serious users, like colleagues in earlier generations who welcomed film, radio, and television, are outnumbered by those who are content to have students leave their classes to go to the computer lab down the hall. The overall picture that emerges after over a decade of advocates' claims and public urgency is that computers play a marginal role in regular instruction in public schools. A one-line summary of the situation to date might be: computers meet classroom; classroom wins.[48]

The educational potential of the computer is already apparent, but the jury is out on how soon and how extensively the computer will be incorporated in everyday instruction. Computers are by far the most powerful teaching and learning machines to enter the classroom. Students and teachers can interact with computers in ways impossible with film, radio, and television. Depending on the software, preschoolers through graduate students can write and edit, learn languages, have a machine "tutor" in algebra, retrieve a great variety of information from electronic disks or distant libraries, receive E-mail from students a continent away, prepare multimedia reports, and use state-of-the-art technology in drafting, auto mechanics, and office work. In special education, computers help blind, deaf, and multiply-disabled students read, write, and communicate in ways that heretofore were unavailable. These various uses of the computer, valuable in themselves, will still require the integration and sense-making that a good teacher can provide. And whether teachers will embrace this new technology depends in good part on the ability of technologically minded reformers to understand the realities of the classroom and to enlist teachers as collaborators rather than regarding them as obstacles to progress.[49]

The Business of Teaching

Like the application of technology, systems analysis, and performance contracting to public education, attempts to model the occupation of teaching on business practices have sometimes ignored the rewards that teachers find most important in their classrooms and in their daily relationships with each other. Outsiders' campaigns to create competition among teachers for merit pay and to erect career ladders for them have rarely succeeded, for they have been out of alignment with the values and practices of teachers.[50]

From time to time, foundation officials, business leaders, school board members, media commentators, university professors, legislators, governors, and other reformers have concluded that existing incentives and career paths in teaching made no sense. Salaries did not reflect performance. Teachers were not equally competent, they thought, and career trajectories were too flat in teaching. Policy talk about merit pay and differentiated staffing has been especially frequent in periods when business efficiency was a popular theme and competitive market solutions were in favor. Treating schools as if they were open-market institutions and teachers as if they were employees in competitive organizations has made sense to outsiders, but teachers have often questioned the assumptions underlying this model and opposed it passively or actively.[51]

Merit pay and hierarchical career ladders contradicted a reform that teachers themselves fought to install in schools from World War I forward: a single salary schedule for all public school teachers, elementary and secondary, male and female. While supporting salaries calibrated to training and years of experience, teachers opposed "class distinctions" in pay based on position or sex and endorsed "the *fundamental intrinsic equality of all good teaching.*" To ensure that all teachers were, in fact, professionals, they worked to require special training and certification as prerequisites for employment in teaching.[52]

The history of teaching as an occupation suggests why the values and perceptions of teachers are different from those of the outsiders who wanted to restructure the profession. In the nineteenth century in small school districts, hiring took place in a more or less open labor market: local school boards basically could hire whomever they wished at whatever was the going wage, for standards of training and certification were low or nonexistent. Most teachers then were not even graduates of secondary schools. Farmers on school committees selected teachers rather the way they would choose a hired hand or a servant to help in the house. Teachers' salaries differed widely from place to place and even in the same one-room school in summer and winter.[53]

From the point of view of those who believe in an open labor market as a guarantee of merit, this was an efficient system. In theory, at least, school boards hired the person who would provide the best service for the least money. In practice, educators complained, committee members were apt to hire inept teachers for extraneous reasons—they might be relatives, or be in debt to a school board member, or be members of the dominant church, or be full of a manly bluster thought to be suitably cowing to the older boys in their classes. Male teachers almost always earned more than did females, though there was growing evidence that women taught at least as well as men.[54]

In large cities, the structure of the labor market in teaching was quite different from that in the countryside. Although there was plenty of nepotism and corruption in the selection of teachers, urban systems were much more bureaucratized. Individual teachers generally did not bargain with lay boards in determining their salaries; instead, most districts published regular salary schedules. These scales explicitly paid men more than women and secondary teachers more than elementary ones.[55]

Reformers in teacher associations disliked both the open-market system of hiring teachers in the countryside and the invidious distinctions in pay in cities. They wanted the same pay for elementary and secondary teachers and for women and men. They also wanted to restrict the labor market by requiring professional training and certification. They hoped thereby to raise the quality of instruction and to increase the inadequate pay of teachers. In the early twentieth century, this notion of professional training and state certification rapidly gained ground.

Especially after the women's suffrage amendment in 1920, the NEA's Department of Classroom Teachers lobbied state legislatures and local school boards to adopt single salary schedules that paid women and men and elementary and secondary teachers the same. By 1930 ten states had adopted equal-pay laws, and a single salary scale had spread to many cities across the nation. In such places, differential pay depended not on sex or type of school but on years of service and extent of professional preparation. All teachers who made teaching a long-term career and obtained the necessary education could in time receive the top salary.[56]

Educators applauded the fact that well-trained and experienced elementary teachers did not have to move to high schools to receive top pay. Teaching was equally challenging at all levels, they believed. They also found that equal pay improved morale and eliminated or decreased what they called "class distinctions" between secondary and primary teachers. The adoption of single salary scales "throughout the nation," wrote a Seattle principal, "would be a democratizing influence which would make itself felt for the great good of the youth of the Nation; for the work of grade and high-school teachers is so intimately related that close cooperation between them is very necessary."[57]

But the practice of single salary schedules simply did not make sense to many people. At the very time when organized teachers were attempting to create more uniform compensation, in the opening decades of the twentieth century, elite school board members and some superintendents were seeking to make teacher evaluations "scientific" and to link those ratings to salary increases.

How do you motivate large numbers of teachers to perform beyond the minimum expectation? How do you get more teachers to excel when they work in isolated classrooms where inspection is infrequent? These basic questions facing school boards and superintendents led many of them to emulate business by creating the earliest merit-pay programs, which would allegedly pay teachers according to performance. From the beginning, however, the rating of teachers was controversial. "We all agree that one teacher differs from another in merit," wrote a superintendent in 1921, "and yet few practical schoolmen have made the attempt [to rate and pay them by merit], and most of those who have done so have lived to repent of their rashness."[58]

Susan Moore Johnson has commented that each time merit pay became an "educational vogue . . . it was considered a novel reform." The present-day call for differentiating the roles and rewards of teachers is only the latest episode in a long history of attempts by outsiders to attract and retain the most gifted instructors, to create meritocratic standards of performance and pay, and to erect hierarchies among teachers. In recent years, many states have passed laws mandating merit pay, career ladders, and other measures to differentiate the functions and rewards of teachers.[59]

Both in the past and in the present, teachers have mostly resisted such reforms. They have not trusted the ability and fairness of administrators charged with assessing "merit." They have typically regarded merit pay not as an incentive but as a bother, as a threat to professional comity, and as irrelevant to the chief intrinsic rewards they experienced—seeing their pupils grow intellectually and socially.[60]

One instance of open conflict erupted when the school board in Kalamazoo, Michigan, decided to reward teachers differently in 1974. *The American School Board Journal* trumpeted the Kalamazoo plan as the end to lockstep pay and unaccountable staff. "Take it from Kalamazoo," the *Journal* said: "A comprehensive, performance-based system of evaluation and accountability can work." This judgment was premature. The merit scheme, in which "nearly everyone evaluated everyone else," choked on paperwork and provoked frustration, not superior performance. The administrators joined the United Automobile Workers union to fight merit pay, and the teachers' union managed to recall six of the seven board members who had supported differential compensation. But repeated experiences like this one in Kalamazoo did not prevent reformers from proposing merit pay again and again.[61]

The history of performance-based salary plans has been a merry-go-round. In the main, districts that initially embraced merit pay dropped it after a brief trial; only a small number of districts continued to use merit pay for decades. In the 1950s merit pay became a fashionable idea, and by the 1960s about 10 percent of districts had adopted some version of payment by performance. By the early 1970s interest had again declined: just over 5 percent of districts said they had merit pay. A 1978 national survey found 115 districts (4 percent of those with more than three hundred students) with provisions for payment by performance, and many of these did not in fact pay teachers differentially. When two researchers went back to those districts five years later they found only 47 still using performance-based compensation. These districts tended to be small, to have fairly homogenous student populations, and to employ merit pay in inconspicuous ways. Although there was another resurgence of interest in merit pay in the 1980s, in the mid-1980s more than 99 percent of teachers were paid on a uniform salary schedule.[62]

In 1986 Richard Murnane and David K. Cohen described six districts where merit pay had been in existence for more than five years. In these schools, merit pay was a voluntary addition to the established salary, earned by extra work outside the classroom, and seldom amounted to a large bonus. Teachers helped to shape the rules of the plan. Murnane and Cohen argue that what kept these plans going was precisely that these districts avoided making problematic distinctions between teachers based on their classroom performance. Instead, they used the plan to provide chances for teachers to earn extra money by engaging in school-related activities, such as revamping curriculum or evaluation of students' work.[63]

Why have so few schemes to pay teachers for their performance stuck? Murnane and Cohen argue that merit pay seldom works if its intent is to get teachers to excel, for little agreement exists among administrators and teachers about just what effective teaching is and how to measure it. In part, the complexity of the teaching act foils merit pay. Internal strife erupts over administrators' judgments when some teachers win "outstanding" marks and others only "average" grades.

Outsiders who pushed merit pay and career ladders often misperceived what in fact motivates teachers to do a better job. Susan Moore Johnson, who actually did ask teachers about incentives and disincentives, found that teachers had good reasons for their opposition to merit pay:

> Promoting competition among colleagues would reduce rather than increase the productivity of schools because teachers would conceal their best ideas and pursue their own interests rather than the general good. Moreover, performance bonuses might perversely reward teachers for success with able students while discouraging efforts with those who progress more slowly. Finally, teachers resented policymakers' efforts to entice them with the prospects of one-time bonuses for a select few when many teachers held second jobs just to meet basic living expenses. By seeking to provide recognition for exemplary teachers, potentially at the expense of many others, the reforms threatened egalitarian norms that the profession supports.[64]

Teachers are not afraid of evaluation, she insists: "they perform before exacting critics [their students] every day." What they dislike is being pitted in competition with each other or judged according to arbitrary standards by people whom they do not particularly trust. The "egalitarian norms" shared by most teachers contradict the premises of merit pay and hierarchy of the sort represented in career ladders.[65]

Obviously, teachers care deeply about receiving adequate salaries—they rarely do—and appreciate public recognition and status, but they and the public have quite different perceptions of their sources of satisfaction and dissatisfaction. When polled in 1981 about what bothered teachers the most, the general public listed poor discipline first and salaries second; teachers listed unfavorable public attitudes toward education first and salaries fourth. Over the years, many studies have shown that teachers value most highly the intrinsic rewards of the occupation that come from seeing their pupils develop and that they treasure praise from students, parents, and colleagues. In 1975 Dan Lortie found that in Dade County, Florida, teachers reported that the biggest extrinsic reward they received (37 percent) was "Respect from others" and the biggest psychic reward (an overwhelming 86 percent) was "Knowing that I have 'reached' students and that they have learned." Johnson found a similar pattern in the 1980s among the teachers she interviewed, though such rewards of respect and praise were all too infrequent.[66]

Reflections

In a society prone to equating change with progress, it is not surprising that people who promise to reinvent schooling attract followers. Innovators appeal to the faith that Americans have vested in education as an engine of social betterment and to the fear that existing schools cannot fulfill their high hopes. Indeed, the dream of a golden age in the future has often been a central theme in utopian designs to reinvent education in the present.

Setting high goals is an essential stage in reform, but raising expectations to a level likely to be achieved only by "schools that are light years beyond those of today" can quickly lead to discouragement or disillusionment. Perhaps even more than the average citizen, teachers tend to be allergic to utopian claims for reform, for they, the agents supposed to carry out break-the-mold reforms, are often the people blamed when grandiose innovations fail.

Expressions of alarm and overpromising may win public support in the short run, for fear and hope can be strong motivators. But hype can lead to distrust and the "acid rain" of cynicism. In 1991 a representative sample of parents were asked if they thought that some of the utopian goals of *America 2000* would in fact be accomplished in the next nine years. Only 4 percent thought that "every school will be free of drugs and violence"; 14 percent believed that "every American adult will be literate"; and 19 percent agreed that "American students will be first in the world in science and math." What will happen to public confidence in leaders—and in public schools—when these impossible goals are *not* met in the millennial year 2000?[67]

In recent decades, the utopian impulses to reinvent schooling have often flickered and faded. Some who promised Nirvana have been hucksters eager to sell their products. Others have been activists convinced of the need for fundamental change. A few have been politicians driven by the deadlines imposed by elections. But rarely have start-from-scratch reformers with their prefabricated innovations really understood the tenacity of the grammar of schooling or the need to adapt change to local knowledge and needs. An undercurrent in much policy talk about reinventing schools is that existing teachers are a drag on reform, deficient if not dim. Some *are* inadequate, to be sure, and some resist change simply because it may create more work. But across the nation there are teachers who have the wisdom to reject fashionable innovations that violate their sense of what their pupils need and instead to experiment on their own terms with reforms they believe in.[68]

Lighthouse schools often end up standing alone for a time and then regress toward the mean. Model schools can also become boutique schools, out of touch with less favored institutions. Edward J. Meade, Jr., senior program officer of the Ford Foundation, observed in 1991 that "there are lessons that can be learned from past efforts which included the development of 'new schools,' e.g. the Ford Foundation's Comprehensive School Improvement Program in the 1960s and the federal government's Experimental Schools Program of the 1970s . . . rarely do new school 'models' illuminate or instruct other schools."[69]

Rather than starting from scratch in reinventing schools, it makes most sense to us to graft thoughtful reforms onto what is healthy in the present system. Schooling is being reinvented all the time, but not necessarily in ways envisaged in macro planning. Good teachers reinvent the world every day for the children in their classes. Vicki Matthews-Burwell, a fifth-grade teacher in the New Plymouth Elementary School in Caldwell, Idaho, finds that "my students don't know about the Goals 2000 education reform act. . . . To them, Chapter I is a room by the library." But they do know that they "stood on a model of a Tenochitlan causeway and fended off the enemy, we touched three-million-year-old stromatolites and mammoth-tooth fossils and we composed E-mail for a school in Pennsylvania." "We fell through the day," she wrote, "like Alice in Wonderland, soaking up ideas, experimenting with and stretching our talents."[70]

Epilogue: Looking toward the Future

Earlier, we expressed cautious optimism about improving American public schools. We do not expect some magical Phoenix to arise from the "ashes" of the current system. We do not believe in educational Phoenixes and do not think that the system is in ashes. Here, drawing on the twin themes of utopia and tinkering, we suggest that reformers take a broader view of the aims that should guide public education and focus on ways to improve instruction from the inside out rather than the top down.

The concepts of progress and decline that have dominated discourse about educational reform distort the actual development of the educational enterprise over time. The ahistorical nature of most current reform arguments results in both a magnification of present defects in relation to the past and an understatement of the difficulty of changing the system. Policy talk about the schools has moved in cycles of gloomy assessments of education and overconfident solutions, producing incoherent guidance in actual reform practice. Hyperbole has often produced public cynicism and skepticism among teachers.

The typical rational and instrumental assumptions of educational reformers fail to give due weight to the resilience of schools as institutions. This institutional structure probably has more influence on the implementation of policy than policy has on institutional practice. The grammar of schooling is the result of previous reforms that had, and continue to have, powerful political constituencies and a strong foundation in the social expectations about schooling held both by educators and by the general public. To bring about improvement at the heart of education—

classroom instruction, shaped by that grammar—has proven to be the most difficult kind of reform, and it will result in the future more from internal changes created by the knowledge and expertise of teachers than from the decisions of external policymakers.

Better schooling will result in the future—as it has in the past and does now—chiefly from the steady, reflective efforts of the practitioners who work in schools and from the contributions of the parents and citizens who support (while they criticize) public education. This might seem to be just common sense. But in planning reforms in recent years, policy elites have often bypassed teachers and discounted their knowledge of what schools are like today. Consider the section "Who Does What?" in former President Bush's education program, *America 2000:* it lists federal and state officials, the business community, and parents as key actors, while relegating teachers to one among many groups active "at the community level."[1]

To the degree that teachers are out of the policy loop in designing and adopting school reforms, it is not surprising if they drag their feet in implementing them. Teachers do not have a monopoly on educational wisdom, but their first-hand perspectives on schools and their responsibility for carrying out official policies argues for their centrality in school reform efforts. As "street-level bureaucrats," teachers typically have sufficient discretion, once the classroom doors close, to make decisions about pupils that add up over time to de facto policies about instruction, whatever the official regulations. In any case, then, teachers will make their imprint on educational policy as it becomes translated into practice.[2]

Reform of instruction by remote control has rarely worked well. Some reformers have believed that teachers were so deeply mired in ruts that it was necessary to devise "teacher-proof" instruction (through technology, for example). The notion of teacher-proof instruction, however, is as foolish as student-proof learning. Educators have often responded to flurries of reforms imposed from the outside—often inconsistent in philosophy and program—by hunkering down and reassuring themselves that this, too, shall pass. We have explored some institutional reasons for this reaction. The hold of traditional practices on teachers and students is strong, often with good reason, and the public tends to share traditional cultural beliefs about what constitutes a "real school."

Reforms should be designed to be hybridized, adapted by educators working together to take advantage of their knowledge of their own diverse students and communities and supporting each another in new ways of teaching. It is especially important to engage the understanding and support of parents and the public when reforms challenge cultural beliefs about what a "real school" should be and do.[3]

Reform of education needs to be anchored in a realistic understanding of the institutional character of schools, but this alone is not enough. School reform is also a prime arena for debating the shape of the future of the society. Such debate is a broad civic and moral enterprise in which all citizens are stake-holders. In recent years, however, discourse about the purposes of education has been impoverished by linking it insistently to the wealth of nations. The underlying rationale of most recent reforms—to use schooling as an instrument of international economic competitiveness—is not new, but its dominance in policy talk is unprecedented.

How might one go about improving schools from the inside out, a kind of adaptive tinkering that preserves what is valuable and remedies what is not? What is the central goal of such reform?

On occasion, in talking about school reform with civic groups, we have asked people to recall their best experiences as students in public schools. Almost always they remember the influence of a teacher who challenged them to develop their potential, who made a subject come alive, or who gave caring advice at a stressful time. There is a striking parallel here with what teachers have said are their chief satisfactions and rewards in their work: seeing their students grow intellectually and mature as persons.[4]

The central purpose of reform, we believe, is to make such encounters between students and teachers more common. This suggests that the major aim of reform is to improve *learning,* generously construed as rich intellectual, civic, and social development, not simply as impressive test scores. Here policymakers outside the schools can go only so far. "Policy can *set the conditions* for effective administration and practice," Richard F. Elmore and Milbrey W. McLaughlin note, "but it can't predetermine how those decisions will be made."[5]

Legislators, officials, and courts can do a great deal to equalize school finance across states and districts, establish policies of racial or gender equity, or provide added resources for children with special needs. Experts in cognitive psychology, curriculum, and the cultures of diverse communities can suggest new and effective ways to teach. These are necessary but not sufficient steps in improving instruction. Unless practitioners are also enlisted in defining problems and devising solutions adapted to their own varied circumstances and local knowledge, lasting improvements will probably not occur in classrooms.

Socialized to familiar institutional practices, teachers have responded in myriad ways to reforms. Sometimes they have spent a good deal of energy in coopting, minimally complying with, or resisting reforms that they did not want from legislators eager to regulate their activity, politicians wanting quick results to help them get reelected, or district entrepreneurs keen to install new programs. But teachers also embraced ideas and practices that they saw as useful and interesting, often incorporating them in unanticipated ways into their daily routines. The resulting hybrids were often well adapted to the local terrain.

Consider an architectural parallel to this hybridizing of instructional reforms. In New York City in the early 1990s, a group of architects responsible for planning six new elementary schools recognized that innovations imposed on teachers frequently created more problems than solutions. In the 1960s, one architect explained, "the 'in' thing in educational design was the open classroom," imported from California and "predicated on infinite optimism. You never knew, these educators thought, what the school would be or what it could become." Large floor spaces with movable partitions would enable teachers to shape instruction to any pattern they wanted. "Well," he said, "it was a disaster in New York . . . you would sometimes have three classes going on, and one disruptive or unhappy student could destroy the day for all three classes."[6]

Instead of starting from scratch, with some mold-breaking design, the architects started with the cell of the organism called the public school system: the classroom. They took the square floor plan (on the left in the diagram on page 138) that the district had used as a prototype for most of the last century and gave it a jolt, producing a design for instructional hybrids (on the right in the diagram). The resulting bay windows would give more light, and the niches would provide space for small groups and computers—opportunities to incorporate new ways of teaching. But most important, the architects believed, the design ensured that "the teacher would remain the real focus of the room, instead of only being a bit player." By combining both tradition and flexibility in their design, with teachers at the center, the architects promoted reform from the inside out rather than imposing it from the top down.[7]

When we talked earlier about what it means for a reform to be successful, we suggested problems with some of the conventional "ra-

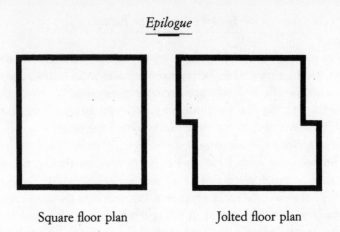

Square floor plan   Jolted floor plan

tional" criteria. Fidelity to plan implies that the initiators of the reform know best; longevity may be a dubious virtue if the change creates new problems; and meeting preset goals may direct attention away from positive or negative consequences that were unanticipated by the original reformers. Note what is lacking in all these criteria: adaptability to local circumstance.

Under a hybridizing model of instructional reform—in which innovations are regarded as resources a teacher may adapt to improve instruction—a "successful" innovation may look quite different in practice from school to school or classroom to classroom. In this approach, new curriculum frameworks, teaching methods, technology, diagnostic tests, strategies for cooperative learning in small groups, and other innovations are regarded not as mandates from outsiders but as resources that teachers can use, with help from each other and outsiders, to help students learn better.

With all the institutional demands on their time, energies, and attention, teachers need help in adapting or developing new instructional practices. Some changes are very hard to make alone. Developing and locally adapting a challenging new curriculum and mode of teaching, for example, is an extraordinarily difficult tasks that requires collaboration. It can energize participants, expose them to new ideas, and encourage them to take pedagogical risks in a supportive environment.

Teachers face serious obstacles, however, to improving instruction from the inside out. The remnants of the hierarchical command structure installed in schools by the administrative progressives early in the century still undermine teacher autonomy. So do the federal and state regulations that have mushroomed in the last decade, often giving mixed signals to practitioners. Facing reams of forms to fill out, overworked educators often feel more like professional accountants than like accountable professionals. Funds for new curricular materials or staff development are often minuscule. Few schools give teachers the incentives or the time necessary for curricular planning. Meetings supposedly designed to "empower" teachers can frustrate them instead if the agendas are vague or conflicting. And many teachers, accustomed to a familiar grammar of schooling and to solitary instruction in self-contained classrooms, lack the confidence and collegial support needed to try out new instructional ideas as well as the knowledge and skills needed to make them work well in their classrooms.[8]

Nonetheless, in many districts—especially those with ample resources and flexible leaders—teachers have led the way in reshaping instruction. The choice does not have to be between top-down reform or solitary efforts of individual teachers; many of the best programs of instructional change involve close collaboration between practitioners who share common purposes but adapt them flexibly to their local circumstances. In high schools across the country, academic departments have served as learning communities for teachers. Networks of teachers in professional groups such as the National Council of Teachers of Mathematics and the Bay Area Writing Project have worked together to transform both content and pedagogy in their fields. In reform programs such as the community-based schools of James P. Comer, Henry Levin's Accelerated Schools, and Theodore R. Sizer's Coalition of Essential Schools, shared general principles guide the renewal of schooling and assist teachers to collaborate with each other and with parents. All these efforts taken together might be regarded as a broad-based social movement to improve learning and to promote greater equality in schooling.[9]

A strategy of educational reform from the inside out requires much greater efforts to recruit talented people into teaching, to revise programs of teacher education to make them challenging and realistic, to induct new teachers in ways that ensure that they have careful support and a chance to succeed, and to winnow out inadequate teachers and retain effective ones. All these tasks demand an understanding of what most strongly motivates and discourages teachers. One place to start is to ask teachers what bothers them the most and to begin reforms there.

We do not want to suggest that the kind of teacher-centered reform sketched here—working from the classroom outward—is a panacea for improving instruction. We do believe that it would produce more improvement of instruction than most forms of innovation that proceed from the top down or the outside in. We are convinced that assisting teachers to adapt new ideas to their own circumstances and students could increase the number of positive encounters with learning that citizens recall and cherish as adults.[10]

In recent times, it has become obvious that those who are committed to public schooling need to confront not just gripes about particular defects but also a widespread malaise about the state of the schools. Like many others, we have spent much of our professional lives criticizing the gap between the ideal and the actuality of public education and working for reform. Now we sometimes feel like the railroad buff who complains about dirty cars, poor food, and bumpy roadbeds on Amtrak only to find some people nodding and suggesting that passenger trains be replaced by airplanes and cars. But abandoning public education because it has flaws was hardly what we had in mind.

It is time to meet the challenge of that general malaise—a symptom, perhaps, that the belief system that undergirds public education has fragmented. A crucial need today is to negotiate a common ground of purpose sufficiently generous, compelling, and plausible that it can unify citizens in support of public schooling. We have been critical of the utopian bent in American thinking that has resulted in great expectations and subsequent disillusionment. But the American faith in education has also been a powerful force for advancing the common good.

In the last generation, discourse about public schooling has become radically narrowed. It has focused on international economic competition, test scores, and individual "choice" of schools. But it has largely neglected the type of choices most vital to civic welfare: collective choices about a common future, choices made through the democratic process about the values and knowledge that citizens want to pass on to the next generation. "While public education may be useful as an industrial policy," Deborah Meier says, "it is *essential* to healthy life in a democracy."[11]

From subways to mental hospitals to national parks to schools, the public sphere has become degraded. It can by no means be taken for granted that people take pride in what they hold in common. Deinstitutionalization and deregulation have become panaceas for the ills of public agencies. The public schools, once both products and creators of shared broad social and political purposes, have become instruments to serve restricted ends.

When the purposes of education become narrowed to economic advantage, and the main measure of success is higher test scores, an easy next step is to regard schooling as a consumer good rather than a common good. Then it is logical to propose alternatives to the common school such as an open-market system of schooling in which parents are given vouchers to send their children to any school of their choice, whether private or public. One of the claims of voucher advocates is that the market system would eliminate the supposed inefficiencies of democratic governance. Critics have attacked the agencies of local democratic governance—in the form of elected school boards—as a cause of alleged decline in schooling, going so far as to suggest the abolition of local school committees.[12]

In recent years, poor education has been blamed for economic decline and tougher education proposed as a solution. This crisis mentality may have served public schools in the short run, for it has brought increased funding for schooling. Dollars in return for scapegoating, unrealistic expectations instead of apathy—these seemed, for a while, not a bad bargain. But they are hardly solid foundations for democratic schooling.

For over a century Americans have linked public schooling to prosperity, both national and individual. In 1909 Ellwood P. Cubberley announced, in terms echoed later by *A Nation at Risk,* that "whether we like it or not, we are beginning to see that we are pitted against the world in a gigantic battle of brains and skill, with the markets of the world, work for our people, and internal peace and contentment as the prizes at stake." But Americans' sense of education as a public good has traditionally included much more than merely economic advantage, individual or national.[13]

Almost a quarter of Americans work in public schools as students or staff. Schoolhouses are everywhere, a visible emblem of the commitment of the society to make learning accessible to all its young citizens. Schools are familiar places to the adults who once attended them, and in comparison with many other institutions, they foster public participation in decision making. American adults have used public debate about educating the young as a forum to decide what sort of future they wanted for the nation as well as for their own children and their immediate community.

During most of the past century, discussion of the purposes of public schools has stressed comprehensive social and political goods more than narrow, instrumental ends. In Horace Mann's time, the common school crusaders believed that the main function of schooling was to produce literate, moral citizens capable of fulfilling the millennial hope of making the United States God's country. As immigrants from incredibly diverse cultures filled the land, citizens discussed how public schools could shape a new people from newcomers from distant shores, and immigrants developed their own concepts and practice of cultural democracy in education. Political philosophers like John Dewey enormously enriched understanding of the links between democracy and education. In the two decades following the *Brown* decision in 1954, Americans ardently discussed how public schooling could promote racial and economic justice.

At its best, debate over purpose in public education has been a continuous process of creating and reshaping a democratic institution that, in turn, helped to create a democratic society. To be sure, there were elites who wanted to decree rather than debate policy. Some interest groups have focused only on their own narrow aims, seeing the politics of education as simply an arena of winners and losers. But to the degree that discourse about purpose in public education concerned itself with the public good, it can be understood as a kind of *trusteeship,* an effort to preserve the best of the past, to make wise choices in the present, and to plan for the future.

In continuing this tradition of trusteeship of the public good, this engaged debate about the shape of the future, all citizens have a stake, not only the students who temporarily attend school or their parents. And this is the main reason that Americans long ago created and have continually sought to reform public education.

THESIS

Notes
Acknowledgments
Index

Notes

Prologue

1. On the dramaturgic quality of debate over education, see David K. Cohen and Bella H. Rosenberg, "Functions and Fantasies: Understanding Schools in Capitalist America," *History of Education Quarterly* 17 (1977): 132, 113–137.

2. Horace Mann, *Life and Works* (Boston: Walker, Fuller, and Co., 1865–1868), vol. 4, pp. 345, 354, 364–365; Robert H. Wiebe, "The Social Functions of American Education," *American Quarterly* 21 (Summer 1969): 147–164; National Commission on Excellence in Education, *A Nation at Risk: The Imperative for Educational Reform* (Washington, D.C.: GPO, 1983); Thomas S. Popkewitz, "Educational Reform: Rhetoric, Ritual, and Social Interest," *Educational Theory* 38 (Winter 1988): 77–93.

3. Michael Sadler, "Impressions of American Education," *Educational Review* 25 (March 1903): 219; David Tyack, "Forming the National Character: Paradox in the Educational Thought of the Revolutionary Generation," *Harvard Educational Review* 35 (Winter 1966): 29–41.

4. Hannah Arendt, "The Crisis in Education," *Partisan Review* 25 (Fall 1958): 493–513; Bernard J. Weiss, ed., *American Education and the European Immigrant, 1840–1940* (Urbana: University of Illinois Press, 1982); Paula Fass, *Outside In: Minorities and the Transformation of American Education* (New York: Oxford University Press, 1989).

5. Johnson is quoted in Henry Perkinson, *The Imperfect Panacea: American Faith in Education, 1865–1965* (New York: Random House, 1979), frontispiece.

6. Richard C. Paddock, "Lobbyists Greet Class in Ethics with Yawns," *Los Angeles Times,* December 6, 1990, p. A3.

7. Jesse K. Flanders, *Legislative Control of the Elementary Curriculum* (New York: Teachers College Press, 1925); Jane Bernard Powers, *The "Girl Question" in Education: Vocational Education for Young Women in the Progressive Era* (Washington, D.C.: Falmer Press, 1992), ch. 2; David Tyack, Thomas James, and Aaron Benavot, *Law and the Shaping of Public Education, 1785–1954* (Madison: University of Wisconsin Press, 1987), ch. 6.

8. Paul R. Mort and Francis G. Cornell, *American Schools in Transition: How Our Schools Adapt Their Practices to Changing Needs* (New York: Teachers College Press, 1941), chs. 1–3.

9. Mort and Cornell, *American Schools in Transition,* p. 53; Paul R. Mort, "Studies in Educational Innovation from the Institute of Administrative Research: An Overview," in Matthew B. Miles, ed., *Innovation in Education* (New York: Bureau of Publications, Teachers College, Columbia University, 1964) pp. 317–328.

10. On the attack on "fads and frills" in the Great Depression, see George Strayer, "Educational Economy and Frontier Needs," in Department of Superintendence, *Official Report,* 1933 (Washington, D.C.: NEA, 1933), pp. 138–146; David Tyack, Michael Kirst, and Elisabeth Hansot, "Educational Reform: Retrospect and Prospect," *Teachers College Record* 81 (Spring 1980): 253–269.

11. Diane Ravitch, *The Troubled Crusade: American Education, 1945–1980* (New York: Basic Books, 1983).

12. There are many valuable ways to examine educational reforms historically. Scholars have analyzed, for example, individual reforms such as vocational education or individual reformers such as John Dewey. They have linked transformations in the political economy to changes in the schools. They have assessed the impact on schools of movements such as progressive education or broad social and political reforms such as civil rights. They have written illuminating monographs on reform in one school district or even one school. While we have benefited from all these types of research, we have written this book as a broad interpretive work aimed at a variety of readers rather than as a monograph primarily for specialists.

13. As Richard E. Neustadt and Ernest R. May observe, "the future has no place to come from but the past, hence the past has predictive value." See *Thinking in Time: The Uses of History for Decision Makers* (New York: The Free Press, 1986), p. 251.

14. Margaret O'Brien Steinfels, *Who's Minding the Children? The History and Politics of Child Care in America* (New York: Simon and Schuster, 1973).

15. Harold Silver and Pamela Silver, *An Educational War on Poverty: American and British Policy-Making* (Cambridge: Cambridge University Press, 1991), pp. 119, 266–268.

16. On the concept of a "real school" and cultural constructions of schooling, see Mary Hayward Metz, "Real School: A Universal Drama amid Disparate Experience," in Douglas E. Mitchell and Margaret E. Goertz, eds., *Education Politics for the New Century* (New York: Falmer Press, 1990), pp. 75–91; John W. Meyer and Brian Rowan, "Institutionalized Organizations: Formal Structure as Myth and Ceremony," *American Journal of Sociology* 83 (September 1977): 340–363; John W. Meyer and Brian Rowan, "The Structure of Educational Organizations," in Marshall W. Meyer, ed., *Environments and Organizations* (San Francisco: Jossey-Bass, 1978), pp. 78–109.

17. Ira Katznelson and Margaret Weir, *Schooling for All: Class, Race, and the Decline of the Democratic Ideal* (New York: Basic Books, 1985); W. Lloyd Warner, Robert J. Havighurst, and Martin B. Loeb, *Who Shall Be Educated? The Challenge of Unequal Opportunities* (New York: Harper and Brothers, 1944).

18. Diane Ravitch, *The Great School Wars: New York City, 1805–1973* (New York: Basic Books, 1974); Herbert M. Kliebard, *The Struggle for the American Curriculum, 1893–1958* (New York: Routledge & Kegan Paul, 1987); Michael W. Apple, *Ideology and Curriculum* (London: Routledge & Kegan Paul, 1979); David Tyack, "Construct-

ing Difference: Historical Reflections on Schooling and Social Diversity," *Teachers College Record* 95 (Fall 1993): 9–34.

19. *Public Schools and Their Administration: Addresses Delivered at the Fifty-Ninth Meeting of the Merchants' Club of Chicago, Saturday, December 8, 1906* (Chicago: The Merchants' Club, 1906); Corinne Gilb, *Hidden Hierarchies: The Professions and Government* (New York: Harper & Row, 1966); David Tyack and Elisabeth Hansot, *Managers of Virtue: Public School Leadership in America, 1820–1980* (New York: Basic Books, 1982), pt. 2.

20. Willard Waller, *The Sociology of Teaching* (New York: Russell and Russell, 1961).

21. Metz, "Real School"; Meyer and Rowan, "Institutionalized Organizations."

1. Progress or Regress?

1. W. W. Carpenter, "Is the Educational Utopia in Sight?" *The Nation's Schools* 8 (September 1931): 71, 72, 71–73.

2. Henry Perkinson, *The Imperfect Panacea: American Faith in Education, 1865–1965* (New York: Random House, 1968); the notion of progress was, and is, so pervasive in educational writing that it has appeared in book titles as if axiomatic—see, for example, Ellwood P. Cubberley, *Readings in Public Education in the United States: A Collection of Sources and Readings to Illustrate the History of Educational Practice and Progress in the United States* (Boston: Houghton Mifflin, 1934), or U.S. Department of Education, *Progress of Education in the United States of America, 1980–81 through 1982–83: Report for the Thirty-Ninth International Conference of Education, Sponsored by UNESCO* (Washington, D.C.: U.S. Department of Education, 1983); the recent program to assess academic achievement sponsored by the federal government since the late 1970s is called the National Assessment of Educational Progress.

3. Harlan Logan, "The Failure of American Education," *Look,* May 28, 1946, pp. 28–32, 34; "How Good Is Your School? 'Life' Test Will Tell You," *Life,* October 16, 1950, pp. 54–55; David K. Cohen, "Willard Waller: on Hating School and Loving Education," in Donald J. Willower and William Lowe Boyd, eds., *Willard Waller on Education and Schools: A Critical Appraisal* (Berkeley: McCutchan, 1989), ch. 5. For a penetrating critique of the notion of a golden educational age in the past, see Patricia Albjerg Graham, *S.O.S.: Sustain Our Schools* (New York: Hill and Wang, 1992).

4. *What People Think about Youth and Education,* National Education Association (NEA) Research Bulletin no. 5, November 1940 (Washington, D.C.: NEA, 1940), pp. 195–196; George H. Gallup, *The Gallup Poll: Public Opinion, 1935–1971* (New York: Random House, 1972), vol. 1, p. 597; Hadley Cantril and Mildred Strunk, *Public Opinion, 1935–46* (Princeton: Princeton University Press, 1951), p. 178.

5. Gallup, *Gallup Poll,* vol. 1, pp. 598; vol. 2, pp. 1366, 1513.

6. Ibid., vol. 1, p. 597; Cantril and Strunk, *Public Opinion,* p. 178.

7. Stanley M. Elam, ed., *A Decade of Gallup Polls of Attitudes toward Education, 1969–1978* (Bloomington, Ind.: Phi Delta Kappa, 1978); Stanley Elam, ed., *The Gallup / Phi Delta Kappa Polls of Attitudes toward Public Schools, 1969–88: A Twenty-Year Compilation and Educational History* (Bloomington, Ind.: Phi Delta

Kappa Educational Foundation, 1989), p. 5; Hans N. Weiler, "Education, Public Confidence, and the Legitimacy of the Modern State: Do We Have a Crisis?" *Phi Delta Kappan* 64 (September 1982): 9; *New York Times,* April 11, 1983, p. A18.

8. National Commission on Excellence in Education, *A Nation at Risk: The Imperative for Educational Reform* (Washington, D.C.: GPO, 1983), p. 11, passim.

9. Ibid.; John Chubb and Terry Moe, *Politics, Markets and America's Schools* (Washington, D.C.: Brookings Institution, 1990).

10. David K. Cohen and Barbara Neufeld, "The Failure of High Schools and the Progress of Education," *Daedalus* 110 (Summer 1981): 69–90; for a broad analysis of the idea of progress in America, see Rush Welter, "The Idea of Progress in America," *Journal of the History of Ideas* 16 (June 1955): 401–415; for a critique of liberal notions of progress, see Christopher Lasch, *The True and Only Heaven: Progress and Its Critics* (New York: W. W. Norton, 1991).

11. Weiler, "Public Confidence"; Arthur Alphonse Ekirch, Jr., *The Idea of Progress in America, 1815–1860* (New York: Columbia University Press, 1944).

12. Ernest Tuveson, *Redeemer Nation: The Idea of America's Millennial Role* (Chicago: University of Chicago Press, 1968).

13. Fletcher B. Dresslar, *American School Buildings,* U.S. Bureau of Education Bulletin no. 17, 1924 (Washington, D.C.: GPO, 1924), pp. 11–14, 66–67, 89–90, 32; for a summary of progress made during the nineteenth century, see William T. Harris's report to the Paris Exposition of 1900—*Elementary Education* (Albany: J. B. Lyon Co., 1900); on the congruence between the Protestant-republican notion of millennial progress and faith in educational "science," see David Tyack and Elisabeth Hansot, *Managers of Virtue: Public School Leadership in America, 1820–1980* (New York: Basic Books, 1982), pts. 1 and 2.

14. Otis W. Caldwell and Stuart A. Courtis, *Then and Now in Education, 1845–1923: A Message of Encouragement from the Past to the Present* (Yonkers-on-Hudson: World Book Co., 1925), pp. vi, 118, 47.

15. For one leader's view of progress, see David Snedden, "The High School of Tomorrow," *The School Review* 25 (January 1917): 1–15; on declining public participation in school decision making, see Ronald E. Butchart, "The Growth of an American School System: The Coconino County, Arizona, Experience" (M.A. thesis, Northern Arizona University, 1973); for a study of innovations regarded as necessary for progress and their gradual implementation, see Paul R. Mort and Francis G. Cornell, *American Schools in Transition: How Our Schools Adapt Their Practices to Changing Needs* (New York: Teachers College Press, 1941), chs. 1–3.

16. William Bullough, "'It Is Better to Be a Country Boy': The Lure of the Country in Urban Education in the Gilded Age," *The Historian* 35 (February 1973): 183–195; when a leading architect of reform, Charles H. Judd of the University of Chicago, wrote a book on educational trends in the first third of the twentieth century, he organized his chapters into what he called "problems," but it was obvious that progress was on the way: *Problems of Education in the United States* (New York: McGraw-Hill, 1933).

17. Ellwood P. Cubberley, *Changing Conceptions of Education* (Boston: Houghton Mifflin, 1909); James Russell, *Founding Teachers College: Reminiscences of the Dean Emeritus* (New York: Teachers College Press, 1937); George D. Strayer, "Progress in City School Administration during the Past Twenty-Five Years," *School and Society* 32 (September 1930): 375–378.

18. "Shall Education Be Rockefellerized?" *American Federationist* 24 (March 1917): 206–209; Institute for Public Service, *Rainbow Promises of Progress in Education* (New York: Institute for Public Service, 1917); Robert Rose, "Career Sponsorship in the School Superintendency" (Ph.D. diss., University of Oregon, 1969); Henry Pritchett, "Educational Surveys," in Carnegie Foundation for the Advancement of Teaching, *Ninth Annual Report of the President and Treasurer* (New York: Merrymount Press, 1914), pp. 118–123; Hollis L. Caswell, *City School Surveys: An Interpretation and Appraisal* (New York: Teachers College Press, 1929).

19. William G. Carr, "Legislation as a Factor in Producing Good Schools," *American School Board Journal* 81 (December 1930): 37–38.

20. Charles H. Judd, "School Boards as an Obstruction to Good Administration," *The Nation's Schools* 13 (February 1934): 13–15.

21. Ellwood P. Cubberley, *Public School Administration: A Statement of the Fundamental Principles Underlying the Organization and Administration of Public Education* (Boston: Houghton Mifflin, 1916); David B. Tyack, *The One Best System: A History of American Urban Education* (Cambridge: Harvard University Press, 1974), pt. 4.

22. National Center for Educational Statistics (NCES), *Digest of Educational Statistics, 1974* (Washington, D.C.: GPO, 1975) p. 53 (hereafter cited as NCES, *Digest,* by date); NCES, *Digest, 1988,* table 67; for a discussion of the rationale for consolidation of rural schools and the demand for professional supervision of them, see Ellwood P. Cubberley, *Rural Life and Education: A Study of the Rural-School Problem* (Boston: Houghton Mifflin, 1914); William B. McElhenny, "Where Do We Stand on School District Reorganization?" *Journal of the Kansas Law Association* 16 (November 1947): 245–251.

23. Lynn Dumenil, "The Insatiable Maw of Bureaucracy: Antistatism and Education Reform in the 1920s," *The Journal of American History* 77 (September 1990): 499–524; U.S. Bureau of Education, *A Manual of Educational Legislation for the Guidance of Committees on Education in the State Legislatures,* Bulletin no. 4, 1919 (Washington, D.C.: GPO, 1919); The National Institute of Education, *State Legal Standards for the Provision of Public Education: An Overview* (Washington, D.C.: GPO, 1978); Judd, *Problems,* p. 116.

24. NCES, *Digest, 1988,* table 61; John W. Meyer et al., *Bureaucratization without Centralization: Changes in the Organizational System of American Public Education, 1940–1980,* Project Report no. 85-A11, Institute for Research on Educational Finance and Governance, Stanford University, 1985, table 1; we are indebted to Jane Hannaway for information on the California code.

25. Edith A. Lathrop, *The Improvement of Rural Schools by State Standardization* (Washington, D.C.: GPO, 1925), pp. 10–13, 34; George J. Collins, *The Constitutional and Legal Bases for State Action in Education, 1900–1968* (Boston: Massachusetts Department of Education, 1968); on the needs of rural schools, see Newton Edwards and Herman G. Richey, *The School in the American Social Order: The Dynamics of American Education* (Boston: Houghton Mifflin, 1947), p. 689; for differences between urban and rural schools, see Harlan Updegraff and William R. Hood, *A Comparison of Urban and Rural Common-School Statistics,* U.S. Bureau of Education Bulletin no. 21, 1912 (Washington, D.C.: GPO, 1912); for samples of school laws, see National Education Association, Educational Research Service, *State School Legislation, 1934,* Circular no. 3, March 1935 (Washington, D.C.: 1935).

26. Caswell, *Surveys*.

27. Larry Cuban and David Tyack, "Match and Mismatch—Schools and Children Who Don't Fit Them," in Henry M. Levin, ed., *Accelerated Schools*, forthcoming; Strayer, "Progress"; Lewis M. Terman, ed., *Intelligence Tests and School Reorganization* (Yonkers-on-Hudson: World Book Co., 1922); Charles H. Judd, "Education," in *Recent Social Trends in the United States: Report of the President's Research Committee on Social Trends* (New York: McGraw-Hill, 1933), pp. 330, 338.

28. Judd, "Education," pp. 345–346; Lewis Terman, *The Hygiene of the School Child* (Boston: Houghton Mifflin, 1929); Robert W. Kunzig, *Public School Education of Atypical Children*, U.S. Bureau of Education Bulletin no. 10, 1931 (Washington, D.C.: GPO, 1931), p. 74; NCES, *Digest, 1990*, p. 63.

29. NCES, *Digest, 1988*, table 67.

30. National Center for Educational Statistics, *120 Years of American Education: A Statistical Portrait* (Washington, D.C.: GPO, 1993), pp. 14, 21, 34–35 (hereafter cited as NCES, *120 Years*); NCES, *Digest, 1990* p. 66.

31. American Association of School Administrators, *The American School Superintendency* (Washington, D.C: American Association of School Administrators, 1952), p. 444; NCES, *Digest, 1990*, p. 48.

32. For the opinion of one fascinating "trouble-maker" on the regime of the administrative progressives, see Margaret Haley, "Why Teachers Should Organize," NEA, *Addresses and Proceedings, 1904* (Washington, D.C.: NEA, 1905), pp. 145–152 (hereafter cited as NEA, *Addresses and Proceedings*, by date); of course, the administrative progressives were not the only interest group influencing legislation and educational philosophy—see Jesse H. Newlon, *Educational Administration as Social Policy* (New York: Charles Scribner's Sons, 1934).

33. On blacks' self-help in education, see James D. Anderson, *The Education of Blacks in the South, 1860–1935* (Chapel Hill: University of North Carolina Press, 1988); Michael B. Katz, *Reconstructing American Education* (Cambridge: Harvard University Press, 1987); W. Lloyd Warner, Robert J. Havighurst, and Martin B. Loeb, *Who Shall Be Educated? The Challenge of Unequal Opportunities* (New York: Harper and Brothers, 1944).

34. George S. Counts, *The Social Composition of Boards of Education* (Chicago: University of Chicago Press, 1927); David Tyack, Robert Lowe, and Elisabeth Hansot, *Public Schools in Hard Times: The Great Depression and Recent Years* (Cambridge: Harvard University Press, 1984), chs. 3–4; for an outstanding example of an educator who did attend to inequalities, see Leonard Covello, *The Heart Is the Teacher* (New York: McGraw-Hill, 1958).

35. Edwards and Ritchey, *Social Order*, pp. 635, 688–699; disparities of local wealth still frustrate meaningful equality in education, as Jonathan Kozol has documented in *Savage Inequalities: Children in America's Schools* (New York: Crown, 1991).

36. Henry S. Shryock, Jr., "1940 Census Data on Numbers of Years of School Completed," *Milbank Memorial Fund Quarterly* 20 (October 1942): 372; Paul R. Mort, *Federal Support for Public Education: A Report of an Investigation of Educational Need and Relative Ability of States to Support Education as They Bear on Federal Aid to Education* (New York: Teachers College, Bureau of Publications, 1936); for an account of the virtues of rural schools, often downplayed by educators,

see Wayne E. Fuller, *The Old Country School: The Story of Rural Education in the Middle West* (Chicago: University of Chicago Press, 1982).

37. The visitor to the Texas school is quoted in Doxey Wilkerson, *Special Problems of Negro Education* (Washington, D.C.: GPO, 1939), p. 99—see also pp.15–49; Horace Mann Bond, *The Education of the Negro in the American Social Order* (New York: Prentice Hall, 1934); Charles S. Johnson, *Shadow of the Plantation* (Chicago: University of Chicago Press, 1934); Harvey Kantor and Barbara Brenzel, "Urban Education and the 'Truly Disadvantaged': The Historical Roots of the Contemporary Crisis, 1945–1990," in Michael B. Katz, ed., *The "Underclass" Debate: Views from History* (Princeton: Princeton University Press, 1993), pp. 366–402.

38. Edwards and Ritchey, *Social Order,* p. 703; Howard M. Bell, *Youth Tell Their Story: A Study of the Conditions and Attitudes of Young People in Maryland between the Ages of Sixteen and Twenty-Four* (Washington, D.C.: American Council on Education, 1938), pp. 59–60.

39. August Hollingshead, *Elmtown's Youth: The Impact of Social Classes on Adolescents* (New York: John Wiley, 1949), chs. 6, 8; "What People Think about Youth and Education," *NEA Research Bulletin* 18 (November 1940): 215; Bernard D. Karpinos and Herbert J. Sommers, "Educational Attainment of Urban Youth in Various Income Classes," *Elementary School Journal* 42 (May 1942): 677–687; Jeannie Oakes, *Keeping Track* (New Haven: Yale University Press, 1985).

40. David Tyack and Elisabeth Hansot, *Learning Together: A History of Coeducation in American Public Schools* (New Haven: Yale University Press and the Russell Sage Foundation, 1990), ch. 7.

41. Naomi J. White, "Let Them Eat Cake! A Plea for Married Teachers," *Clearing House* 13 (September 1938): 135–139; there was a conscious program to recruit more men into teaching—see "Teaching: A Man's Job," *Phi Delta Kappan* 20 (March 1938): 215; Elisabeth Hansot and David Tyack, "The Dream Deferred: A Golden Age for Women Administrators?" (Stanford, Calif.: Institute for Research on Educational Finance and Governance, 1981); Tyack and Hansot, *Learning Together,* chs. 7–9.

42. John G. Richardson, "Historical Expansion of Special Education," in Bruce Fuller and Richard Rubinson, eds., *The Political Construction of Education: The State, School Expansion, and Economic Change* (Westport, Conn.: Praeger, 1992), pp. 207–221; Kunzig, "Atypical Children"; Frank M. Phillips, *Schools and Classes for Feeble-Minded and Subnormal Children, 1926–1927,* U.S. Bureau of Education Bulletin no. 5, 1928 (Washington, D.C.: GPO, 1928); James H. Van Sickle, James H. Witmer, and Leonard P. Ayres, *Provision for Exceptional Children in Public Schools,* U.S. Bureau of Education Bulletin no. 14, 1911 (Washington, D.C.: GPO, 1911); NCES, *120 Years,* p. 44.

43. Joseph L. Tropea, "Bureaucratic Order and Special Children: Urban Schools, 1890s–1940s," *History of Education Quarterly* 27 (Spring 1987): 29–53; Barry M. Franklin, "Progressivism and Curriculum Differentiation: Special Classes in the Atlanta Public Schools, 1898–1923," *History of Education Quarterly* 29 (Winter 1989): 571–593.

44. Gunnar Myrdal, *An American Dilemma: The Negro Problem and American Democracy* (New York: Harper and Brothers, 1944), pp. xlvi-xlviii.

45. Frances Piven and Richard Cloward, *Poor Peoples' Movements: Why They Succeed, How They Fail* (New York: Pantheon, 1977).

46. Brown v. Board of Education, 347 U.S. 493 (1954); Richard Kluger, *Simple Justice: The History of Brown v. Board of Education and Black America's Struggle for Equality* (New York: Vintage Books, 1977); Kantor and Brenzel, "Urban Education"; David Neal and David L. Kirp, *The Allure of Legalization Reconsidered: The Case of Special Education* (Stanford, Calif.: Institute for Research on Educational Finance and Governance, 1983).

47. Joseph Gusfield, ed., *Protest, Reform, and Revolt: A Reader in Social Movements* (New York: John Wiley, 1970); Anthony Obershall, *Social Conflict and Social Movements* (Englewood Cliffs, N.J.: Prentice Hall, 1973).

48. Robert Newby and David Tyack, "Victims without 'Crimes': Some Historical Perspectives on Black Education," *Journal of Negro Education* 40 (Summer 1971): 192–206; Lawrence A. Cremin, *Popular Education and Its Discontents* (New York: Harper & Row, 1990), ch. 3; Nancy Frazier and Myra Sadker, *Sexism in School and Society* (New York: Harper & Row, 1973); Susan S. Klein, ed., *Handbook for Achieving Sex Equity through Education* (Baltimore: Johns Hopkins University Press, 1985).

49. Gary Orfield, *Public School Desegregation in the United States, 1968–1980* (Washington, D.C.: Joint Center for Policy Studies, 1983), pp. 12, 15–19; NCES, *Digest, 1991,* pp. 110, 181; Harold Hodgkinson, "What's Right with Education," *Phi Delta Kappan* 61 (November 1979): 160–162; Jennifer O'Day and Marshall S. Smith, "Systemic School Reform and Educational Opportunity," in Susan Fuhrman, ed., *Designing Coherent Education Policy: Improving the System* (San Francisco: Jossey-Bass, 1993), pp. 233–267.

50. Jonathan Kozol, *Savage Inequalities: Children in America's Schools* (New York: Crown, 1991); Nat Hentoff, *Our Children Are Dying* (New York: Viking, 1966); Jonathan Kozol, *Death at an Early Age: The Destruction of the Hearts and Minds of Negro Children in the Boston Public Schools* (Boston: Houghton Mifflin, 1972).

51. Henry M. Levin, ed., *Community Control of Schools* (Washington, D.C.: Brookings Institution, 1970); Madeline Arnot, "A Cloud over Coeducation: An Analysis of the Forms of Transmission of Class and Gender Relations," in Stephen Walker and Len Barton, eds., *Gender, Class, and Education* (New York: Falmer Press, 1983), pp. 69–92.

52. On public concerns about the schools, see Elam, *Gallup Polls, 1969–88;* George R. Kaplan, *Images of Education: The Mass Media's Version of America's Schools* (Washington, D.C.: National School Public Relations Association and the Institute for Educational Leadership, 1992).

53. Cohen and Neufeld, "Failure," p. 70.

54. James S. Coleman et al., *Equality of Educational Opportunity* (Washington, D.C.: GPO, 1966); Christopher Jencks et al., *Inequality: A Reassessment of the Effect of Family and Schooling in America* (New York: Basic Books, 1972); Donald M. Levine and Mary Jo Bane, eds., *The "Inequality Controversy": Schooling and Distributive Justice* (New York: Basic Books, 1975).

55. Elam, *Gallup Polls, 1969–88,* p. 9; Weiler, "Public Confidence"; Daniel E. Griffiths, "The Crisis in American Education," *New York University Education Quarterly* 14 (Fall 1982): 1–10.

56. Weiler, "Public Confidence"; Elam, *Gallup Polls, 1969–88,* p. 9; Griffiths, "Crisis."

57. Elam, *Gallup Polls, 1969–88,* pp. 220, 221, 5; Stanley M. Elam, Lowell C.

Rose, and Alex M. Gallup, "The Twenty-Fourth Gallup/Phi Delta Kappa Poll of the Public's Attitudes toward the Public Schools," *Phi Delta Kappan* 74 (September 1992): 45.

58. Stanley M. Elam, Lowell C. Rose, and Alec M. Gallup, "The Twenty-Third Annual Gallup Poll of the Public's Attitudes toward the Public Schools," *Phi Delta Kappan* 73 (September 1991): 55; Stanley M. Elam and Alec M. Gallup, "The Twenty-First Annual Gallup Poll of the Public's Attitudes toward the Public Schools," *Phi Delta Kappan* 71 (September 1989): 49.

59. Elam, *Gallup Polls, 1969–88,* pp. 172–173, 186.

60. Ibid., p. 5.

61. Ibid., pp. 3–5.

62. Ibid., p. 3; Gene Maeroff, "Reform Comes Home: Policies to Encourage Parental Involvement in Children's Education," in Chester E. Finn and Theodor Rebarber, eds., *Education Reform in the Nineties* (New York: Macmillan, 1992), pp. 158–159; Susan Chira, "What Do Teachers Want Most? Help from Parents," *New York Times,* June 23, 1993, p. B6.

63. "Teachers Are Better Educated, More Experienced, But Less Satisfied than in the Past: NEA Survey," *Phi Delta Kappan* 62 (May 1982): 579; National Center for Educational Statistics, *Condition of Education, 1982* (Washington, D.C.: GPO, 1983), pp. 104–105.

64. Elam, Rose, and Gallup, "Twenty-Fourth Gallup Poll," p. 46.

65. Elam, Rose, and Gallup, "Twenty-Third Gallup Poll," pp. 43–44.

66. Elam, *Gallup Polls, 1969–88,* pp. 187–188; Elam and Gallup, "Twenty-First Gallup Poll," pp. 45, 49.

67. National Commission on Excellence in Education, *A Nation at Risk,* p. 5; for a critique of conventional interpretations of school achievement data and the reforms based on them, see Daniel Koretz, "Educational Practices, Trends in Achievement, and the Potential of the Reform Movement," *Educational Administration Quarterly* 24 (August 1988): 350–359.

68. Cremin, *Popular Education,* p. 103; The Carnegie Foundation for the Advancement of Teaching, *An Imperiled Generation: Saving Urban Schools* (Princeton: Carnegie Foundation for the Advancement of Teaching, 1988).

69. Lawrence C. Stedman and Marshall S. Smith, "Recent Reform Proposals for American Education," *Contemporary Education Review* 2 (Fall 1983): 85–104; Lawrence C. Stedman and Carl F. Kaestle, "Literacy and Reading Performance in the United States, from 1880 to the Present," *Reading Research Quarterly* 27 (Winter 1987): 8–46; Carl F. Kaestle, "The Decline of American Education: Myth or Reality?" (Ms., University of Wisconsin, November 1992); Gerald W. Bracey, "Why Can't They Be like We Were?" *Phi Delta Kappan* 73 (October 1991): 104–117.

70. David C. Berliner, "Educational Reform in an Era of Disinformation," paper presented at the meeting of the American Association of Colleges of Teacher Education, San Antonio, Texas, February 1992, pp. 7–15; Bracey, "Why?" pp. 108–110.

71. Carl F. Kaestle et al., *Literacy in the United States: Readers and Reading since 1880* (New Haven: Yale University Press, 1991), p. 130, chs. 3–4.

72. Kaestle, *Literacy,* 75–76; William Celis III, "Study Says Half of Adults in U.S. Can't Read or Handle Arithmetic," *New York Times,* September 9, 1993, pp. A1, A16; Paul Copperman, *The Literacy Hoax: The Decline of Reading, Writing, and Learning in the Public Schools and What We Can Do about It* (New York: William

Morrow, 1978); Frank E. Armbruster, *Our Children's Crippled Future: How American Education Has Failed* (New York: Quadrangle Books, 1977).

73. Daniel P. Resnick and Lauren B. Resnick, "The Nature of Literacy: An Historical Exploration," *Harvard Educational Review* 47 (August 1977): 370–385.

74. E. D. Hirsch, Jr., *Cultural Literacy: What Every American Needs to Know* (Boston: Houghton Mifflin, 1987), p. 8; see also Allan Bloom, *The Closing of the American Mind: How Higher Education Has Failed Democracy and Impoverished the Souls of Today's Students* (New York: Simon and Schuster, 1987).

75. *New York Times,* June 21, 1942, p. 1; *New York Times,* May 2, 3, 4, 1976; Allan Nevins, "American History for Americans," *New York Times Magazine,* May 3, 1942, pp. 6, 28; Dale Whittington, "What Have Seventeen-Year-Olds Known in the Past?" *American Educational Research Journal* 28 (Winter 1992): 759–783; Chester E. Finn, Jr., and Diane Ravitch, "Survey Results: U.S. Seventeen-Year-Olds Know Shockingly Little about History and Literature," *American School Board Journal* 174 (October 1987): 31–33. In Kaestle, *Literacy,* pp. 80–89, Lawrence C. Stedman and Carl F. Kaestle discuss the conceptual and technical problems with then-and-now studies and conclude that "our educated guess is that schoolchildren of the same age and socioeconomic status have been performing at similar levels throughout most of the twentieth century" (p. 89).

76. Berliner, "Disinformation." pp. 37–43.

77. Iris C. Rotberg, "I Never Promised You First Place," *Phi Delta Kappan* 72 (December 1990): 297, 296–303; Ian Westbury, "Comparing American and Japanese Achievement: Is the United States Really a Low Achiever?" *Educational Researcher* (June/July 1992): 18–24; Gerald W. Bracey, "The Second Bracey Report on the Condition of Public Education," *Phi Delta Kappan* 74 (October 1992): 108.

78. National Assessment of Educational Progress, *Accelerating Academic Achievement* (Princeton: Educational Testing Service, 1990); Bracey, "Condition"; Stedman and Smith, "Proposals"; O'Day and Smith, "Systemic Reform."

79. Bracey, "Why Can't They Be like We Were?" p. 112; Berliner, "Disinformation," p. 28. Bracey and Berliner question the meaning of rising per-pupil costs. They point out that public schools are legally and morally bound to provide an appropriate education for all children who come to their doors, and that the computation of educational costs typically includes sharply rising expenditures for special education. When U.S. expenditures for K–12 schooling were expressed as a percent of per capita income in 1985, the United States came fourteenth in a list of sixteen industrialized nations.

80. Office of Educational Research and Improvement, *Youth Indicators, 1988: Trends in the Well-Being of Youth* (Washington, D.C.: GPO, 1988); "Social Well-Being," *Education Week,* October 21, 1992, p. 3.

81. Berliner, "Disinformation," p. 21; Bracey, "Second Bracey Report," pp. 112–113.

82. Robert Rothman, "Revisionists Take Aim at Gloomy View of Schools," *Education Week,* November 13, 1991, pp. 1, 12–13.

83. Cremin, *Popular Education,* p. 103; Clark Kerr, "Is Education Really All That Guilty?" *Education Week,* February 27, 1991, p. 30; Henry M. Levin and Russell W. Rumberger, "The Low Skill Future in High Tech," *Stanford Educator,* Summer 1983, pp. 2–3; Peter T. Kilborn, "Job Security Hinges on Skills, Not on an Employer for Life," *New York Times,* March 12, 1994, pp. A1, A7.

84. Robert Kuttner, "Training Programs Alone Can't Produce $20-an-Hour Workers," *Business Week,* March 8, 1993, p. 16; Reich is quoted in Peter T. Kilborn, "New Jobs Lack the Old Security in Time of 'Disposable Workers,'" *New York Times,* March 3, 1993, pp. A1, A6.

85. Elam, *Gallup Polls, 1969–88,* pp. 9, 222.

2. Policy Cycles and Institutional Trends

1. Carl F. Kaestle has pointed out that a key task "for the historian is to distinguish between . . . cyclical and linear developments"—"Social Reform and the Urban School," *History of Education Quarterly* 12 (Summer 1972): 218, 211–228; in Chapter 4 we discuss a third issue, why the organization of instruction has remained relatively constant amid cycles of policy talk and trends that diversified the institutional structure of schools.

2. Susan Fuhrman, William H. Clune, and Richard F. Elmore, "Research on Education Reform: Lessons on the Implementation of Policy," *Teachers College Record* 90 (Winter 1988): 237–257; Larry Cuban, "Reforming Again, and Again, and Again," *Educational Researcher* 19 (January-February 1990): 3–13.

3. Robert J. Taggart, *Private Philanthropy and Public Education: Pierre S. DuPont and the Delaware Schools, 1890–1940* (Newark: University of Delaware Press, 1988), ch. 4.

4. Julius Gordon, "School Reform Again? (Sigh)," *New York Times,* January 29, 1990, p. A19; James W. Guthrie and Julia Koppich, "Exploring the Political Economy of National Education Reform," in William Boyd and Charles Kershner, eds., *The Politics of Excellence and Choice in Education* (Philadelphia: Falmer Press, 1987), p. 26; David N. Plank, "Why School Reform Doesn't Change Schools: Political and Organizational Perspectives," in Boyd and Kershner, eds., *Politics,* pp. 143–152.

5. Robert Slavin, "Pet and the Pendulum: Faddism in Education and How to Stop It," *Phi Delta Kappan* 90 (June 1989): 750–758; Richard E. Elmore and Milbrey W. McLaughlin, *Steady Work: Policy, Practice, and the Reform of American Education* (Santa Monica: Rand Corporation, 1988), p. v.

6. Carl F. Kaestle, "The Public Schools and the Public Mood," *American Heritage* 41 (February 1990): 68, 66–81.

7. David K. Cohen and Bella H. Rosenberg, "Functions and Fantasies: Understanding Schools in Capitalist America," *History of Education Quarterly* 17 (Spring 1977): 113–137.

8. Amy Gutmann, *Democratic Education* (Princeton: Princeton University Press, 1987).

9. Herbert H. Kliebard, *Success and Failure in Educational Reform: Are There Historical Lessons?* (East Lansing, Mich.: The Holmes Group, 1989); David Tyack, Michael W. Kirst, and Elisabeth Hansot, "Educational Reform: Retrospect and Prospect," *Teachers College Record* 81 (Spring 1980): 253–269.

10. David Tyack and Elisabeth Hansot, "Conflict and Consensus in American Public Education," *Daedalus* 110 (Summer 1981), 1–25.

11. William J. Reese, *Power and the Promise of School Reform* (Boston: Routledge & Kegan Paul, 1986).

12. Arthur M. Schlesinger, Jr., *The Cycles of American History* (Boston: Houghton Mifflin, 1986).

13. As a sample of popular articles on the "crisis" in education, see *U.S. News and World Report,* November 30, 1956, pp. 68–69; *Time,* September 7, 1953, p. 68; and *Life,* March 24, 1958, pp. 25–33; see also Thomas James and David Tyack, "Learning from Past Efforts to Reform the High School," *Phi Delta Kappan,* 64 (February 1983): 400–406, and Michael W. Kirst, *The Progress of Reform: An Appraisal of State Education Initiatives* (New Brunswick, N.J.: Center for Policy Research in Education, 1989), pp. 10, 13.

14. Tyack and Hansot, "Conflict and Consensus"; David Tyack, Robert Lowe, and Elisabeth Hansot, *Public Schools in Hard Times: The Great Depression and Recent Years* (Cambridge, Mass.: Harvard University Press, 1984), ch. 3; William Lowe Boyd, "How to Reform Schools without Half Trying," *Educational Administration Quarterly* 24 (August 1988): 299–309.

15. Chester E. Finn, Jr., and Theodor Rebarber, "The Changing Politics of Education Reform," in Finn and Rebarber, eds., *Education Reform in the Nineties* (New York: Macmillan, 1992), pp. 190–191; Kirst, *Progress of Reform.*

16. Rick Ginsberg and Robert Wimpelberg, "Educational Change by Commission: Attempting 'Trickle Down' Reform," *Educational Evaluation and Policy Analysis* 9 (Winter 1987): 344–360; for a perceptive critique of recent reports of such commissions, see Paul E. Peterson, "Did the Education Commissions Say Anything?" *The Brookings Review* 2 (Winter 1983): 3–11.

17. Jeffrey E. Mirel, "Progressive School Reform in Comparative Perspective," in David N. Plank and Rick Ginsberg, eds., *Southern Cities, Southern Schools: Public Education in the Urban South* (New York: Greenwood Press, 1990), pp. 151–174; Paul E. Peterson, *The Politics of School Reform, 1870–1940* (Chicago: University of Chicago Press, 1985); John Dewey, "An Undemocratic Proposal," *Vocational Education* 2 (March 1913): 374–377; David Tyack, "Constructing Difference: Historical Reflections on Schooling and Social Diversity," *Teachers College Record* 95 (Fall 1993): 8–31. Historians frequently debate what periods *mean* but rarely question whether they *exist;* Peter F. Filene has questioned whether there was either a coherent "progressive" program or "progressive" movement—Peter F. Filene, "An Obituary for the 'Progressive Movement,'" *American Quarterly* 22 (Spring 1970): 20–34.

18. NCES, *Digest, 1990,* p. 48; J. Harvie Wilkerson III, *From Brown to Bakke: The Supreme Court and School Integration, 1954–1978* (New York: Oxford University Press, 1979).

19. Kaestle, "Public Schools," pp. 78–80; Arthur G. Powell, Eleanor Farrar, and David K. Cohen, *The Shopping Mall High School: Winners and Losers in the Educational Marketplace* (Boston: Houghton Mifflin, 1985), pp. 281–283; David K. Cohen, "Educational Technology and School Organization," in R. Nickerson and P. Zodhiates, eds., *Technology and Education in the Year 2020* (Hillsdale, N.J.: Lawrence Erlbaum Associates, 1988), ch. 11.

20. NCES, *120 Years,* p. 55; this section is adapted from James and Tyack, "Learning from Past Efforts."

21. Edward L. Thorndike, "A Neglected Aspect of the American High School," *Educational Review* 33 (1907): 254; Robert Hampel, *The Last Little Citadel: American High Schools since 1940* (Boston: Houghton Mifflin, 1986).

22. NCES, *120 Years,* p. 50; Logan C. Osterndorf and Paul J. Horn, *Course Offerings, Enrollments, and Curriculum Practices in Public Secondary Schools, 1972–73* (Washington, D.C.: GPO, 1976), pp. 5, 6, 13, 11, 4–21; NCES, *120 Years,* p. 50.

23. Stanley M. Elam, ed., *A Decade of Gallup Polls of Attitudes toward Education, 1969–78* (Bloomington, Ind.: Phi Delta Kappa, 1978), p. 121; Edward A. Krug, *The Shaping of the American High School, 1920–1941* (Madison: University of Wisconsin Press, 1972); Charles Burgess and Merle L. Borrowman, *What Doctrines to Embrace: Studies in the History of American Education* (Glenview, Ill.: Scott, Foresman, 1969), ch. 5; Harvey Kantor and David Tyack, eds., *Work, Youth, and Schooling: Historical Perspectives on Vocationalism in American Education* (Stanford: Stanford University Press, 1982).

24. Herbert M. Kliebard identifies four competing philosophies of secondary schooling that dominated professional discourse during the years from 1890 to 1958: a *humanist* group, which stressed high academic and cultural standards based on the traditional subjects; a *child development* group, which proposed a child-centered curriculum based on the interests and developing capacities of the young; a *social efficiency* group, which wanted to sort out and train students for differing adult roles; and the *social reconstructionists,* who hoped to use the schools to bring about a more equal and just social order—*The Struggles for the American Curriculum, 1890–1958* (Boston: Routledge & Kegan Paul, 1986).

25. For the views of two educators who drew different lessons from such changes, see John Dewey, *The School and Society* (Chicago: University of Chicago Press, 1899), and Ellwood P. Cubberley, *Changing Conceptions of Education* (Boston: Houghton Mifflin, 1909).

26. Powell, Farrar, and Cohen, *Shopping Mall High School* p. 240.

27. Theodore R. Sizer, *Secondary Schools at the Turn of the Century* (New Haven: Yale University Press, 1964).

28. Charles W. Eliot, "The Gap between the Elementary Schools and the Colleges," NEA, *Addresses and Proceedings, 1890,* pp. 22–33; Edward A. Krug, *The Shaping of the American High School* (New York: Harper & Row, 1964), chs. 1–3.

29. NEA, *Report of the Committee of Ten on Secondary School Studies* (New York: American Book Co., 1894), pp. 41, 46–47.

30. John Dewey, "The Influence of the High School upon Educational Methods," in *The Early Works of John Dewey, 1882–1898* (Carbondale: University of Illinois Press, 1972), pp. 270–271.

31. Commission on the Reorganization of Secondary Education, *Cardinal Principles of Secondary Education,* U.S. Bureau of Education, Bulletin no. 35, 1918 (Washington, D.C.: GPO, 1918); Krug, *Shaping,* chs. 13–15.

32. Commission on the Reorganization of Secondary Education, *Cardinal Principles,* pp. 7–8.

33. Powell, Farrar, and Cohen, *Shopping Mall High School,* pp. 275, 260–273.

34. Michael B. Katz, *Reconstructing American Education* (Cambridge: Harvard University Press, 1987); Tyack, "Constructing Difference."

35. Arthur Bestor, *Educational Wastelands: The Retreat from Learning in Our Schools* (Urbana: University of Illinois Press, 1953); Diane Ravitch, *The Troubled Crusade: American Education, 1945–1980* (New York: Basic Books, 1983), ch. 3, pp. 228–232.

36. Albert Lynd, *Quackery in the Public Schools* (Boston: Little, Brown, 1953); Hyman G. Rickover, *Education and Freedom* (New York: E. P. Dutton, 1959).

37. Ira Katznelson and Margaret Weir, *Schooling for All: Class, Race, and the Decline of the Democratic Ideal* (New York: Basic Books, 1985), chs. 7–8; David

Tyack and Elisabeth Hansot, *Managers of Virtue: Public School Leadership in America, 1820–1980* (New York: Basic Books, 1982), pt. 3.

38. Joseph Murphy, *The Educational Reform Movement of the 1980s: Perspectives and Cases* (Berkeley: McCutchan Publishing Co., 1990).

39. David F. Labaree, "Politics, Markets, and the Compromised Curriculum," *Harvard Educational Review* 57 (November 1987): 489, 491, 483–494.

40. Susan Moore Johnson, "Redesigning Teachers' Work," in Richard Elmore et al., *Restructuring Schools: The Next Generation of Educational Reform* (San Francisco: Jossey-Bass, 1990), pp. 127, 125–151.

41. David Tyack and Elisabeth Hansot, *Learning Together: A History of Coeducation in American Schools* (New Haven: Yale University Press, 1990), chs. 3, 6.

42. Fletcher B. Dressler, *American School Buildings,* (U.S. Bureau of Education Bulletin no. 17, 1924 (Washington, D.C.: GPO, 1924).

43. Jane Bernard Powers, *The "Girl Question" in Education: Vocational Education for Young Women in the Progressive Era* (London: Falmer Press, 1992), ch. 2; Michael Imber, "Toward a Theory of Educational Origins: The Genesis of Sex Education," *Educational Theory* 34 (Summer 1984): 275–286.

44. Paul Saettler, *A History of Instructional Technology* (New York: McGraw-Hill, 1968).

45. Paul R. Mort and Francis G. Cornell, *American Schools in Transition: How Our Schools Adapt Their Practices to Changing Needs* (New York: Teachers College Press, 1941), chs. 1–3.

46. Tyack, Lowe, and Hansot, *Public Schools in Hard Times.* p. 3.

47. Horace Mann Bond, *The Education of the Negro in the American Social Order* (New York: Prentice Hall, 1934); Louis Harlan, *Separate and Unequal: Public School Campaigns and Racism in the Southern Seaboard States, 1901–1915* (1958; reprint ed., New York: Athenaeum, 1968).

48. Donald Orlosky and B. Othanel Smith, "Educational Change: Its Origins and Characteristics," *Phi Delta Kappan* 53 (March 1972): 412–414.

49. Tyack, Kirst, and Hansot, "Educational Reform: Retrospect and Prospect"; Michael W. Kirst and Gail R. Meister, "Turbulence in American Secondary Education: What Reforms Last?" *Curriculum Inquiry* 15, no. 2 (1985): 169–185.

50. Larry Cuban, "Enduring Resiliency: Enacting and Implementing Federal Vocational Education Legislation," in Kantor and Tyack, eds., *Work, Youth, and Schooling,* pp. 45–78.

51. Ellwood P. Cubberley, *Public School Administration: A Statement of the Fundamental Principles Underlying the Organization and Administration of Public Education* (Boston: Houghton Mifflin, 1916.

52. Paul Chapman, *Schools as Sorters: Lewis M. Terman, Applied Psychology, and the Intelligence Testing Movement, 1890–1939* (New York: New York University Press, 1988).

3. How Schools Change Reforms

1. Milbrey Wallin McLaughlin, "Learning from Experience: Lessons from Policy Implementation," *Educational Evaluation and Policy Analysis* 9 (Summer 1987): 171–178; Thomas B. Timar, "A Theoretical Framework for Local Responses to

Policy: Implementing Utah's Career Ladder Program," *Educational Evaluation and Policy Analysis* 11 (Winter 1989): 329–341.

2. It is a mistake, say Vicki Eaton Baier, James G. March, and Harald Saetren, to "assume that policy goals and directives are (or can be) clear, that policy makers know what they want, and that what they want is consistent, stable, and unambiguous"—"Implementation and Ambiguity," in James G. March, *Decisions and Organizations* (Oxford: Basil Blackwell, 1988), pp. 157, 150–164; March suggests that "we can treat *goals as hypotheses*"—"The Technology of Foolishness," ibid., pp. 262, 253–265; Carl D. Glickman, "Unlocking School Reform: Uncertainty as a Condition of Professionalism," *Phi Delta Kappan* 69 (October 1987): 120–122.

3. Stephen Brint and Jerome Karabel argue that like other organizations schools, rather than being neutral instruments, are "arenas of power relations" whose interests follow a logic of their own—"Institutional Origins and Transformations," in Walter W. Powell and Paul J. Dimaggio, eds., *The New Institutionalism in Organizational Analysis* (Chicago: University of Chicago Press, 1991), pp. 355, 337–360.

4. On the range of teachers' responses to reforms, see Larry Cuban, *How Teachers Taught: Constancy and Change in American Classrooms, 1890–1980*, 2nd ed. (New York: Teachers College Press, 1993); David K. Cohen and Bella H. Rosenberg, "Functions and Fantasies: Understanding Schools in Capitalist America," *History of Education Quarterly* 17 (Spring 1977): 132.

5. Jane Bernard Powers, *The "Girl Question" in Education: Vocational Education for Young Women in the Progressive Era* (London: Falmer Press, 1992), ch. 2.

6. Paul Lindsay, "The Effect of High School Size on Student Participation, Satisfaction, and Attendance," *Educational Evaluation and Policy Analysis* 4 (Spring 1982): 57–65.

7. Dale Mann, "For the Record," *Teachers College Record* 77 (February 1976): 320.

8. Albert O. Hirschman, *The Rhetoric of Reaction: Perversity, Futility, Jeopardy* (Cambridge: Harvard University Press, 1991), pp. 12, 38; Bruce L. Wison and H. Dickson Corbett, "Statewide Testing and Local Improvement: An Oxymoron?" in Joseph Murphy, ed., *The Educational Reform Movement of the 1980s: Perspectives and Cases* (Berkeley: McCutchan, 1990), pp. 215–242.

9. David Tyack and Elisabeth Hansot, *Learning Together: A History of Coeducation in American Public Schools* (New Haven: Yale University Press, 1990), pp. 291–292.

10. Deirdre Kelly, *Last Chance High* (New Haven: Yale University Press, 1993).

11. Jeannie Oakes, *Keeping Track* (New Haven: Yale University Press, 1985); Paul Chapman, *Schools as Sorters: Lewis M. Terman, Applied Psychology, and the Intelligence Testing Movement, 1890–1939* (New York: New York University Press, 1988).

12. John Dewey, *Experience and Education* (1938; reprint ed., New York: Collier, 1963).

13. David K. Cohen and James P. Spillane, "Policy and Practice: The Relations between Governance and Instruction," in Gerald Grant, ed., *Review of Research in Education,* vol. 18, 1992 (Washington, D.C.: American Educational Research Association, 1992), pp. 3–50; Murphy, *Reform Movement of the 1980s.*

14. Lee S. Shulman, "Knowledge and Teaching: Foundations of the New Reform," *Harvard Educational Review* 57 (1987): 1–22; McLaughlin, "Learning from Experience."

15. Barbara Beatty, "Child Gardening: The Teaching of Young Children in American Schools," in Donald Warren, ed., *American Teachers: Histories of a Profession at Work* (New York: Macmillan, 1989), pp. 65, 70, 65–97; Elizabeth Peabody, *Guide to the Kindergarten and Intermediate Class* (New York: E. Steiger, 1877), p. 35; for an unsympathetic picture of urban elementary instruction, see Joseph Mayer Rice, *The Public School System of the United States* (New York: Century, 1983).

16. The phrase "preventive charity" is from a speech by Felix Adler quoted in John Taylor, *Twentieth-Sixth Annual Report of the Superintendent of Schools* (San Francisco: Department of Public Schools, 1879), p. 361; Nina Vandewalker, *The Kindergarten in American Education* (New York: Macmillan, 1908).

17. Teacher quoted in John Swett, *Annual Report of the Public Schools of the City and County of San Francisco* (San Francisco: San Francisco Public Schools, 1892), p. 71; Beatty, "Child Gardening," pp. 70–80; Michael S. Shapiro, *Child's Garden: The Kindergarten Movement from Froebel to Dewey* (University Park: Pennsylvania State University Press, 1983).

18. Marvin Lazerson, "Urban Reform and the Schools: Kindergartens in Massachusetts, 1870–1915," *History of Education Quarterly* 11 (Summer 1971): 130–132, 115–142; Larry Cuban, "Why Some Reforms Last: The Case of the Kindergarten," *American Journal of Education* 100 (February 1992): 173–176, 166–194.

19. William T. Harris, "The Kindergarten as a Preparation for the Highest Civilization," *Kindergarten Review* 12 (1903): 731; Selwyn K. Troen, *The Public and the Schools: Shaping the St. Louis System, 1838–1920* (Columbia: University of Missouri Press, 1976).

20. Cuban, "Kindergarten," p. 177; on kindergartens for African American children, see Alice D. Cary, "Kindergartens for Negro Children," *Southern Workman* 29 (1900): 461–463.

21. Teacher quoted in Beatty, "Child Gardening," p. 85; Lazerson, "Urban Reform," pp. 130–135; Michael W. Sedlak and Steven Schlossman, "The Public School and Social Services: Reassessing the Progressive Legacy," *Educational Theory* 35 (Fall 1985): 436–467; home visits in a number of cities became the assignment of a new specialist, the "visiting teacher" (or school social worker).

22. Lazerson, "Urban Reform."

23. Almira M. Winchester, *Kindergarten Supervision in City Schools,* U.S. Bureau of Education Bulletin no. 38, 1918 (Washington, D.C.: GPO, 1918), pp. 37–38; Beatty, "Child Gardening," p. 67.

24. Alice Temple, *Survey of the Kindergartens of Richmond, Indiana* (Chicago: University of Chicago Press, 1917), p. 24; the teacher's comment about "flabby kindergarten intellect" quoted in Shapiro, *Child's Garden,* p. 150; Beatty, "Child Gardening," p. 86.

25. Mary Dabney Davis, *General Practice in Kindergarten Education in the United States* (Washington, D.C.: NEA, 1925) p. 16, passim; Grace Parsons, *Cooperation between Kindergarten and Primary Education* (Baltimore: International Kindergarten Union, 1919); Winchester, *Supervision;* Marianne N. Bloch, "Becoming Scientific and Professional: An Historical Perspective on the Aims and Effects of Early Education," in Thomas S. Popkewitz, ed., *The Formation of the School Subjects: The Struggle for Creating an American Institution* (New York: Falmer Press, 1987), pp. 41–49; Cuban, "Kindergarten," pp. 176–190.

26. Bloch, "Scientific and Professional," pp. 47, 51–52; Evelyn Weber, *Ideas*

Influencing Early Childhood Education: A Theoretical Analysis (New York: Teachers College Press, 1984); Dominic Cavallo, "From Perfection to Habit: Moral Training in the American Kindergarten," *History of Education Quarterly* 16 (Summer 1976): 147–161; Margaret Holmes, *Mental Testing Carried on in the New York Public School Kindergartens by Ten Kindergartners* (Louisville: International Kindergarten Union, 1922).

27. For a balanced assessment of the influences of the kindergarten and primary grades' on each other, see Barbara Beatty, *The Culture of Young Children: A History of Policy and Pedagogy in American Preschool Education* (New Haven: Yale University Press, 1994), ch. 6.

28. Vandewalker, *Kindergarten;* Beatty, "Child Gardening," p. 86; Lawrence A. Cremin, *The Transformation of the School* (New York: Vintage Books, 1961); Cuban, "Kindergarten," p. 188; Grace Langdon, *A Study of the Similarities and Differences in Teaching in Nursery School, Kindergarten, and First Grade* (New York: Day, 1933).

29. Leonard P. Ayres, *Laggards in Our Schools: A Study of Retardation and Elimination in City School Systems* (New York: Charities Publication Committee, 1909), p. 4.

30. William F. Book, "Why Pupils Drop Out of School," *Pedagogical Seminary* 12 (June 1904): 209–231; Joseph King Van Denburg. *Causes of the Elimination of Students in Public Secondary Schools of New York* (New York: Teachers College, 1911); Selwyn K. Troen, "The Discovery of the Adolescent by American Educational Reformers, 1900–1920: An Economic Perspective," in Lawrence Stone, ed., *Schooling and Society: Studies in the History of Education* (Baltimore: Johns Hopkins University Press, 1976), ch. 10; Harvey Kantor, *Learning to Earn: School, Work, and Vocational Reform in California, 1880–1930* (Madison: University of Wisconsin Press, 1988).

31. Aubrey Douglass, *The Junior High School,* Fifteenth Yearbook of the National Society for the Study of Education (Bloomington, Ind.: The Public School Publishing Co., 1916); Carole Ford, "The Origins of the Junior High School, 1890–1920" (Ed.D diss., Teachers College, Columbia University, 1982); Daniel Perlstein and William Tobin, "The History of the High School: A Study of Conflicting Aims and Institutional Patterns," paper commissioned by the Carnegie Corporation of New York, 1988; Marvin Lazerson and Norton Grubb, *American Education and Vocationalism: A Documentary History, 1870–1970* (New York: Teachers College Press, 1974), introduction; Sol Cohen, "The Industrial Education Movement, 1906–1917," *American Quarterly* 20 (Spring 1968): 95–110.

32. Charles H. Judd, "Recent Articles and Books on the Junior High School," *The Elementary School Journal* 17 (1917): 679–680; David Snedden, "Reorganization of Education for Children from Twelve to Fourteen Years of Age," *Educational Administration and Supervision* 2 (September 1916): 425–432; Edward V. Robinson, "The Reorganization of the Grades and the High School," *The School Review* 20 (January 1912): 665–687; Herbert Weet, "A Junior High School," *The School Review* 24 (1916): 142–151; Commission on the Reorganization of Secondary Education, *Cardinal Principles of Secondary Education,* U.S. Bureau of Education Bulletin no. 35, 1918 (Washington, D.C.: GPO, 1918); Lawrence A. Cremin, *American Education: The Metropolitan Experience* (New York: Harper & Row, 1988), pp. 305–307.

33. Charles Johnson, "The Junior High School," NEA, *Addresses and Proceedings, 1916,* pp. 145–146; Leonard Koos, "The Peculiar Functions of the Junior High

School: Their Relative Importance," *School Review* 28 (November 1920): 673–681; H. N. McClellan, "The Origins of the Junior High School," *California Journal of Secondary Education* 10 (February 1935): 165–170; there was political opposition, however, to junior high schools, especially from unions, which feared that workers' children might be denied an adequate academic education, a legitimate concern since junior high schools often became sorting agencies—Mary E. Finn, "'Democratic Reform,' Progressivism, and the Junior High Controversy in Buffalo (1918–1923)," *Urban Education* 18 (January 1984): 477–489.

34. NCES, *120 Years,* pp. 36–37; NCES, *Digest, 1975,* p. 54.

35. David L. Angus, Jeffrey E. Mirel, and Maris A. Vinovskis, "Historical Development of Age Stratification in Schooling," *Teachers College Record* 90 (Winter 1988): 211–236; NCES, *120 Years,* pp. 26–27; Harvey Kantor and David B. Tyack, eds., *Work, Youth, and Schooling: Historical Perspectives on Vocationalism in American Education* (Stanford: Stanford University Press, 1982).

36. Thomas Briggs, *The Junior High School* (Boston: Houghton Mifflin, 1922), pp. v-vi, and Briggs, "Possibilities of the Junior High School," *Education* 37 (January 1917): 289.

37. Aubrey Douglass, "The Persistent Problems of the Junior High School," *California Journal of Secondary Education* 20 (February 1945): 117.

38. Task Force on the Education of Young Adolescents, *Turning Points: Preparing American Youth for the Twenty-First Century* (Washington, D.C.: Carnegie Corporation of New York, 1989), p. 32; Kenneth Tye, *The Junior High School in Search of a Mission* (Lanham, Md.: University Press of America, 1985), pp. 8–10, 320–325, 338–339; John Lounsbury and Harlan Douglass, "Recent Trends in Junior High School Practices," in M. Brough and R. Hamm, eds., *The American Intermediate School* (Danville, Ill.: The Interstate Printers and Publishers, 1974), pp. 171–175; Larry Cuban, "Why Reforms Last: The Case of the Junior High School," *American Educational Research Journal* 29 (Summer 1992): 227–251.

39. John Meyer, "Organizational Structure as Signalling," *Pacific Sociological Review* 22 (1980): 481–500; Mary Hayward Metz, "Real School: A Universal Drama amid Disparate Experience," in Douglas E. Mitchell and Margaret E. Goertz, eds., *Education Politics for the New Century* (New York: Falmer Press, 1990), pp. 75–91; Paul J. DiMaggio and Walter W. Powell, "The Iron Cage Revisited: Institutional Isomorphism and Collective Rationality in Organizational Fields," *American Sociological Review* 48 (April 1983): 147–160.

40. Geraldine Jonçich Clifford, "Man/Woman/Teacher: Gender, Family, and Career in American Educational History," in Donald R. Warren, ed., *American Teachers: Histories of a Profession at Work* (New York: Macmillan, 1989), pp. 293–343; David Tyack and Elisabeth Hansot, *Learning Together: A History of Coeducation in American Public Schools* (New Haven: Yale University Press, 1990), ch. 7.

41. David Tyack attended this junior-senior high school at that time.

42. A. K. Loomis, Edwin Johnson, and B. Lamar, *The Program of Studies* (Washington, D.C.: U.S. Office of Education, 1932), pp. 7–8, 51–54, 58–60, 266–271; Warren Coxe, "When Is a School a Junior High School?" *Junior-Senior High School Clearing House* 5 (October 1930): 72–79.

43. Fred M. Hechinger, "Schools for Teenagers: A Historic Dilemma," *Teachers College Record* 94 (Spring 1993): 522–539; Task Force on the Education of Young Adolescents, *Turning Points,* pp. 9–10.

44. David L. Kirp and Donald N. Jensen, eds., *School Days, Rule Days: The Legalization and Regulation of Education* (Philadelphia: Falmer Press, 1986); Cohen and Spillane, "Governance and Instruction."

45. Diane Ravitch, *The Great School Wars* (New York: Basic Books, 1974).

46. David C. Hammack, "The Centralization of New York City's Public School System, 1896: A Social Analysis of a Decision" (M.A. thesis, Columbia University, 1969); Joseph M. Cronin, *The Control of Urban Schools: Perspectives on the Power of Educational Reformers* (New York: The Free Press, 1973).

47. Nicholas Murray Butler, "Editorial," *Educational Review* 12 (September 1896): 196–207; Selma Berrol, "William Henry Maxwell and a New Educational New York," *History of Education Quarterly* 8 (Summer 1968): 215–228.

48. Critic quoted in Donald H. Ross, ed., *Administration for Adaptability: A Source Book Drawing Together the Results of More Than 150 Individual Studies Relating to the Question of Why and How Schools Improve* (New York: Metropolitan School Study council, 1958), p. 205; David Rogers, *110 Livingston Street* (New York: Random House, 1968).

49. Melvin Zimet, *Decentralization and School Effectiveness* (New York: Teachers College Press, 1973); Boulton H. Demas, *The School Elections: A Critique of the 1969 New York City School Decentralization,* a report of the Institute for Community Studies (New York: Queens College, City University of New York, 1971).

50. John W. Meyer, W. Richard Scott, David Strang, and Andrew Creighton, *Bureaucratization without Centralization: Changes in the Organizational System of American Public Education, 1940–1980,* Project Report no. 85-A11, Institute for Research on Educational Finance and Governance, Stanford University, 1985.

51. *New York Times,* January 6, 1990, pp. A1, 16; January 19, 1990, p. A16; March 9, 1990, pp. A-1, 16; for discussion of Fernandez's work in decentralizing the Miami schools, see Jane L. David, "Restructuring in Progress: Lessons from Pioneering Districts," in Richard F. Elmore et al., *Restructuring Schools: The Next Generation of Educational Reform* (San Francisco: Jossey-Bass, 1990), pp. 212–215, 209–250.

52. John W. Meyer, *The Impact of the Centralization of Educational Funding and Control of State and Local Educational Governance,* Institute for Research on Educational Finance and Governance, Stanford University, 1980; on the problems induced by incremental and cumulative changes in governance, see David K. Cohen, "Governance and Instruction: The Promise of Decentralization and Choice," in William H. Clune and John F. Witte, eds., *Choice and Control in American Education: The Theory of Choice and Control in Education* (Philadelphia: Falmer Press, 1990), pp. 337–386.

53. The administrator is quoted in Jane L. David and Paul D. Goren, *Transforming Education: Overcoming Barriers* (Washington, D.C.: National Governors' Association, 1993), p. 27; "Ten Lessons about Regulation and Schooling," *CPRE Policy Briefs* (New Brunswick, N.J.: Rutgers University, 1992); on the ambiguous connection between changes in instruction and reforms in governance, see Cohen, "Governance and Instruction."

54. Elmore et al., *Restructuring,* pp. 290–292; Milbrey W. McLaughlin, Scott Pfeiffer, Deborah Swanson-Owens, and Sylvia Yee, *State Policy and Teaching Excellence* (Stanford, Calif.: Institute for the Study of Educational Finance and Governance, 1985).

55. Marshall S. Smith and Jennifer O'Day, "Systemic School Reform," in Susan

Fuhrman and Betty Malen, eds., *The Politics of Curriculum and Testing* (Philadelphia: Falmer Press, 1991), pp. 233–267; U.S. Congress, Office of Technology Assessment, *Testing in American Schools: Asking the Right Questions,* (Washington, D.C.: GPO, 1992), ch. 3.

56. Bruce L. Wilson and H. Dickson Corbett, "Statewide Testing and Local Improvement: An Oxymoron?" in Joseph Murphey, ed., *The Educational Reform Movement of the 1980s: Perspectives and Cases* (Berkeley: McCutchan, 1990), pp. 261–262, 243–264.

57. Thomas R. Timar and David L. Kirp, "Educational Reform and Institutional Compliance," *Harvard Educational Review* 57 (August 1987): 319–326, 308–330; Thomas B. Timar and David L. Kirp, *Managing Educational Excellence* (New York: Falmer Press, 1988).

58. "Cavazos Issues 'Terrible' Report on U.S. Schools," *Los Angeles Times,* May 3, 1990, p. A3; Alan L. Ginsburg, Jay Noell, and Valena White Plisco, "Lessons from the Wall Chart," *Educational Evaluation and Policy Analysis* 10 (Spring 1988): 1–12.

59. Timar and Kirp, *Excellence;* Toch, *Excellence;* McLaughlin, "Learning from Experience."

60. The veteran reformer John Goodlad thinks that "we are rapidly moving toward the use of the word 'restructuring' whenever we talk about school reform at all. And if we have enough conferences on it, we'll assume that the schools have been restructured." But what does it signify? Goodlad is quoted in Lynn Olson, "The 'Restructuring' Puzzle: Ideas for Revamping 'Egg-Crate' Schools Abound, But to What Ends?" *Education Week,* November 2, 1988, pp. 7, 7–11.

61. Elmore et al., *Restructuring,* p. 4; William A. Firestone, Susan H. Fuhrman, and Michael W. Kirst, *The Progress of Reform: An Appraisal of State Education Initiatives* (New Brunswick, N.J.: Center for Policy Research in Education, 1989), pp. 10, 13. Michael Kirst observes that "restructuring" is "almost a Rorschach test. It's all in the eye of the beholder" (quoted in Olson, p. 7).

62. *New York Times,* October 1, 1989, sect. 4, pp. 1, 22 (emphasis added to *radical*).

63. Michael W. Kirst, "Who Should Control Our Schools: Reassessing Current Policies," Center for Educational Research at Stanford, School of Education, Stanford University, 1988; *New York Times,* March 23, 1990, p. A9.

64. David and Goren, *Barriers.*

65. Elmore et al., *Restructuring,* pp. 290–292.

66. Joan E. Talbert, Milbrey W. McLaughlin, and Brian Rowan, "Understanding Context Effects on Secondary School Teaching," *Teachers College Record* 95 (Fall 1993): 45–68.

67. David K. Cohen and Deborah Loewenberg Ball, "Relations between Policy and Practice: A Commentary," *Educational Evaluation and Policy Analysis* 12 (Fall 1990): 251–252.

68. Ibid., pp. 252–253.

69. Milbrey W. McLaughlin and Joan E. Talbert, *Contexts That Matter for Teaching and Learning: Strategic Opportunities for Meeting the Nation's Educational Goals* (Stanford, Calif.: Center for Research on the Context of Secondary School Teaching, 1993), p. 21.

4. Why the Grammar of Schooling Persists

1. John Dewey, *The Educational Situation* (Chicago: University of Chicago Press, 1902), pp. 22–23; on the "regularities" of schools as institutions, see Seymour B. Sarason, *The Predictable Failure of Educational Reform* (San Francisco: Jossey-Bass, 1990), pp. 173–175; on the difficulty of changing practice in teaching, see David K. Cohen, "Teaching Practice: Plus Ça Change . . ." in Philip Jackson, ed., *Contributing to Educational Practice: Perspectives on Research and Practice* (Berkeley: McCutchan, 1988), pp. 27–84.

2. Both schools and language are, of course, in flux—for example, as new words or institutional features are added—but we are arguing that changes in the basic structure and rules of each are so gradual that they do not jar. "Grammar" in this sense might be thought of both as descriptive (the way things are) and prescriptive (the way things ought to be). We appreciate the advice of the linguist Shirley Brice Heath in thinking about these parallels.

3. Larry Cuban, *How Teachers Taught: Constancy and Change in American Classrooms, 1890–1980* (New York: Longman, 1984); Annette Hemins and Mary Hayood Metz, "Real Teaching: How High School Teachers Negotiate Societal, Local Community, and Student Pressures When They Define Their Work," in R. Page and L. Valli, eds., *Interpretive Studies in U.S. Secondary Schools* (Albany: State University of New York Press, 1990), ch. 5.

4. On the political construction of schooling, see Ira Katznelson and Margaret Weir, *Schooling for All: Class, Race, and the Decline of the Democratic Ideal* (New York: Basic Books, 1985); Herbert M. Kliebard, *The Struggle for the American Curriculum, 1893–1958* (New York: Routledge & Kegan Paul, 1987); and Michael W. Apple, *Ideology and Curriculum* (London: Routledge & Kegan Paul, 1979). We thank David Labaree for suggesting the importance of the timing of reforms in the organizational life cycle—letter of November 10, 1993.

5. On the relation of a "real school" to concepts of equality, see Mary Hayward Metz, "Real School: A Universal Drama amid Disparate Experience," in Douglas E. Mitchell and Margaret E. Goertz, eds., *Education Politics for the New Century* (New York: Falmer Press, 1990), pp. 75–91; John W. Meyer and Brian Rowan, "Institutionalized Organizations: Formal Structure as Myth and Ceremony," *American Journal of Sociology* 83 (September 1977): 340–363; Meyer and Rowan, "The Structure of Educational Organizations," in Marshall W. Meyer, ed., *Environments and Organizations* (San Francisco: Jossey-Bass, 1978), pp. 78–109; Paul J. DiMaggio and Walter W. Powell, "The Iron Cage Revisited: Institutional Isomorphism and Collective Rationality," and Stephen Brint and Jerome Karabel, "Institutional Origins and Transformations: The Case of American Community Colleges," in DiMaggio and Powell, eds., *The New Institutionalism in Organizational Analysis* (Chicago: University of Chicago Press, 1991), pp. 63–82, 337–360.

6. Donald Orlosky and B. Othanel Smith, "Educational Change: Its Origins and Characteristics," *Phi Delta Kappan* 53 (March 1972): 412–414.

7. Wilfred M. Aiken, *The Story of the Eight-Year Study* (New York: Harper & Row, 1942).

8. Ellwood P. Cubberley, *Rural Life and Education: A Study of the Rural-School Problem as a Phase of the Rural-Life Problem* (Boston: Houghton Mifflin, 1914); Wayne E. Fuller, *The Old Country School* (Chicago: University of Chicago Press,

1982); Andrew Gulliford, *America's Country Schools* (Washington, D.C.: Preservation Press, 1986).

9. Henry Barnard, "Gradation of Public Schools, with Special Reference to Cities and Large Villages," *American Journal of Education* 2 (December 1856): 455–464.

10. John D. Philbrick, "Report of the Superintendent of Common Schools to the Assembly [of Connecticut], May 1856," *American Journal of Education* 2 (September 1856): 261–264; David L. Angus, Jeffrey E. Mirel, and Maris A. Vinovskis, "Historical Development of Age Stratification in Schooling," *Teachers College Record* 90 (Winter 1988): 211–236; Willard Waller, *The Sociology of Teaching* (New York: John Wiley, 1965).

11. William J. Shearer, *The Grading of Schools* (New York: H. P. Smith, 1898); Frank Forest Bunker, *Reorganization of the Public School System,* U.S. Bureau of Education Bulletin no. 8, 1916 (Washington, D.C.: GPO, 1916).

12. William T. Harris, "The Early Withdrawal of Pupils from School—Its Causes and Its Remedies," NEA, *Addresses and Proceedings, 1874,* pp. 260–72; E. E. White, "Several Problems in Graded-School Management," NEA *Addresses and Proceedings, 1874,* pp. 255–263; Felix Adler, "Educational Needs," *North American Review* 136 (March 1883): 290–291; John I. Goodlad and Robert H. Anderson, *The Non-Graded Elementary School,* rev. ed. (New York: Harcourt, Brace and World, 1963), ch. 3.

13. Leonard P. Ayres, *Laggards in Our Schools: A Study of Retardation and Elimination in City School Systems* (New York: Charities Publication Committee, 1909).

14. Angus, Mirel, and Vinovskis, "Age Stratification"; David B. Tyack, *The One Best System: A History of American Urban Education* (Cambridge: Harvard University Press, 1974), pp. 198–216.

15. Goodlad and Anderson, *The Non-Graded Elementary School.*

16. The Carnegie Foundation for the Advancement of Teaching (CFAT), *First Annual Report of the President and Treasurer* (New York: Carnegie Foundation for the Advancement of Teaching 1906), p. 38 (CFAT annual reports are hereafter cited by short title and date); on the origins and consequences of "the credit system," see Dietrich Gerhard, "The Emergence of the Credit System in American Education Considered as a Problem of Social and Intellectual History," Presidential Address to the Historical Association of Greater St. Louis, May 1953.

17. Ellen Condliffe Lagemann, *Private Power for the Public Good: A History of the Carnegie Foundation for the Advancement of Teaching* (Middletown, Conn,: Wesleyan University Press, 1983), ch. 3.

18. CFAT, *First Annual Report, 1906,* pp. 38, 42.

19. CFAT, *First Annual Report, 1906,* pp. 39–47, and *Second Annual Report, 1907,* pp. 66–70; Leslie Santee Siskin, *Realms of Knowledge: Academic Departments in Secondary Schools* (Philadelphia: Falmer Press, 1994).

20. Ellsworth Tompkins and Walter H. Gaumnitz, *The Carnegie Unit: Its Origin, Status, and Trends,* U.S. Department of Health, Education, and Welfare Bulletin no. 7, 1954 (Washington, D.C.: GPO, 1954); Lagemann, *Private Power,* p. 95.

21. CFAT, *Second Annual Report, 1907,* p. 69.

22. U.S. Commissioner of Education, *Report for 1903* (Washington, D.C.: GPO, 1904), vol. 2, p. 1818.

23. Edward A. Krug, *The Shaping of the American High School, 1920–1941,* vol.

2 (Madison: University of Wisconsin Press, 1972), p. 64; for educators' critiques of the Carnegie unit, see Thompkins and Gaumnitz, *Carnegie Unit,* pp. 53–54.

24. The principal of the Dalton High School, E. D. Jackman, helped Parkhurst develop her reforms—see Jackman, "The Dalton Plan," *The School Review* 28 (March 1920): 688–696.

25. Sylvester Moorhead, "The Dalton Plan in the United States and England" (Ph.D. diss., Stanford University, 1950); Lawrence A. Cremin, *The Transformation of the School: Progressivism in American Education, 1876–1957* (New York: Alfred A. Knopf, 1961).

26. Helen Parkhurst, *Education on the Dalton Plan* (New York: E. P. Dutton, 1922).

27. Ibid.

28. Ibid.

29. Roy O. Billet, *Provisions for Individual Differences, Marking, and Promotion,* U.S. Bureau of Education Bulletin no. 17, 1932 (Washington, D.C.: GPO, 1933), p. 9 and passim; Moorhead, "Dalton Plan," p. 94; Evelyn Dewey, *The Dalton Laboratory Plan* (New York: E. P. Dutton, 1922).

30. Moorhead, "Dalton Plan," pp. 220, 102 (superintendent quoted on p. 273); June Edwards, "To Teach Responsibility, Bring Back the Dalton Plan" *Phi Delta Kappan,* 72 (January 1991):398–401.

31. Teacher quoted in Krug, *High School, 1920–1941,* p. 165; Moorhead, "Dalton Plan," pp. 112–123, 205–212.

32. Committee on Education and Labor, U.S. House of Representatives, *A Compilation of Federal Education Laws* (Washington, D.C.: GPO, 1969), p. 369; John Dale Russell et al., *Vocational Education* (Washington, D.C.: GPO, 1938), pp. 38–40.

33. Nell Lawler, "Experimenting with a Core Curriculum," *Curriculum Journal* 8 (November 1937): 310–312; William B. Brown, "The Core Is Not All of the Curriculum," *Curriculum Journal* 9 (May 1938): 210–212; L. W. Webb, "Ten Years of Curriculum Planning by the North Central Association," *Curriculum Journal* 8 (October 1937): 234–238; Daniel Tanner and Laurel Tanner, *History of the School Curriculum* (New York: Macmillan, 1990), pp. 168–171; Ralph N. D. Atkinson, "South Side High School's Plan of General Education," *The Clearing House* 17 (May 1943): 548–553; Helen Babson, "Progress at Eagle Rock High School," *California Journal of Secondary Education* 16 (May 1941): 299–303; Paul B. Jacobson, "Inaugurating the Core Program," *The Clearing House* 18 (March 1944): 392–395; on the persistence and key role of departments in high schools, see Siskin, "Realms of Meaning."

34. Jesse Newlon, "The Need of a Scientific Curriculum Policy for Junior and Senior High Schools," *Educational Administration and Supervision* 3 (1917–18): 267; Denver Public Schools, *Denver Program of Curriculum Revision,* Monograph 12 (Denver: Denver Public Schools, 1927); Cuban, *How Teachers Taught,* ch. 3.

35. Max McConn, "Freeing the Secondary School for Experimentation," *Progressive Education* 10 (November 1933): 367.

36. Ibid., pp. 368–371; Wilfred D. Aiken, *The Story of the Eight-Year Study* (New York: McGraw-Hill, 1942); Krug, *High School, 1920–1941,* pp. 255–265.

37. Aiken, *Eight-Year Study,* chs. 2–3; Wilfred M. Aiken, "The Eight-Year Study: If We Were to Do It Again," *Progressive Education* 31 (October 1953): 13; Cremin, *Transformation,* pp. 251–257.

38. Progressive Education Association, Commission on the Relation of School and College, *Thirty Schools Tell Their Story,* vol. 5 in *Adventure in American Education* (New York: Harper and Brothers, 1942).

39. Frederick Redefer, "The Eight-Year Study . . . after Eight Years," *Progressive Education* 28 (November 1950): 33, 33–36; for critiques and defenses of the scientific aspects of the college study, see, for example, Helmer G. Johnson, "Some Comments on the Eight-Year Study," *School and Society* 72 (November 25, 1950): 337–339, and Paul E. Diederich, "The Eight-Year Study: More Comments," *School and Society* 73 (January 20, 1951): 41–42.

40. Redefer, "After Eight Years," p. 33.

41. Ibid., pp. 34–35; Frederick L. Redefer, "The Eight-Year Study—Eight Years Later" (Ed.D. diss., Teachers College, Columbia University, 1951).

42. Redefer, "After Eight Years," p. 36.

43. Ibid., Redefer, "Eight Years Later," chs. 3–4.

44. Kliebard, *The Struggle for the American Curriculum* p. 269.

45. Redefer, "After Eight Years," p. 35; for samples of later appreciations of the Eight-Year Study, see Gordon S. Plummer, "Unclaimed Legacy: The Eight-Year Study," *Art Education* 22 (May 1969): 5–6; Charles D. Ritchie, "The Eight-Year Study: Can We Afford to Ignore It?" *Educational Leadership* 28 (February 1971): 484–486; Elaine F. McNally, "The Eight-Year Study," in O. L. Davis, ed., *Perspectives on Curriculum Development, 1776–1976* (Washington, D.C.: Association for Supervision and Curriculum Development, 1976), p. 221.; for afterthoughts on the study by its director, see Aiken, "Eight-Year Study," *Progressive Education* 31 (October 1953): 11–14.

46. Paul Goodman, *Compulsory Mis-Education* (New York: Vintage Books, 1964); Charles Silberman, *Crisis in the Classroom* (New York: Random House, 1970.

47. Allen Graubard, *Free the Children: Radical Reform and the Free School Movement* (New York: Pantheon, 1972).

48. J. Lloyd Trump, *Images of the Future* (Urbana, Ill.: Committee on the Experimental Study of the Utilization of Staff in the Secondary School, 1959); on the relation of architecture to school reform, past and present, see William W. Cutler III, "Cathedral of Culture: The Schoolhouse in American Educational Thought and Practice since 1820," *History of Education Quarterly* 29 (Spring 1989): 1–40.

49. Paul Nachtigal, *A Foundation Goes to School: The Ford Foundation Comprehensive School Improvement Program, 1960–1970* (New York: The Ford Foundation, 1972); J. Lloyd Trump, "How the Project Evolved and Developed," *NASSP Bulletin* 61 (November 1977): 1–4; A. John Fiorino, *Differentiated Staffing: A Flexible Instructional Organization* (New York: Harper & Row, 1972); David W. Beggs III, *Decatur-Lakeview High School: A Practical Application of the Trump Plan* (Englewood Cliffs, N.J.: Prentice Hall, 1964).

50. Nachtigal, *Foundation.*

51. Division of Educational Development, Oregon State Department of Education, *The Oregon Program: Final Report, 1962–1967* (Salem, Oregon State Department of Education 1967) (the quote is from p. 55); Gaynor Petrequin, ed., *Individualizing Learning through Modular-Flexible Scheduling* (New York: McGraw-Hill, 1968).

52. Allen L. Dobbins, "Instruction at Adams," *Phi Delta Kappan* 52 (May 1971): 517, 516; this issue of the *Kappan* had several remarkably candid and self-critical

articles by the team who had created Adams—"Profile of a High school," pp. 514–530.

53. Dobbins, "Adams," 517–519.

54. Robert B. Schwartz, "Profile of a High School: An Introduction" and "The John Adams Team," *Phi Delta Kappan* 52 (May 1971): 515, 514; see also John Guernsey, "Portland's Unconventional Adams High," *American Education* 6 (May 1970): 3–7.

55. Gerald Grant, *The World We Created at Hamilton High* (Cambridge: Harvard University Press, 1988), chs. 2–3; Robert Hampel, *The Last Little Citadel: American High Schools since 1940* (Boston: Houghton Mifflin, 1986), chs. 4–5.

56. Don Glines, "Why Innovative Schools Don't Remain Innovative," *NASSP Bulletin* 57 (February 1973): 1–8; J. Lloyd Trump and William Georgiades, "Retrospect and Prospect," *NASSP Bulletin* 61 (November 1977): 127–133; J. Lloyd Trump and William Georgiades, "Factors that Facilitate and Limit Change—From the Vantage of the NASSP Model Schools Project," 57 (May 1973): 93–102; Richard R. Doremus, "What Ever Happened to . . . John Adams High School?" *Phi Delta Kappan* 83 (November 1981): 199–202; Doremus, "Northwest High School"; John R. Popenfus, Louis V. Paradise, and Kenneth Wagner, "Student Attitudes toward Modular Flexible Scheduling," *The High School Journal* 62 (October 1978): 34–39; Neal C. Nickerson, Jr., "Comments on Research," *NASSP Bulletin* 87 (March 1973): 104–111.

57. A. W. Sturges and Donald Mrdjenovich, "Anticipated and Experienced Problems in Implementing a Flexible-Modular School," *The Journal of Educational Research* 66 (February 1973): 269–273; Scott D. Thompson, "Beyond Modular Scheduling," *Phi Delta Kappan* 52 (April 1971): 484–487.

58. Nachtigal, *Foundation,* pp. 23, 22–26; the *Education Index,* published by H. H. Wilson since 1929, is a cumulative index of subjects and authors that provides a good barometer of policy talk about topics such as flexible scheduling.

59. John D. Philbrick, *City School Systems in the United States,* U.S. Bureau of Education Circular of Information no. 1, 1885 (Washington D.C.: GPO, 1885), p. 47; Patricia Hansen and John Guenther, "Minicourse Programs at the Crossroads," *Phi Delta Kappan* 59 (June 1978): 715–716; the legislator is quoted by Michael W. Kirst, "Recent State Education Reform in the United States: Looking Backward and Forward," *Educational Administration Quarterly* 24 (August 1988): 319–328; William Bennett, *American Education: Making It Work* (Washington, D.C.: GPO, 1988).

60. For evidence that similar problems have arisen in a recent reform movement, see Donna E. Muncey and Patrick J. McQuillen, "Preliminary Findings from a Five-Year Study of the Coalition of Essential Schools," *Phi Delta Kappan* 74 (February 1993): 486–489, and Patricia A. Wasley, "Stirring the Chalkdust: Changing Practices in Essential Schools," *Teachers College Record* 93 (Fall 1991): 28–58.

61. Lawrence A. Cremin, *The Transformation of the School: Progressivism in American Education, 1876–1957* (New York: Alfred A. Knopf, 1962), ch. 9, pp. 350–351; for a discussion of the relation of progressive theories to practice and changing climates of opinion, see Arthur Zilversmit, *Changing Schools: Progressive Education Theory and Practice, 1930–1960* (Chicago: University of Chicago Press, 1993), esp. pp. 169–170.

62. Milbrey Wallin McLaughlin, "Implementation as Mutual Adaptation: Change

in Classroom Organization," *Teachers College Record* 77 (February 1976): 342–343; Orlosky and Smith, "Educational Change"; Neal Gross, Joseph B. Giacquinta, and Marilyn Bernstein, *Implementing Organizational Innovations* (New York: Basic Books, 1971).

63. For three influential examples of powerful middle-level reform movements today, see Henry Levin, *Accelerated Schools: A New Strategy for At-Risk Students,* Policy Bulletin no. 6 (Bloomington, Ind.: Consortium on Educational Policy Studies, School of Education, Indiana University, 1989); Theodore R. Sizer, *Horace's School: Redesigning the American High School* (Boston: Houghton Mifflin, 1992); and James P. Comer, "New Haven's School-Community Connection," *Educational Leadership* 44 (March 1987): 13–16.

5. Reinventing Schooling

1. U.S. Department of Education, *America 2000: An Education Strategy* (Washington, D.C.: U.S. Department of Education, 1991), 15; New American Schools Development Corporation, *Designs for a New Generation of American Schools: Request for Proposals* (Arlington, Va.: New American Schools Development Corporation, 1991), cover, pp. 7, 20–21 (Bush quoted on p. 7); Karen DeWitt, "Bush's Model-School Effort Draws Ideas but Little Money," *New York Times,* May 28, 1992, p. A9; Gary Putka, "Foundation Encourages Firms to Devise a New Class of Schools," *Wall Street Journal,* August 26, 1991, pp. B1–B2; on the millennial American faith in schooling, see Henry J. Perkinson, *The Imperfect Panacea: American Faith in Education, 1965–1990* (New York: McGraw-Hill, 1991).

2. William Celis III, "Private Group Hired to Run Nine Public Schools in Baltimore," *New York Times,* June 11, 1992, p. A9; David A. Bennett, "Rescue Schools, Turn a Profit," *New York Times,* June 11, 1992, p. A19; Mark Walsh, "Whittle Unveils Team to Design New Schools," *Education Week,* March 4, 1992, p. 1 Dinitia Smith, "Turning Minds into Profits," *This World,* September 20, 1992, pp. 8–9, 12; Linda Darling-Hammond, "For-Profit Schooling: Where's the Public Good?" *Education Week,* October 7, 1992, p. 40; Jonathan Kozol, "Whittle and the Privateers," *The Nation,* September 21, 1992, pp. 272–278.

3. Edison quoted in Larry Cuban, *Teachers and Machines: The Classroom Use of Technology since 1920* (New York: Teachers College Press, 1986) p. 9; Virginia Woodson Church, *Teachers Are People, Being the Lyrics of Agatha Brown, Sometime Teacher in the Hilldale High School,* 3rd ed. (Hollywood, Calif.: David Fischer Corporation, 1925), p. 59; for a more recent paean to technology, see William C. Norris, "Via Technology to a New Era in Education," *Phi Delta Kappan* 58 (February 1977): 451–453.

4. Howard Gardner, "The Two Rhetorics of School Reform: Complex Theories vs. the Quick Fix," *Chronicle of Higher Education,* May 6, 1992, pp. 7–8; on the trimming back of Whittle's project from building new for-profit schools to managing public schools, see Geraldine Fabrikant, "Whittle Schools Said to Scale Back Its For-Profit Schools Plan," *New York Times,* July 30, 1993, pp. C1, C5, and Peter Applebome, "The Reasons behind For-Profit Management's Appeal Are Clear. But Will It Really Work?" *New York Times,* November 2, 1994, p. B8; on scaling down NASDC's rhetoric and funding, see James A. Mecklinburger, "The Braking of the 'Break-the-Mold' Express," *Phi Delta Kappan* 74 (December 1992): 280–289.

5. P. Carpenter-Huffman, G. R. Hall, and G. C. Sumner, *Change in Education: Insights from Performance Contracting* (Cambridge, Mass.: Ballinger, 1974), p. 54— they observe about performance contracting in schools that "the competition among firms to sell untested learning systems appears, in fact, to have produced perverse incentives to inflate aspirations."

6. Mecklenburger, "'Break-the-Mold' Express," p. 281; Elisabeth Hansot, *Perfection and Progress: Two Modes of Utopian Thought* (Cambridge: MIT Press, 1974).

7. "Saving our Schools," *Business Week,* September 14, 1992, pp. 70–80; Lonnie Harp, "Group Dissects Education 'Industry' with Eye to Improving Productivity," *Education Week,* November 18, 1992, pp. 1, 13; "Saving Our Schools," special issue of *Fortune,* Spring 1990; H. Thomas James, *The New Cult of Efficiency and Education* (Pittsburgh: University of Pittsburgh Press, 1969); NEA, *In Its Own Image: Business and the Reshaping of Public Education* (Washington, D.C.: NEA, 1990).

8. Gerald N. Tirozzi, "Must We Reinvent the Schools?" in *Voices from the Field: Thirty Expert Opinions on "America 2000," the Bush Administration Strategy to "Reinvent" America's Schools* (Washington, D.C.: William T. Grant Foundation Commission on Work, Family, and Citizenship and the Institute for Educational Leadership, 1991), pp. 9–10.

9. Richard Bumstead, "Performance Contracting," reprinted from *Educate* (October 1970) in J. A. Mecklenburger, J. A. Wilson, and R. W. Hostrop, eds., *Learning C.O.D.* (Hamden, Conn.: Linnet Books, 1972), p. 28.

10. Larry Cuban, "Reforming Again, Again, and Again," *Educational Researcher* 19 (January-February 1990): 3–13.

11. Edward J. Meade, Jr., "Ignoring the Lessons of Previous School Reforms," in *Voices,* p. 46; Robert E. Herriott and Neal Gross, eds., *The Dynamics of Planned Educational Change* (Berkeley: McCutchan, 1979), p. 275; Milbrey W. McLaughlin, "Where's the Community in *America 2000?*" in *Voices,* p. 44. The metaphor "silly putty" appears in Thomas B. Timar and David L. Kirp, *Managing Educational Excellence* (New York: Falmer Press, 1988), p. 127.

12. Susan R. Nevas, "Analytic Planning in Education: Critical Perspectives," *Interchange* 8, no. 3 (1977–78): 13–42; James A. Mecklenberger, "My Visit to BRL," in Mecklenburger, Wilson, and Hostrop, eds., *Learning C.O.D.,* pp. 215–218; Leon Lessinger, *Every Kid a Winner: Accountability in Education* (New York: Simon and Shuster, 1970); James, *The New Cult.*

13. Raymond E. Callahan, *Education and the Cult of Efficiency* (Chicago: University of Chicago Press, 1962); David Tyack and Elisabeth Hansot, *Managers of Virtue: Public School Leadership in America, 1820–1980* (New York: Basic Books, 1982), pt. 2.

14. Cubberley quoted on p. 97 of Callahan, *Cult;* NEA, *In Its Own Image.*

15. David Tyack, Robert Lowe, and Elisabeth Hansot, *Public Schools in Hard Times: The Great Depression and Recent Years* (Cambridge: Harvard University Press, 1984), chs. 1–2.

16. John Brackett, Jay Chambers, and Thomas Parrish, *The Legacy of Rational Budgeting Models in Education and a Proposal for the Future,* Project Report no. 83-A21, Institute for Research on Educational Finance and Governance, Stanford University, 1983.

17. Odiorne quoted in S. J. Knezevich, *Management by Objectives and Results—A Guidebook for Today's School Executive* (Arlington, Va.: American Association of

School Administrators, 1973), p. 4; Carmelo V. Sapone and Joseph L. Guliano, "Management-by-Objectives: Promise and Problems," *Educational Technology* 17 (August 1977): 38; Philip C. Winstead, "Managing by Objectives or Managing by Delusions?" *Educational Technology* 20 (December 1980): 35–37; for a case study of one district's implementation of MBO, see Lee S. Sproull and Kay Ramsey Hofmeister, "Thinking about Implementation," *Journal of Management* 12, no. 1 (1968): 43–60.

18. Aaron Wildavsky, "Rescuing Policy Analysis from PPBS," in R. H. Haveman and J. Margolis, eds., *Public Expenditures and Policy Analysis* (Chicago: Markham, 1970), p. 469; Brackett, Chambers, and Parrish, "Rational Budgeting Models in Education."

19. Michael W. Kirst, "The Rise and Fall of PPBS in California," *Phi Delta Kappan* 56 (April 1975): 536–538.

20. Harry F. Wolcott, *Teachers versus Technocrats: An Educational Innovation in Anthropological Perspective* (Eugene, Or.: Center for Educational Policy and Management, 1977), pp. 14, 241, 244–245.

21. Kirst, "Rise and Fall of PPBS," pp. 536–538.

22. Francis Keppel, "The Business Interest in Education," *Phi Delta Kappan* 18 (January 1967): 188, 187–190; Francis Keppel, "New Relationships between Education and Industry," *Public Administration Review* 30 (July-August 1970): 353–359; on military/corporate/school links see Douglas D. Noble, *The Classroom Arsenal: Military Research, Information Technology, and Public Education* (Philadelphia: Falmer Press, 1991).

23. Stanley Elam, "The Age of Accountability Dawns in Texarkana," *Phi Delta Kappan* 51 (June 1970): 509–514.

24. Quotations from James A. Mecklenburger and John H. Wilson, "Learning C.O.D: Can the Schools Buy Success?" reprinted from *Saturday Review,* September, 18, 1971, in Mecklenburger, Wilson, and Hostrap, *Learning C.O.D.,* p. 2.

25. Mecklenberger, "My Visit to BRL," in Mecklenburger, Wilson, and Hostrap, *Learning C.O.D.,* p. 216; Roald F. Campbell and James E. Lorion, *Performance Contracting in School Systems* (Columbus: Charles E. Merrill Publishing Co., 1972), pp. 33–39.

26. Teacher quoted in Elam, "Texarkana," in Mecklenburger, Wilson, and Hostrop, *Learning C.O.D.,* p. 25; Campbell and Lorion, *Performance Contracting,* ch. 8; for a variety of criticisms, see Mecklenburger, Thomas, and Hostrop, *Learning C.O.D.,* pp. 43–47, 391–324, J. Lawrence McConville, "Evolution of Performance Contracting," *The Educational Forum* 37 (May 1973): 443–452, and Paul Goodman, "The Education Industries," *Harvard Educational Review* 37 (Winter 1967): 107–115.

27. Campbell and Lorion, *Performance Contracting,* ch. 2.

28. Richard Bumstead, "Performance Contracting," in Meckelburger, Thomas, and Hostrop, *Learning C.O.D.,* p. 35; Reed Martin and Peter Briggs, "Private Firms in the Public Schools," *Education Turnkey News,* February-March 1971, quoted in Mecklenburger, Thomas, and Hostrop, *Learning C.O.D.,* p. 226; Green quoted in Campbell and Lorion, *Performance Contracting,* p. 16.

29. Bumstead, "Performance Contracting," pp. 34–39; Campbell and Lorion, *Performance Contracting,* p. 29–33.

30. *Education Daily,* October 1, 1975, p. 5; Campbell and Lorian, *Performance*

Contracting, pp. 111–135; Carpenter-Huffman, Hall, and Sumner, *Change,* p. 53; Battelle Columbus Laboratories, *Final Report on the Office of Economic Opportunity Experiment in Educational Performance Contracting* (Columbus: Battelle Memorial Institute, 1972).

31. Myron Lieberman, *Privatization and Educational Choice* (New York: St. Martin's Press, 1989), ch. 4; Kozol, "Whittle"; for other criticisms of the evaluations, see Carpenter-Huffman, Hall, and Sumner, *Change;* for a critique and analysis of performance contracting as a social experiment, see Edward M. Gramlich and Patricia P. Koshel, *Educational Performance Contracting* (Washington, D.C.: Brookings Institution, 1975).

32. Josiah F. Bumstead, *The Blackboard in the Primary Schools* (Boston: Perkins and Marvin, 1841), p. viii, and Andrews & Co., *Illustrated Catalogue of School Merchandise* (Chicago, 1881), p. 73, as quoted in Charnel Anderson, *Technology in American Education, 1650–1900* (Washington, D.C.: GPO, 1962), pp. 18, 32; David Tyack, "Educational Moonshot?" *Phi Delta Kappan* 58 (February 1977): 457; Philip W. Jackson, *The Teacher and the Machine* (Pittsburgh: University of Pittsburgh Press, 1967).

33. By 1931 twenty-five states and many large cities had departments devoted to audiovisual instruction—Cuban, *Teachers and Machines* p. 12; Paul Saettler, *A History of Instructional Technology* (New York: McGraw-Hill, 1968), ch. 7; David Tyack and Elisabeth Hansot, "Futures That Never Happened: Technology and the Classroom," *Education Week,* September 4, 1985, pp. 40, 35.

34. Cuban, *Teachers and Machines;* Anthony Oettinger and Selma Marks, "Educational Technology: New Myths and Old Realities," *Harvard Educational Review* 38 (Fall 1968): 697–717; the *Education Index,* described earlier, charts the rise and decline of hyperbolic claims about instruction by various technologies.

35. Larry Cuban, "Determinants of Curriculum Change and Stability," in Jon Schaffarzick and Gary Sykes, eds., *Value Conflicts and Curriculum Issues* (Berkeley: McCutchan, 1979), pp. 139–196.

36. Anderson, *Technology.*

37. Saettler, *History,* pp. 110–111, 127.

38. Cuban, *Teachers and Machines.* ch. 1; Saettler, *History,* p. 302–303.

39. Mark May and Arthur Lumsdaine, *Learning from Films* (New Haven: Yale University Press, 1958), p. 206.

40. William Levenson, *Teaching through Radio* (New York: Farrar and Rinehart, 1945), p. 181; Norman Woelfel and Keith Tyler, *Radio and the School* (Yonkers-on-Hudson: World Book Co., 1945), pp. 3, 4–5.

41. *Decade of Experiment: The Fund for the Advancement of Education, 1951–1961* (New York: The Ford Foundation, 1962); Cuban, *Teachers and Machines,* ch. 2.

42. Cuban, *Teachers and Machines,* pp. 38–39 (advocate quoted on p. 50).

43. Ibid., ch. 3.

44. Ibid.

45. U.S. Department of Commerce, *Statistical Abstract of the United States, 1991* (Washington, D.C.: GPO, 1991), p. 150; Peter West, "Survey Finds Gaps in U.S. Schools' Computer Use," *Education Week,* December 15, 1993, p. 8; Gina Boubion, "Technology Gap Frustrates Schools," *San Jose Mercury,* March 14, 1993, pp. 1, 8A; Charles Pillar, "Separate Realities: The Creation of the Technological Underclass in America's Public Schools," *Macworld,* September 1992, pp. 218, 218–231.

46. Pillar, "Separate Realities," pp. 218–219.

47. U.S. Congress, Office of Technology Assessment, *Power On: New Tools for Teaching and Learning* (Washington, D.C.: GPO, 1988), p. 6, passim.

48. Larry Cuban, "Computers Meet Classroom; Classroom Wins," *Teachers College Record* 95, no. 2 (Winter 1993): 185–210.

49. Susan Russell, *Beyond Drill and Practice: Expanding the Computer Mainstream* (Reston, Va.: The Council for Exceptional Children, 1989); Office of Technology Assessment, *Power On.*

50. For discussions of the different worlds of teachers and many policymakers, see Neal Gross, Joseph B. Giacquinta, and Marilyn Bernstein, *Implementing Organizational Innovations* (New York: Basic Books, 1971), and Milbrey McLaughlin, "Learning from Experience: Lessons from Policy Implementation," *Educational Evaluation and Policy Analysis* 9 (Summer 1987): 172, 171–178.

51. Linda Darling-Hammond and Barnett Berry, *The Evolution of Teacher Policy* (Washington, D.C.: Center for the Study of the Teaching Profession, 1988); William R. Johnson, "Teachers and Teacher Training in the Twentieth Century," in Donald Warren, ed., *American Teachers: Histories of a Profession at Work* (New York: Macmillan, 1989), pp. 237–256; U.S. Department of Education, *America 2000,* p. 13.

52. "The Single Salary Schedule," *School and Society* 20 (July 5, 1924): 9, 9–13; "An Unjust Discrimination," *The Journal of the National Education Association* 12 (February 1923): 48; in 1921 and in successive years the NEA resolved in favor of a single salary schedule—NEA *Addresses and Proceedings, 1921,* p. 27.

53. Wayne E. Fuller, "The Teacher in the Country School," in Warren, ed., *Teachers,* pp. 98–117; Michael W. Sedlak, "'Let Us Go and Buy a School Master': Historical Perspectives on the Hiring of Teachers in the United States, 1750–1980," in Warren, ed., *Teachers,* pp. 257–290.

54. David Tyack and Elisabeth Hansot, *Learning Together: A History of Coeducation in American Public Schools* (New Haven: Yale University Press and the Russell Sage Foundation, 1990), pp. 57–69.

55. Willard A. Ellsbree, *The American Teacher: Evolution of a Profession in a Democracy* (New York: American Book Co., 1939); David Tyack, *The One Best System: A History of American Urban Education* (Cambridge: Harvard University Press, 1974), pp. 59–65, 255–294.

56. NEA, *Addresses and Proceedings, 1922,* p. 45; Vaughan MacCaughey, "The Single Salary Schedule," *School and Society* 20 (July 5, 1924): 9–13; Ellsbree, *Teacher,* p. 451.

57. Dio Richardson, "Single-Salary Schedules," *The Journal of the National Education Association* 11 (June 1922): 226; Cora B. Morrison, "Single Salary Schedules," NEA, *Addresses and Proceedings,* 1924, pp. 480–486.

58. Henry D. Hervey, "The Rating of Teachers," NEA, *Addresses and Proceedings, 1921,* p. 825; Callahan, *Cult;* Richard J. Murnane and David K. Cohen, "Merit Pay and the Evaluation Problem: Why Most Merit Pay Plans Fail and a Few Survive," *Harvard Educational Review* 56 (February 1986): 2, 1–17.

59. Susan Moore Johnson, "Merit Pay for Teachers: A Poor Prescription for Reform," *Harvard Educational Review* 54 (May 1984): 179, 175–185; William A. Firestone, Susan H. Fuhrman, and Michael W. Kirst, *The Progress of Reform: An Appraisal of State Education Initiatives* (New Brunswick, N.J.: Center for Policy Research in Education, 1989).

60. Johnson, "Merit Pay."

61. Richard R. Doremus, "Kalamazoo's Merit Pay Plan," *Phi Delta Kappan* 63 (February 1982): 409–410.

62. Johnson, "Merit Pay"; P. J. Porwoll, *Merit Pay for Teachers* (Arlington, Va.: Educational Research Service, 1979); Susan M. Johnson, "Incentives for Teachers: What Motivates, What Matters?" *Educational Administration Quarterly* 22 (Summer 1986): 54–79; Murnane and Cohen, "Merit Pay," p. 2.

63. Murnane and Cohen, "Merit Pay," pp. 12–15.

64. Susan Moore Johnson, "Redesigning Teachers' Work," in Richard Elmore et al., *Restructuring Schools: The Next Generation of Educational Reform* (San Francisco: Jossey-Bass, 1990), pp. 125, 128.

65. Susan Moore Johnson, *Teachers at Work: Achieving Success in Our Schools* (New York: Basic Books, 1990), ch. 10.

66. Jerry Duea, "School Officials and the Public Hold Disparate Views on Education," *Phi Delta Kappan* 63 (March 1982): 479; Dan C. Lortie, *Schoolteacher: A Sociological Study* (Chicago: University of Chicago Press, 1975), p. 105; Johnson, *Teachers at Work.*

67. Karen De Witt, "Most Parents in Survey Say Education Goals Can't Be Met," *New York Times,* November 13, 1991, p. B7.

68. As Sarah Lawrence Lightfoot shows, good schools come in a great variety of patterns to fit the local context: *The Good High School: Portraits of Character and Culture* (New York: Basic Books, 1983).

69. Milbrey W. McLaughlin, "Where's the Community in *America 2000?*" in *Voices,* p. 44; Edward J. Meade, Jr., "Ignoring the Lessons of Previous School Reforms," in *Voices,* p. 46; on the short-lived federal programs of model and experimental schools, see Harold Howe II, "Seven Large Questions for *America 2000's* Authors," in *Voices,* p. 27, and Michael W. Kirst, "Strengthening Federal-Local Relationships Supporting Educational Change," in Robert E. Herriott and Neal Gross, eds., *The Dynamics of Planned Educational Change* (Berkeley: McCutchan, 1979), p. 275.

70. Vicki Matthews-Burwell, "Drinking It All In," *New York Times,* February 12, 1994, p. 15.

Epilogue

1. U.S. Department of Education, *America 2000: An Education Strategy* (Washington, D.C.: U.S. Department of Education, 1991), p. 2; Milbrey W. McLaughlin, "Where's the Community in *America 2000?*" in *Voices from the Field: Thirty Expert Opinions on "America 2000,"* the Bush Administration Strategy to "Reinvent" America's Schools (Washington, D.C.: William T. Grant Foundation Commission on Work, Family, and Citizenship and the Institute for Educational Leadership, 1991), pp. 43–44.

2. Richard F. Elmore and Milbrey Wallin McLaughlin, *Steady Work: Policy, Practice, and the Reform of American Education* (Santa Monica: Rand Corporation, 1988); Michael Lipsky, *Street Level Bureaucracy: Dilemmas of the Individual in Public Services* (New York: Russell Sage Foundation, 1980); Milbrey McLaughlin, "Learning from Experience: Lessons from Policy Implementation," *Educational Evaluation and Policy Analysis* 9 (Summer 1987): 172.

3. Milbrey W. McLaughlin and Joan E. Talbert, *Contexts That Matter for Teaching and Learning: Strategic Opportunities for Meeting the Nation's Goals* (Stanford, Calif.: Center for Research on the Context of Secondary School Teaching, 1993); Joan E. Talbert, Milbrey McLaughlin, and Brian Rowan, "Understanding Context Effects on Secondary School Teaching," *Teachers College Record* 95 (Fall 1993): 45–68.

4. Daniel Lortie, *Schoolteacher* (Chicago: University of Chicago Press, 1975).

5. Elmore and McLaughlin, *Steady Work,* p. v.

6. *New Yorker,* August 12, 1991, pp. 22–23.

7. Ibid.

8. Jane L. David and Paul D. Goren, *Transforming Education: Overcoming Barriers* (Washington, D.C.: National Governors' Association, 1993); Harold Howe II, *"America 2000:* A Bumpy Ride on Four Trains," *Phi Delta Kappan* 73 (November 1991): 192–203.

9. Leslie Siskin, *Realms of Knowledge: Academic Departments in Secondary Schools* (Philadelphia: Falmer Press, 1994); David K. Cohen, Milbrey W. McLaughlin, and Joan E. Talbert, eds., *Teaching for Understanding: Challenges for Policy and Practice* (San Francisco: Jossey-Bass, 1993); Katherine C. Boles, "School Restructuring by Teachers," *Journal of Applied Social Science* 28 (June 1992): 173–203; James P. Comer, "Educating Poor Minority Children," *Scientific American,* November 1988, pp. 42–48; Henry M. Levin, "Accelerated Schools for Disadvantaged Students," *Educational Leadership* 44 (March 1987): 19–21; Theodore R. Sizer, *Horace's School: Redesigning the American High School* (Boston: Houghton Mifflin, 1992).

10. We have emphasized the importance of focusing school reform on improving what students learn—broadly defined—and on the critical importance of teachers. The current movement for "systemic reform" of schooling is partially compatible with these principles: It does focus on what students learn and proposes bottom-up as well as top-down strategies. To bring new standards of learning alive in the classroom, many of the advocates of systemic reform also incorporate a creative role for teachers in meeting these standards. In this neo-progressive subtext for systemic change, reformers advocate a challenging pedagogy that stresses active learning and teaching for understanding. But national standards and tests have the potential of determining crucial decisions about *what* to teach and becoming a sophisticated nationalized version of the old "one best system" of the administrative progressives, in which the experts planned what to teach and teachers had little say over curriculum. See Marshall S. Smith and Jennifer O'Day, "Systemic School Reform," in Susan Fuhrman and Betty Malen, eds., *The Politics of Curriculum and Testing* (New York: Falmer Press, 1991), pp. 233–267.

11. Deborah Meier, "Choice Can Save Public Education," *The Nation,* March 4, 1991, pp. 270, 253, 266–271.

12. John E. Chubb and Terry M. Moe, *Politics, Markets, and America's Schools* (Washington, D.C.: Brookings Institution, 1990); Chester E. Finn, "Reinventing Local Control," *Education Week,* January 23, 1991, pp. 40, 32; Dennis P. Doyle and Chester E. Finn, "American Schools and the Future of Local Control," *The Public Interest* 77 (Fall 1984): 77–95.

13. Ellwood P. Cubberley, *Changing Conceptions of Education* (Boston: Houghton Mifflin, 1909), p. 78.

Acknowledgments

We are deeply grateful to the Spencer Foundation for sponsoring this study, to the Stanford Humanities Center for a sabbatical-year fellowship and lively intellectual community, and to the Stanford Center for the Study of Families, Children, and Youth for funding research assistants and providing a forum for discussing ideas.

We thank the *American Educational Research Journal* for permission to adapt (in Chapter 4) the essay "The 'Grammar' of Schooling: Why Has It Been So Hard to Change?" which appeared in volume 31 (Fall 1994); we also are grateful to The Johns Hopkins University Press for permission to reprint, in revised form in Chapter 5, the essay "Reinventing Schooling," in Diane Ravitch and Maris Vinovskis, eds., *Historical Perspectives on the Current Education Reforms* (© 1994 by The Johns Hopkins University Press). We appreciate the *New Yorker*'s permission to reproduce the cartoon on page 15.

This book would have seen print much earlier had we had not had so many helpful colleagues eager to improve it, and we would not have had nearly so much stimulation and pleasure in the work without those exchanges. A number of scholars gave us critical and helpful readings of different versions of the whole manuscript: Richard Elmore, Susan Moore Johnson, Carl Kaestle, Harvey Kantor, David Labaree, Kim Marshall, Jeffrey Mirel, and Mike Rose. Elisabeth Hansot and John Meyer gave us invaluable advice and key ideas at every stage of the writing. William Tobin, coauthor with Tyack of an earlier version of Chapter 4, assisted us perceptively in both research and writing. As coauthor with Tyack of an essay on reforming the high school and an astute historical analyst of educational policy, Tom James contributed to our understanding of the complex relationship between policy talk and institutional trends. We were extremely fortunate to have Nancy Clemente as our editor at Harvard University Press.

Several colleagues assisted in our research or criticized individual chapters: Lucy Bernholz, Jane David, Michael Kirst, Gerald Letendre, Robert Lowe, Milbrey McLaughlin, Daniel Perlstein, Dorothy Shipps, Decker Walker, and Diane Wood. In a book of this sort, which seeks to integrate our own research with that of many scholars, we stand much in debt to the published work we cite in our notes. We have also had many discussions about school reform with practitioners, school board members, policy makers, parents, and public school students, and these experiences kept reminding us that educational policy is of deep concern to citizens across the nation and must be answerable to them.

During our work on this book we co-taught a course on the history of educational reform. Our students contributed a great deal to our thinking about the subject. Our debt to them, and our pleasure in working with them, is reflected in the dedication of this book. We might equally have dedicated it to friendship, for our close friendship of many years not only survived coauthorship but was strengthened by the process of exploring, in writing together, the values that give meaning to our lives and work.

Index

Index

Race, 17, 28, 46, 47, 52, 66, 136
Rand Corporation, 120
Reagan administration, 33, 37, 45
"Real schools," 7, 9, 10, 108, 109, 135; features of, 86, 88, 97, 101; and grades, 91, 94; and students, 107
Rebarber, Theodor, 45
Redefer, Frederick L., 99, 100, 101
Reform: and tinkering, 1, 5, 111, 113, 134, 136; of education, 1; through education, 2–3; definition of educational, 4; and changes in schools, 5, 9, 53, 54, 60, 75, 78; and public schools, 5; cycles of, 5, 40–42, 47; gradual, 5; hybridizing of ideas in, 5, 9, 64, 69, 78, 83, 88, 97, 109, 135, 137, 138; success in, 5, 61–63; institutional analysis of, 7, 9–10, 102; agenda of, 8, 17, 46, 58, 59; implementation of, 17, 40, 44, 54–58, 60, 80, 84, 86; systemic, 19, 81; activist, 26, 53; calls for, 33, 38; rhetoric of, 42, 59, 61; periods of, 43; different impact of on social groups, 55; time lag in, 55; uneven penetration of, 55–56; influential constituencies in, 57; legally mandated, 57; structural add-ons in, 57; plans vs. practice in, 60, 64, 82–83; definition of failure in, 61; unintended consequences of, 61, 62, 80; interactive, 63–64, 76, 78; by accretion, 83; opposition to, 101; and business, 110–112, 114–120, 127, 141; hyperbole in, 132, 134
Regulations, 19–20, 26, 78, 81; and score cards, 20; school board, 40; and policy elites, 41, 86, 107; conflicting, 64, 138; and change, 109
Reich, Robert B., 39
Republican Party, 45
Restructuring, 80, 81–82, 83
Rockefeller, John D., 18
Roosevelt, Teddy, 17
Rotberg, Iris C., 36
Rousseau, Jean-Jacques, 102

SAT. *See* Scholastic Aptitude Test
Schlesinger, Arthur M., Jr., 44
Scholastic Aptitude Test (SAT), 35, 37, 82
School boards, 18–19, 21, 22, 26, 42, 77, 109, 115, 127, 141
School buildings, 16, 23–24, 141
School funding: equalizing, 22, 33, 56; differences in, 23; inadequacy of, 31, 139; increase in, 47
Schooling: importance of, 14, 30, 39; differ-

entiated instruction in, 20, 54; increased access to, 21; and economy, 34, 38, 53; effectiveness of, 44; aim of, 107; malaise about, 140. *See also* Education
Schooling, grammar of, 9, 84, 85–109, 134; durability of, 5, 85, 87–88; and policy elites, 86; and teachers, 86, 139; reforms in, 87, 92–93, 132; challenges to, 94–107
School prayer, 29, 45
Schools: graded vs. ungraded, 4, 62–63, 64, 70, 85, 87, 88–89, 90, 97, 107; urban, 8, 18, 20, 23, 89–90; criticism of, 13; ranking of, 13; and economic competitiveness, 14, 38–39, 43, 136, 140; one-room, 19, 21, 58, 63, 88–89, 90, 127; rural, 19, 21, 23, 127–128; summer, 20; increase in size of, 21; supplies in, 23; Afrocentric, 28, 42; single-sex, 28; religion in, 29; confidence in, 30–32; inner-city, 33; success of, 37, 38; in the nineteenth century, 38, 46, 54, 68; experimental, 45; continuation, 62, 87, 91; middle, 75; evolution of, 76; community control of, 77; reinventing, 78, 111, 113, 132, 133; elementary, 85, 88, 103, 107; progressive, 99, 100, 101; model, 101, 112, 133; free, 102; without walls, 102; lighthouse, 103, 112, 114, 133; for-profit, 110; boutique, 114, 133; factory as model for, 115, 144; open classrooms in, 137. *See also* "Real schools"
Search, Preston, 94
Sex education, 2, 42, 55
Sexism, institutional, 24, 28
Shulman, Lee, 64
Sizer, Theodore R., 139
Smith-Hughes Act (1918), 72
Social engineering, 2, 17, 51–52, 65, 112, 114, 117
Socialization: institutional, 9, 17; efficiency in, 51, 70; compensatory, 65, 66, 69
Social protest, 26, 28, 43, 53
South, school systems in, 22, 23, 47, 56
Soviet Union, 44, 47, 52
Special education, 20–21, 22, 26, 27, 42, 54, 87, 136; and misfits, 21, 25; and computers, 126
Sputnik, 44, 52, 113
Standardization, 17, 19, 20, 29, 88
Students, 50–52, 102, 106–107; social promotion of, 72, 90; health of, 75; retarded, 90; and decision making, 104–105
Superintendents, 8, 10, 19, 21, 54, 77; state, 20; and reform, 58, 98, 114, 115